The effective measurement and management of IT costs and benefits

The effective measurement and management of IT costs and benefits

Second edition

Dan Remenyi

Arthur Money

Michael Sherwood-Smith

With

Zahir Irani

OXFORD AUCKLAND BOSTON JOHANNESBURG MELBOURNE NEW DELHI

Butterworth-Heinemann
Linacre House, Jordan Hill, Oxford OX2 8DP
225 Wildwood Avenue, Woburn, MA 01801-2041
A division of Reed Educational and Professional Publishing Ltd

Ⓡ A member of the Reed Elsevier plc group

First published as *A Guide to Measuring and Managing IT Benefits* by
    NCC Blackwell 1991
First published by Butterworth-Heinemann 1995. (Revised, updated and
    re-edited by Dan Remenyi)
Second edition 2000

British Library Cataloguing in Publication Data
A catalogue record for this book is available from the British Library

Library of Congress Cataloguing in Publication Data
A catalogue record for this book is available from the Library of Congress

ISBN 0 7506 4420 6

Typeset by MCI Ltd
Printed and bound in Great Britain

Coventry University

Contents

Butterworth-Heinemann/
Computer Weekly Professional Series

There are few professions which require as much continuous updating as that of the IT executive. Not only does the hardware and software scene change relentlessly, but also ideas about the actual management of the IT function are being continuously modified, updated and changed. Thus keeping abreast of what is going on is really a major task.

The Butterworth-Heinemann/*Computer Weekly* Professional Series has been created to assist IT executives keep up-to-date with the management ideas and issues of which they need to be aware.

Aims and objectives

One of the key objectives of the series is to reduce the time it takes for leading edge management ideas to move from the academic and consulting environments into the hands of the IT practitioner. Thus, this series employs appropriate technology to speed up the publishing process. Where appropriate some books are supported by CD-ROM or by additional information or templates located on the publisher's web site (http://www.bh.com/samples).

This series provides IT professionals with an opportunity to build up a bookcase of easily accessible but detailed information on the important issues that they need to be aware of to successfully perform their jobs as they move into the new millennium.

Would you like to be part of this series?

Aspiring or already established authors are invited to get in touch with me if they would like to be published in this series:

Dr Dan Remenyi, Series Editor (Remenyi@compuserve.com)

Series titles
Published

IT investment – Making a business case

The Effective measurement and management of IT – Costs and benefits (second edition)

Stop IT project failures through risk management

Understand the Internet

Prince version 2: A practical handbook

Considering computer contracting?

David Taylor's Inside Track

A hackers guide to project management

Forthcoming

Corporate politics for IT managers: how to get streetwise

Delivering business value from IT

Revitalising the IT department

Delivering IT strategies

Knowledge management for IT professionals

Information warfare

Strategies for the virtual organisation

How to become a successful IT consultant

How to manage the IT help desk call center

About the authors

Dan Remenyi has spent more than 25 years working as a management consultant in areas related to the effective implementation of corporate performance improvements based on information technology. His work in this field began during his time with IBM, with Barclays Bank and Barclays Merchant Bank and with the management consultants, Turquand Young and Layton-Bennett (subsequently merged and eventually became part of Ernst and Young). In recent years he has worked as an information technology management advisor for major clients both in the United Kingdom and abroad.

Other recent books written by him are *Achieving Maximum Value from Information Systems – A Process Approach*, and *Stop IT Project Failure through Risk Management* and *IT Investment – Making a Business Case*. He regularly conducts management seminars and briefings for both senior and operational management on how to use the information systems resource to make their organisations more efficient and effective, as well as to give themselves a competitive advantage.

Arthur Money PhD, is Director of Studies specialising in doctoral research at Henley Management College where his main area of interest is supervising a wide range of business research topics, both in the United Kingdom and abroad. Since obtaining his PhD in 1972 he has assisted several hundred postgraduate students as a supervisor or mentor. He has published extensively in the field of quantitative methods as well as in the measurement of information systems benefits. He regularly conducts seminars and workshops on research statistics in the UK and abroad.

Michael Sherwood-Smith PhD, FICS, is currently based in the Department of Computer Science at University College Dublin (UCD). He worked for 25 years in data processing and management with international companies (Nestlé, W.R. Grace & Unilever). Since 1981 he has been in the Computer Science Department at UCD involved in teaching and research. He has been a Project Director on European Commission research projects for ten years. His doctoral research was in the field of evaluation of information systems. He has published several papers as well as lectured and consulted in this field. He is a past Chairman of the Irish Computer Society (ICS) and formally the Head of the Department of Computer Science at University College Dublin.

Zahir Irani PhD, lectures on Information Systems and is the director of industrial placements in the Department of Information Systems and Computing, Brunel University (UK). He is also a member of the senior staff management committee within the department. Having worked for several years as a project manager, Zahir retains close links with industry, and also advises the European Union (EU) on the Fifth framework. His doctoral research was in the field of evaluation of information systems. He has published several papers as well as lectured and consulted in this field.

How to use this book

This book offers a combination of theory and practice. The theoretical chapters discuss the nature of IT investment and the benefits to be derived from it, while the practical chapters provide guidelines about issues such as business case accounting, ranking and scoring techniques and user information systems surveys.

In general Chapters 1 through 6 can be considered to be theoretical chapters as well as Chapters 12 and 14.

Chapters 7 and 8 address in detail the practical ins and outs of both deterministic and stochastic business case accounting. In Chapter 9 the use of a measuring instrument to assess user satisfaction is described in detail. Chapters 10 and 11 both address the issues of ranking and scoring, with Chapter 11 exploring how this is used specifically in a value for money study.

Chapter 13 takes the user through the practical steps of using evaluation as a project management tool.

Finally, Chapter 14 offers some final thoughts on these complex issues.

All the forms needed for the practical hands-on type sections are provided in the appendices as well as being available in electronic form on the publisher's web-site at www.bh.com/samples

Preface to the first edition

So far no comprehensive economics of information has been developed.

By 'economics of information' is meant a systematic series of concepts and theories which explain the role which information plays in assisting the firm in its conception, production and delivery of goods and services in order to create wealth in society. Although much work has been done in the field of cost benefit analysis of information technology as well as user satisfaction with specific systems, little attempt has been made to produce a comprehensive approach to understanding the economics of how information is used to either boost the efficiency or the effectiveness of the firm. Also, the economics of the way information may be focused so that it becomes the basis of a new business strategy, or even how information can itself be used to establish a new enterprise, has not been well addressed.

A definition of information economics is not a trivial matter. A traditional definition of economics states that economics is the science of how wealth is created and managed and how this is achieved through exchange. A non-traditional definition of information would state that it is the presentation of facts and figures in such a way that decisions may be easily and quickly made. Therefore, it may be said that the economics of information is concerned with how facts and figures may be used to create, manage and exchange wealth. This is a very wide subject area, which overlaps with many other aspects of business management.

As will be seen in the first chapter, IT has been used to help manage wealth creation for quite some time. This has been done through the processes referred to as automate and informate. However, the use of IT to create wealth is a relatively new process sometimes referred to as Transformate, which has only been understood for a decade or so.

There are probably several reasons why the economics of information has not been properly developed. One of the most important reasons is that the subject of information economics is a very difficult one and most practitioners respond to the challenges it offers by either attempting to ignore it, i.e. just get on with the day to day job, or by understating its importance. Unfortunately for IT practitioners and professionals, top management has begun to insist that much more attention be paid to the economic aspects of information systems than ever before and this has lead to an increasing demand for a comprehensive and reliable IT metric.

This book provides a basic framework for understanding the main issues concerning the economics of information as well as some suggestions as to how the firm's IT efforts may be appraised. The book discusses a number of different evaluation concepts as well as reviewing several approaches to cost benefit measurement. It takes a management approach to both investment proposals and to post implementation audits and describes how separate departments may be set up to specifically measure and manage IT benefits. In the final chapters an approach towards a number of IT Assessment Metrics (ITAM) is proposed which allows firms to measure their progress towards obtaining maximum value from their information technology efforts.

In all, this book provides a significant step towards an economic of information, but cannot be regarded as a definitive work of this enormous subject. It is a potpourri of ideas and approaches which most IT professionals and many business executives will find both stimulating and useful. Perhaps this book might be considered a guide to measuring and managing IT benefits.

Dan Remenyi

remenyi@compuserve.com

Preface to the current edition

The original work in writing this book began in 1990 when I developed a two-day executive briefing on the subject of how to manage IT benefits. The course turned out to be very popular and was conducted scores of times in a dozen different countries. From that work we developed a measuring instrument to determine the effectiveness of IT investment and this has now been used in a variety of different organisations in various parts of the world.

This book is today quite a different book to how it started out, having been published by NCC Blackwell and Butterworth-Heinemann in various printings/editions. The book and all the activities which surround it has been a major learning experience for all of us involved in this field of study and the further we advance generally the more we realise that the subject is almost limitless.

All this work makes me feel that in a certain sense a considerable amount of progress has been made in understanding the issues involved with the effective measuring and management of IT costs and benefits. On the other hand when I talk to those who claim to know about this subject I am often surprised that basic misunderstandings occur time and again. There is clearly still a lot of learning to be done.

I hope that this book will offer some insights to practitioners, academics, consultants and of course students, who are looking to improve their understanding and their ability to effectively measure and manage IT costs and benefits.

Dan Remenyi
Remenyi@Compuserve.com

Foreword

Dan Remenyi and his co-authors stand out for their deep insight into the real world, and challenges, being faced by IT directors and departments, every single day. This is evidenced in this book, which represents a major step forward in understanding the issues involved in the effective measurement and management of IT costs and benefits.

The identification of IT costs and benefits and knowing how to manage them effectively has been a persistent problem for IT directors, suppliers, consultants and academics for too many years.

Although much progress has been made, most organisations struggle to translate IT investment into real business financial benefits.

This new edition of an already well established book combines detailed research with the authors' consulting practices, and as such cuts through much of the hype and theory, and reaches the heart of the key issues to be addressed.

I welcome this book as another step in the steady move forward to have better control over these very thorny areas of information systems management.

I wish the authors every success with this new edition.

David Taylor

President CERTUS

1 The elusive nature of IT benefits

Nowadays people know the price of everything and the value of nothing

Oscar Wilde, *The Picture of Dorian Gray* (1891)

Long run is a misleading guide to current affairs. In the long run we are all dead.

John Maynard Keynes, *A Tract on Monetary Reform* (1923)

1.1 Introduction

The amount of corporate funds spent on IT investment has always been controversial. For many years it has been thought by some executives that too much has been spent and not enough return has been obtained from this IT expenditure. Robert Solow (1987) the famous Nobel Prize winning economist has suggested that in business one could see computers everywhere but in the productivity statistics. Brynjolfsson (1993) pointed out that there was a productivity paradox, which meant that computers were not delivering the value promised. The *Economist* in 1991, claimed the return on IT was so poor that organisations:

would have done better ... to have invested that same capital in almost any other part of their businesses.

But was the performance of the investment made in IT really so terribly bad?

The business community wanted to be able to see the benefits of IT in the same way as you see a big colourful brass band coming down the street. They wanted their IT benefits right up in their faces, as the modern idiom would say. However it is not clear why the business community should have expected IT benefits to be so glaringly obvious. Maybe this expectation was just unreasonable and unrealistic. There are many aspects of business investment where the benefits are really rather subtle, but are no less real for that. Examples are corporate head offices, prestige motorcars for executives to mention only two. Maybe, such is the case with IT investment.

In addition to this, the business community generally demanded that IT benefits be always expressed in terms of financial values, i.e. how much money was saved or how much extra money was made as a result of the IT investment. Some IT investment benefits however cannot be satisfactorily stated in monetary terms. Nonetheless they are real business benefits and need to be taken into account in any development of the investment evaluation equation.

1.2 Economics of information

The measuring and managing of IT benefits is a difficult business challenge that has plagued the IT industry, IT professionals, consultants and academics, for many years. The main reason for this is that despite the considerable amount of research conducted by academics and consultants so far no comprehensive or rigorous economics of information has been developed.

By economics of information[1] is meant a systematic series of concepts and theories that explain the role which information and information systems play in assisting individuals or organisations in their conception, production and delivery of

---

[1] The term economics of information should not be confused with information economics, which is a specific concept derived by Parker and Benson (1987, 1989).

goods and services both in the private and public services. There are probably several reasons why the economics of information has not been developed. One of the most important reasons is that the subject of the economics of information is a very difficult one both from a theoretical and a practical point of view and most practitioners respond to the challenges it offers by either attempting to ignore it, i.e. just get on with the day-to-day highly pressurised job, or by understating its importance. The view which practitioners often tried to assert was that relatively speaking IT expenditure was low and should be seen as an 'act of faith' (Lincoln 1990). If this view was a reasonable one, it is certainly no longer the case, as IT investment has become an important part of corporate expenditure.

Fortunately top management have begun to insist that much more attention be paid to the economic aspects of information systems than ever before and this has lead to an increasing demand for a comprehensive and reliable IT performance evaluation.[2]

1.3   Some progress in understanding information systems

During the past decade some progress has been made in understanding and articulating the role and function of information systems in organisations (Symons 1991; Walsham 1993; Willcocks and Lester 1993; Farbey *et al.* 1995; Remenyi 1996, 1999; Strassmannn 1985, 1990, 1997; Ward *et al.* 1996).

Business computing is nearly 50 years old and for most of that period the subject has been perceived as essentially a technical

---

[2] It would not be true to say that IS academics or even consultants have ignored the challenges offered by this demanding area. However although much work has been done and hundreds of academic papers published there has been very little attention paid to attempting to consolidate this work into a coherent theory.

one.[3] And although technical issues have frequently been of paramount or central importance to the success of business computing, this emphasis has been largely at the expense of a business and management understanding of information systems and what their potential and actual benefits are likely to be.

1.4   The problems with IT benefit measurement and management

There have been four major areas that have contributed to the problems with IT benefit measurement and management. These are:

1 Benefits and identifiable performance improvements

2 The issue of information systems reach

3 Tangible and intangible benefits

4 Benefit evolution.

---

[3] It is easy enough to identify the start of business computing with the introduction of computers to the Bureau of Census in the United States of America by Eckert and Mauchly, and to the J. Lyons Organisation in the United Kingdom by Cambridge University in 1952 (Evans 1981). It is more difficult to be specific about the roots of information systems management. Sometimes it is argued that the first semblance of information systems management may be recognised in the work of Dick Nolan published in the Harvard Business Review in 1973 and 1974. Thus this represents a 20-year lag between the time computers were introduced until they became of serious object of management study. But even today many IT executives will say that their organisations still perceive them to be 'techies', although they have actually become in their day-to-day work quite far removed from the detail of how the technology works. As was recently pointed out to the authors in a discussion with a senior business consultant, some IT executives hardly know more than how to switch *on* and *off* their personal computers and some of them are actually proud of this.

1.4.1 Benefits and identifiable performance improvements

For information systems project success potential benefits need to be identified as early as possible in the systems development cycle. In fact, in an ideal world benefits would be identified and quantified before the information systems development project began. However, although this does happen for some projects it is seldom possible to produce a definitive statement of all the benefits that an information systems development project will produce. In fact a high degree of success at early benefit identification is often quite elusive.

This situation may be complicated when attempts are made to use special IT benefit metrics. No special metrics are required. General business performance metrics are adequate for the identification of IT benefits.

1.4.2 The issue of information systems reach

Information systems even when they are simple stand-alone systems often, if not usually, play an important integrating type role in organisations. If one thinks of information as the glue that holds together the structure of an organisation, then information systems may be seen as *inter alia*, the conduit of that glue or the tracks over which the glue is laid and business activities or processes flow. This integrating type role brings together a number of different corporate issues, problems and resources. Even for the most straightforward information systems applications it is never simple to understand exactly what the results will be of bringing together information about different business issues. There will nearly always be knock-on effects associated with the introduction of any substantial information system especially when such a system has the effect of integrating business processes or even simply integrating reports about business processes.

For example, a payroll system where the primary objective is to automate a series of routine and simple clerical type tasks, will frequently be used as an interface to a human resource management application which could include details of training, salary benchmarks, succession planning, etc. Also a payroll system may have connections with various costing systems which show actual and standard costs, drawing on the actually amounts paid each week or month. The payroll system may also be interfaced with staff loans accounting. Of course a payroll system will need to be able to transfer data to the corporate general ledgers. So a relatively simple system such as a payroll can have substantial tentacles that penetrate into a number of different aspects of the organisation. Clearly it is a challenge to visualise all the different identifiable performance improvements such a system can have.

When more complex business applications are considered such as sales order processing, production planning and control or vehicle scheduling it becomes even more difficult to identify all the possible benefits of such systems.[4] The point is that information is at the heart and soul of the business and our ability to build useful information systems directly affects the way the business itself is or may be operated.

The importance of information is well described by Evans and Wurster when they said:

When managers talk about the value of customer relationships, for example, what they really mean is the proprietary information which they have about their customers and what their customers have about the company and its products. Brands, after all, are nothing but the information – real or imaginary, intellectual or emotional – that consumers have in their heads about a product. And the tools used to build brands – advertising, promotion, and even shelf space – are themselves information or ways of delivering information. (Evans and Wurster 1999)

---

[4] When it comes to really complex systems such as Enterprise Resource Planning (ERP) then this problem become even trickier and benefits have to be, in a sense, discovered as the implementation progresses.

When seen in this light the issue of being able to identify all the benefits in advance becomes a virtually insurmountable challenge. Often the situation is just too complex.

1.4.3   Tangible and intangible benefits

Some aspects of an information system may produce hard or tangible benefits[5] which will directly improve the performance of the firm, such as reducing costs, and will therefore be seen in the accounts of the organisation as an improvement in profit and perhaps in return on investment (ROI). These benefits are of course relatively easy to identify and to quantify both in physical terms, i.e. the number of people employed or the number of widgets used, and in financial terms, the number of pounds or dollars saved or earned. But other aspects of an information system may only create soft or intangible benefits, which might improve the general circumstances of the staff and thus make life easier in the organisation, but will not directly lead to identifiable performance improvements and as such will not be easily seen in the company accounts.

However, although difficult to be precise about their actual value, especially in financial terms, intangible benefits can make a critical contribution to the success of an organisation. Intangible benefits may often be quantified by measuring instruments such as questionnaires, but it is quite difficult to make a creditable connection between what can be measured with such devices and the impact on the corporate financial results. This whole area of intangible benefits is one of the major problems that make benefit measurement and management difficult or elusive.

---

[5] There are several different definitions of tangible and intangible benefits. For the purposes of this paper a tangible benefit is one that affects the organisation's bottom line and an intangible benefit does not.

1.4.4   Benefit evolution

But there is a third issue that makes benefit identification and especially early benefit identification even more elusive and that is the propensity for benefits to evolve. The benefits of IT are just not stable, some benefits dry up while others which may originally not have been foreseen, materialise. In short when planning an IT investment it is extremely difficult to look into the future to create a comprehensive catalogue of potential benefits. No matter how thoroughly the feasibility study or the business case is produced it is usually nearly impossible to foresee all the future ramifications of the proposed information system in advance. Forecasting is simply notoriously difficult and thus it is perhaps unrealistic to expect a high degree of success at future benefit identification to be anything other than elusive. This is especially true in the current environment in which business is rapidly changing.

Every information system will have some easy-to-identify or obvious benefits that will be sustainable over a period of time. However, as the development project proceeds and the ramifications of the system are more fully understood, new ideas about potential benefits will become apparent. This will have been due to the process of creative dialogue between the principal stakeholders, which will bring to light new business processes and practices. In short, potential benefits should not be seen as being static, but rather to evolve, as a greater understanding is gained of the organisation and the role that the system will play in it. Of course it is necessary to point out that in the same way as new benefits surface during the development project, other benefit suggestions that were originally identified may turn out to be illusory and not really exist.

These three issues are at the centre of why IT benefits have been so difficult to identify and are the prime reasons why benefits and value have been so elusive in the past.

Of course, this problem of business and management understanding and thus of computer evaluation has not been purely limited to individual systems. A lack of understanding has also applied to the more general area of the whole information systems function itself. According to Lacity and Hirschheim (1995) 'The problem is that meaningful measures of departmental efficiency do not exist for IS'. Fortunately we are seeing some changes to this unsatisfactory state of affairs. For the past decade, business executives, as opposed to information systems executives, have been demanding, by expressing their dissatisfaction at the way in which information systems departments or functions have been operated, a new approach to the management of information systems. The message is beginning to arrive that information systems are an important aspect of many organisations and new ideas as to how to manage them are well under development and a number of different approaches to this problem are discussed here.

1.5 Investment, value and economics

One of the first issues that needs to be addressed in coming to terms with a new approach to IT management is the fact that IT investment has no direct value in its own right. IT investment has a potential for derived value. Furthermore it is widely agreed that IT benefits are not directly a technology issue as such, but are to do with business initiatives. Therefore, they need to be measured and managed by P&L[6] people focusing on business processes and practices. The value of the IT invest-

---

[6] A P&L (profit and loss) person is someone who has corporate responsibility to make all or part of the organisation's profit. This role is contrasted with a staff or specialist person who does not has the responsibility to make profit, such as a personnel manager or an information systems manager.

ment depends entirely upon the way in which it is able to make the organisation more efficient and effective.[7]

To understand how this actually works in an organisation it is useful to rethink the role of information systems investment by going back to some fundamental concepts. To use classical economic language, an information system is a capital or producer or investment good. A capital, producer or investment good is something that is not acquired or valued for the utility it delivers by itself in its own right. Simply, capital goods do not have any intrinsic utility or value in their own right, as a television set, a jacket, a meal in a fine restaurant, listening to a guitar concerto, a tennis racket, a holiday in the sun, etc, do.

A capital, producer or investment good is desired because it can be used to produce other goods and services, which in turn may offer us utility and value such as the television set, a jacket, a meal or a holiday. Capital, producer or investment goods are essentially tools. A bulldozer is a clear example of a capital or producer or investment good. A bulldozer on its own has no intrinsic value. In fact to many individuals and organisations a bulldozer could be seen as a huge liability as it takes up much space, is costly to move about, requires expensive maintenance and needs a highly skilled and costly operator. It has to be clearly understood that a bulldozer's value is only derived as a result of its use, i.e. the hole in the ground, the levelling of the old building or the preparing of the ground for a new road or motorway surface. The value potential of the bulldozer is thus linked to the result that may be obtained by its appropriate use.[8] The same principle applies to IT or to information systems

---

[7] An important by-product of this view of the role of IT in an organisation is the fact that to measure its performance it is not necessary to create any IT specific metrics. General business performance metrics are perfectly adequate as measures of the success or failure of IT investment.

[8] Of course it is possible that some extraordinarily eccentric and very wealthy individuals might actually collect bulldozers and in such a case a bulldozer would indeed become in classical economic terms, a consumer durable good.

and is illustrated in Figure 1.1, which shows a similar logic to that developed by Soh and Markus (1995).

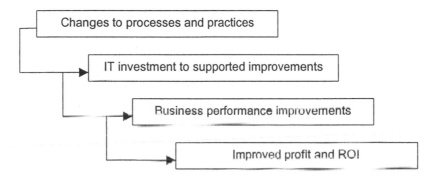

Figure 1.1: The relationship between business process and IT investment

1.5.1   IT and derived value

As a producer good, IT has a derived or second-order value that is realised when it is used as a component of an organisational or business process or practice. In fact for the value of IT to be generated or realised, it is necessary that the business process or practice to which it contributes actually improve the effectiveness or efficiency of the enterprise. In as far as these organisational or business processes or practices produce improvements to the business they will, at least in the medium term, positively affect one or more of the corporate performance variables. In turn this will show in the corporate performance indicators and thus will be regarded as delivering value.

Quite specifically, if the process innovation and improvement which is to be supported by an IT investment is to improve productivity then the IT investment will be judged primarily on whether that productivity improvement has been achieved. An improvement in productivity would mean that more goods and services are produced for the same amount of input, or that the same number of products or services is produced for less input. This is essentially a cost or pricing issue (Handy 1998). However such a system might also improve the quality of the products being produced and perhaps also have a positive impact on the morale of the manufacturing workers. If this were the case then it would be appropriate to evaluate the process innovation and improvement on all three of these variables.

On the other hand, if the process innovation and improvement was to improve customer satisfaction then the IT investment needs be judged on whether that has been achieved. Some instrument such as a ServQual scale (Parasuraman *et al.* 1988) could measure an improvement in customer satisfaction. In such a case it might not be all that useful to try to reduce these benefits to monetary values. But nonetheless, these benefits are clearly measurable and they can give the organisation a major competitive advantage in the marketplace. However such a system might also improve the cost effectiveness of serving customers and if this were the case then it would be appropriate to evaluate this process innovation and improvement also in terms of its financial impact on the organisation.

In practice it will seldom be appropriate to evaluate a process innovation or improvement in terms of one metric alone. Thus this type of evaluation really requires multi-metric analysis, which needs to be managed by the principal stakeholders.

To ensure that the value of the innovation or improvement is fully exposed, a process approach needs to be taken to its assessment. This is similar to the process perspective suggested by researchers such as Brynjolfsson and Hitt (1995), Barua *et al.* (1995), McKeen *et al.* (1999), and Mooney *et al.* (1995).

At the outset of the business intervention the process owners need to be quite specific about their objectives and goals and these need to be stated in a business case, a value proposition, or a business model. They need to be quantified where possible and a timetable needs to be established as to when they can realistically be achieved. The next step is to identify in some detail the exact changes to the current procedures and practices that need to take place, and which individuals will be affected by these changes. Then responsibility has to be allocated for these changes taking place together with the necessary resources including time for training, etc. Finally a review mechanism needs to be established, along with a procedure to follow if the proposed changes are not actually happening.

As a consequence of the above, it is clear that IT investment only derives its value to the organisation though its business applications, which can only be effected in the hands of the systems' principal stakeholders. It is these individuals who need to manage the evaluation of the investment.

1.6   IT investment as an asset

The question of whether an organisation's management of its IT resources is improved if it regards the funds which are spent on this activity to be in the accumulation of an asset as opposed to simple being part of recurrent expenditure is an interesting one. It has been argued that by emphasising the asset nature of IT investment the organisation will somehow manage it more attentively. There does not appear to be much ground for this assertion. In fact, from the above it may be argued that an information system has no intrinsic value in its own right. This is certainly what Strassmannn (1990) was saying when he pointed out 'a computer is worth only what it can fetch at an auction'. This type of argument espoused by Strassmannn suggests that by itself an information system is nothing more than a sunk cost that has been spent on a collection of hardware, software and communications equipment. And the cost of this 'kit' is normally a very large amount indeed. In fact it may be argued that there is really no overriding reason to see information systems as assets,[9] except for the fact that they are reusable i.e. not in-

---

[9] For some organisations there are several issues involved here including the fact that traditionally purchased hardware has been treated as an asset and thus capitalised. Sometimes purchased software was also handled from an accounting point of view as a capitalisable item. On the other hand software

stantly consumed. Today many personal computers and other small systems are being written off immediately and thus do not appear in the balance sheet, being treated merely as an operating cost.

But once the computer is successfully integrated into a business process then the whole picture changes and to be fair to Strassmann he did recognise this in his book. Thus, it is generally agreed that an information system really only acquires value when it is used in collaboration with other resources as part of a business process or practice that will result in the enhancement of the effectiveness or the efficiency of the organisation. This conclusion begs the question of which business processes or practice should be supported by IT and how should this actually happen.

1.7 Processes, practices and people

Business processes or practices are made to function by people working in groups, or individuals mostly in line or profit and loss (P&L) positions.[10] In the private sector these people make, sell and support the products or services for which the organisation was created. But this argument does not only apply to profit-orientated business. In the public sector, governmental or not-for-profit organisations focus on services at the national, re-

---

that was produced internally was seldom treated as an asset and thus it was quite rare to see it being capitalised in the accounts. To make this issue even more complex Keen (1991) points out that the value of an organisation's data may be worth just as much as all the hardware and software together. Maybe in the past too much has been made of the distinction between assets and cost and investment and expenditure.

[10] It is perhaps important to note that information systems are not in any way restricted to line or P&L positions within the organisation but are used in all sorts of functions and processes including staff or support activities. However the value arguments will be more easily seen in functions where the organisation's profit is at stake.

gional or local level. It is these line or P&L people who know what is required by their organisations to succeed. These individuals also know how information systems can best support their private or public sector efforts.

In effect these groups or individuals use the information systems as tools or producer goods to achieve organisational results. It is the efforts of these people that make the IT investment a success or a failure. Furthermore they intrinsically know what benefits are actually being delivered and if the information system should actually be regarded a success.

1.8   Looking for benefits and value

The main implication of this notion of the derived value of IT is that the actual benefits of an IT investment cannot be perceived directly or on their own. Only when IT is coupled with other resources, and especially the principal stakeholders, can any benefits or value be perceived. There is no standard way of combining IT with other resources or with people. Davenport pointed out the importance of people in information systems success when he wrote:

Information and knowledge are quintessentially human creations, and we will never be good at managing them unless we give people a primary role. (Davenport 1997)

Combinations of information systems, people and other resources are entirely dependent on the context of the business process or practice but in general unless IT is an integral part of a greater programme of process innovation and improvement it is quite unlikely that much value or benefits will be derived.

1.9   Primary stakeholders

The P&L people are the primary or principal stakeholders of the IT investment. By 'primary stakeholder of the IT investment' is meant the individual or group of people who have the most to gain or the most to lose if the investment is or is not a success. The characteristic of the principal or primary stakeholder that is of most interest is the fact that he or she or they can directly influence the success or failure of the information systems. Most often the principal or primary stakeholders are in fact the user-owners and it is the user-owners who makes all the difference between success and failure. Strassmannn supports this view when he said:

The lack of correlation of information technology spending with financial results has led me to conclude that it is not computers that make the difference, but what people do with them. Elevating computerization to the level of a magic bullet of this civilization is a mistake that will find correction in due course. It leads to the diminishing of what matters the most in any enterprise: educated, committed, and imaginative individuals working for organizations that place greater emphasis on people than on technologies. (Strassmannn 1997)

The recognition of these line people as the principal or primary stakeholders[11] in any information system is a fundamental change in approach or paradigm shift for many organisations. In the 'old days' it was naturally thought that the systems belonged to the information systems people. Having information systems people as systems owners produced a most unsatisfactory state of antagonism between P&L people and IT people, which has sometimes been described as the culture gap.

This new approach largely eliminates that culture gap. It is however important to point out that this does not in any way diminish the contribution of the information systems professional to the successful use of business computing. It simply changes the locus of responsibility for the IT investment deci-

---

[11] Svendsen (1998) provides a general definition of the word stakeholder as follows: 'The term "stakeholders" refers to the individual or group who can affect or be affected by a corporation's activities. In the information systems environment the stakeholders are all those individuals and groups who can affect or be affected by the information system'.

sion and the locus of responsibility for ensuring that the new business process is a success.

1.10 The locus of responsibility

Placing the principal or primary stakeholders at the centre of the information systems investment does indeed reposition the locus of responsibility[12] for the success of the information system and put it squarely where it should be, with the line mangers and user-owners. There are several reasons why the user-owners need to be centre stage in any information systems investment, but by far the most important is that the chances of the information systems delivering the type of support required by the business process or practice, i.e. being relevant, are substantially increased. The problems that arise when the user-owners are not regarded as the primary stakeholders are well articulated by Davenport who said, when talking as an information systems professional:

We have spent a great deal of time and money bringing water to the horse, but we don't even know if he is thirsty, and we have no idea how to get him to drink. (Davenport 1997)

1.10.1 The user-owner – not the only stakeholder

But the user-owners are not the only stakeholders in an information systems investment. The group of IT professionals who will work with the technical development of the information systems are clearly stakeholders of some considerable importance. They supply the IT expertise that will make the technology aspects of the new processes work. Traditionally in-house IT professionals have accepted a large part of the respon-

---

[12] The idea of locus of responsibility is similar to that of IT governance. The locus of responsibility would include issues such as how money is allocated to investment, who can give the go-ahead for IT investment and who are able to comment on the success of these investments.

sibility for the success of the IT investment. It was not uncommon for IT professionals to develop information systems for their so-called end-users. Sometimes this was done without adequate consultation, as IT professionals have been known to believe that they knew what the user requirements were, at least as well as the users themselves. Clearly this was not very satisfactory, and as mentioned above, there have been problems of communications between IT professionals and users, as well as the development of what is sometimes referred to as the culture gap. Increasingly it is thought that the users-owners need to play a greater role in ensuring the success of the IT investment.

However the IT professional still has a totally indispensable role to play in any IT investment project. The IT professional should be seen as a critical adviser to the users-owners who will ensure that the appropriate technology is acquired and employed. The role of the IT professional has also been complicated by the fact that some organisations have outsourced the supply of IT expertise.

Outsourcing has been a familiar aspect of the supply of IT competencies in many organisations over the past years. Few organisations have never used contractors or from time to time employed consultants. However it has only been in recent years that organisations have outsourced all, or the major part of the IT operation. Today organisations increasingly use a portfolio of IT expertise, which includes both internal and external people and organisations. All these sources of IT expertise may be stakeholders in their own right and are shown in Figure 1.2. In fact there are usually several of these groups involved as stakeholders in any given IT investment.

The third group of principal or primary stakeholders are the financial managers and administrators. Financial managers and administrators are always stakeholders in any corporate investment as they are instrumental in making the funds available for the purchase of the equipment, etc.

IT Professionals
♦ Internal staff
♦ Departmental IT staff
♦ Contractors
♦ Consultants
♦ Outsource contractors

Figure 1.2: The more usual sources of IT expertise

They will arrange the contracts and ensure that goods are received and that payments are made, etc. Financial managers and administrators are often involved with the detail of the business case accounting, as users-owners may not be familiar with the costing approaches required. IT investments that are made to improve business processes and practices can affect the internal controls within the organisation, and for this reason both internal and external auditors may be required to advise on the propriety of new proposals. Figure 1.3 lists some of the stakeholders that fall into this category.

Financial Services
♦ Financial managers
♦ Accountants
♦ Capital budgeting staff
♦ Corporate treasury staff
♦ Corporate planners
♦ Corporate strategists
♦ Internal auditors
♦ External auditors

Figure 1.3: Some of the financial managers and administrator stakeholders

1.10.2   Re-focus the traditional role of the IT professional

Thus the traditional role of the information systems professionals needs to be re-focused. They need to become primarily advisors and educators. However the information systems professionals, of course, do not lose all their action-orientated role of doers, as they still need to play a role in making the technology work. But information systems professionals should not try to initiate the innovative processes and practices that are responsible for the benefit creation and delivery. Also the information systems professionals should not be responsible for identifying benefits or justifying the expenditure on the systems. The business case for information systems development needs to be created by the line manager, maybe with the help of the other principal stakeholders who will use the system to improve their personal or group efficiency and effectiveness.

1.11   Summary

The way forward in reducing the degree to which IT investment benefits have been elusive requires the recognition that IT investment needs to be an integral part of a greater programme of process innovation and improvement. The success of the IT investment is then tightly coupled with the success of the process innovation and improvement. In fact the IT investment cannot be evaluated independently of it.

If the process innovation and improvement was to improve productivity then the IT investment will be judged on whether that has been achieved. On the other hand, if the process innovation and improvement was to improve customer satisfaction then the IT investment needs be judged on whether that has been achieved. It is also necessary to accept that some IT investment benefits cannot be satisfactorily stated in monetary terms. Nonetheless they are real business benefits and need to be taken into account in any development of any investment evaluation equation.

Having established the process innovation and improvement element of an IT investment it then follows that IT professionals may not be the most appropriate individuals to initiate or lead such projects. The principal stakeholder of these IT-enabled or even IT-driven process improvements needs to be a P&L manager, who is at the same time the information system user-owner.

It is important to recognise the fact that IT investment benefits have been difficult to identify because of the issue of information systems reach, the nature of tangible versus intangible benefits and the question of benefit evolution. A process approach is required to both the delivery and the assessment of IT benefits.

Finally the locus of responsibility issue needs to be clearly focused if IT benefits are to be identified and evaluated.

2 | Why evaluate information technology investments?

Business has a freedom to experiment missing in the public sector and often in not for profit organizations. It also has a clear bottom line, so that experiments can be evaluated, at least in principle, by objective criteria.

Peter Senge, *The Fifth Discipline* (1990)

The real trouble with this world of ours is not that it is an unreasonable world, nor even that it is a reasonable one. The commonest kind of trouble is that it is nearly reasonable, but not quite. Life is not an illogicality; yet it is a trap for logicians. It looks just a little more mathematical and regular than it is; its exactitude is obvious, but its inexcatitude is hidden; its wildness lies in wait.

G.K. Chesterton, *Orthodoxy – The Romance of Faith* (1990)

2.1   Introduction

A question continually asked by both practitioners and general managers is ' why evaluate IT?' The evaluation of IT is at best a difficult process, which in certain circumstances can be quite costly and therefore it should be made clear to everyone why this process is being undertaken.

The main reason why so many firms have recently taken an interest in IT evaluation is because there is considerable doubt in many circles that investment in IT has proved economically successful at all. It is clear that investment in IT is high and in many organisations it represents the highest ongoing capital expenditure. In fact many observers claim that more than 50% of all corporate investment is spent on IT, directly or indirectly. It is therefore essential for senior management to be sure that this investment is economically justifiable and that a sound return is being made on these funds. Furthermore, in the same way that IT is only one of many claims made on a firm's resources, there are many claims to be made on the IT resource and it is important to evaluate these in order to prioritise different IT projects.

As mentioned in Chapter 1, there is no little dissatisfaction about the performance of IT investment and this has been so for quite some time. And this questionable performance has led to an increasing demand for the detailed scrutiny, evaluation and assessment of IT investment.

Another reason why it is important to evaluate IT investment is that the evaluation process is in itself a learning experience. By conducting an IT evaluation the organisation will learn how well it used its funds. This will give the organisation the opportunity to understand how IT may be better employed in its business processes and a feedback process may be put in place in the hope that better decisions are made next time around.

Before looking at the detail of IT evaluation it is worth mentioning that evaluation is an intrinsic part of our society. It is deeply inbred in our culture to ask which is the better player, team, actor, motorcar, computer, etc. In fact this relentless search for the better, or best performer, team, motor vehicle model etc., often leads to questions that are essentially unanswerable. For example, the question 'What is the best computer?' has no meaningful answer. The notion of the best computer has got to be placed in a very specific context. Thus it is meaningful for one to ask which is the best computer for the XYZ Company in terms of the firm's requirements, its budgets, its expertise in IT, etc.

Although it is likely that some form of evaluation is constantly taking place in the IT environment of most organisations, in many cases this is on an informal basis, with managers making judgements based only on their own perceptions. Indeed, sometimes these judgements are based on the level of complaints made about a computer system. In such cases the decisions of those members of staff who are most verbal or animated get to be known and they receive an inordinate amount of the IT support or investment resources. This is usually regarded as being unsatisfactory. It is important, therefore, to establish a formal evaluation process whereby managers can, together, make decisions on the actions most appropriate to the organisation.

2.2 Different approaches to evaluation

There are a number of evaluation taxonomies. The following sections examine two of the primary categories of evaluation, which are ex-ante and ex-post evaluations and summative and formative evaluations.

IT investment evaluation will normally require an analyst to be familiar with the concepts underlying all of these approaches.

2.2.1 Ex-ante and ex-post evaluation

Predictive evaluations performed to forecast and evaluate the impact of future situations are sometimes referred to as ex-ante evaluations. Post-implementation evaluations that assess the value of existing situations are sometimes referred to as ex-post evaluations. Ex-ante evaluations are normally performed using financial estimates, which may be either single point estimates of costs and benefits or range estimates of such figures. In either case this type of analysis attempts to forecast the outcome of the IT investment in terms of an indicator or set of indicators such as the payback, the net present value or the internal rate of return, to mention only three. The purpose of ex-ante evaluation is to support IT investment justification.

The purpose of ex-post evaluation is to assess and confirm, or refute, the value of an IT investment. The ex-post or the post-implementation evaluations investigate and analyse an established IT investment to examine 'what is' against some previously suggested situation. This is done to confirm the value of the investment and support operational decisions about improvements. Ex-post evaluations may be made on the basis of financial indicators such as those described for the ex-ante situation above or they may be made using other non-financial measures such as user satisfaction surveys.

Ex-ante or predictive evaluations are complex. The evaluator has to understand the existing system in order to predict and understand the future investment, as well as be able to estimate the potential impact of the future situation. On the other hand ex-ante evaluations only require estimates of likely costs and benefits while ex-post evaluation require actual costs and actual benefits which are sometimes very difficult to determine.

2.2.2   Formative and summative evaluation

Evaluation activities may also be categorised as *formative* and *summative*. Formative evaluation, or learning evaluation has been explained by Finne *et al.* as:

Formative evaluation approaches typically aim at improving program performance, take place while the program is in operation, rely to a large extent on qualitative data and are responsive to the focusing needs of program owners and operators. (Finne *et al.* 1995)

The term formative is taken from the word *form*, ' to mould by discipline and education' . Formative evaluation is viewed as an iterative evaluation and decision-making process continually influencing the social programme and influencing the participants, with the overall objective of achieving a more acceptable and beneficial outcome from the programme. The idea of formative evaluation has its roots in the nineteenth century in both the United Kingdom and the United States of America, but it is relatively new to business, especially IT investment management. Originally formative evaluation was a technique developed to help improve the performance of government and social initiatives especially in the field of education and health.

Summative evaluation on the other hand, derived from the word *sum*, is viewed as an act of evaluation assessing the final (sum) impact of the social programme. Adelman (1996) points out that summative and formative are conditions of the evaluator in contrast to process and product, which are conditions of the evaluation.

It is recognised that with IT investments both formative and summative evaluation takes place. Hewett describes this:

As applied to development of computer systems, formative evaluation involves monitoring the process and products of system development and gathering user feedback for use in the refinement and further system development. Summative evaluation involves assessing the impact, usability and effectiveness of the system; the overall performance of user and system. (Hewett 1986)

Hewett goes on to point out that in systems development these two types of evaluation are required in mixes of different proportions at different stages in the development cycle. In practice there is an overlap of the two conditions. The adoption of either summative or formative evaluation approaches depends on the preferences and needs of those performing the evaluation of the IT investment.

Formative evaluation is not only about measuring the contribution, but also about the inclusion of the views of a wide range of the stakeholders. It does not stop at summary statistics, but probes the reality behind the numbers in order to understand what is really going on, i.e. what is being achieved, what is to be achieved and what the current and potential problems are. Adelman suggests:

that formative admits more representational equity than summative and giving equal voice to all stakeholders also admits diversity. (Adelman 1996)

The terms formative and summative do not in themselves imply participation for formative evaluation and non-participation for summative evaluation. From its definition 'moulding by discipline and education' there is at least an expectation that stakeholders are involved in a formative evaluation process. But it is also clear that a participatory summative evaluation can take place.

2.3 Establish the costs

The process of evaluation is not seen as easy due to a lack of consistency in the way IT investments develop and evolve. It can be difficult to allocate costs to specific projects when a product will be utilised throughout the organisation, such as in the case of a corporate database or the installation of a corporate communications network. And it has proved notoriously difficult to accurately estimate the cost of developing such systems. Those in favour of the project will frequently initially underestimate the costs in the hope of having the project accepted. The investment cost is then escalated during the development or implementation phase to a more realistic amount. This practice, which is not an uncommon technique for obtaining authorisation for IT projects, is sometimes referred to as creeping commitment.[1]

Ongoing costs can also be difficult to estimate over time due to the fact that the ultimate lifespan of an IT investment is frequently unknown – technological advances can render a system out-of-date sooner than the developers could ever have imagined. On the other hand, some IT investments continue to work for much longer periods than was ever envisaged. This phenomenon is at the heart of the issues that have been responsible for the Year 2000 problem.

---

[1] There is considerable debate about what constitutes creeping commitment or scope creep, which is a variation on this subject. Generally in IT development it is sometimes regarded as a mistake to look too far ahead as it is almost certain that the systems requirement will change over time.

The arrival of desktop or end user computing with the decentralisation of the purchasing of hardware, software and support has not made the establishment of IT costs any easier. As a result there are few organisations today that can claim to know accurately the full cost of its IT. This refers to both the cost of the purchase of hardware and software as well as the full (three- to five-year or more) ownership cost of the equipment.

Thus it is not always a simple matter to be able to identify IT costs, especially on going cost and considerable care needs to be giving to understanding how the IT investment will be used in the organisation in order to create reliable estimations of these amounts.

2.4   The problems of benefit evaluation

It is often said, with considerable justification that IT investment benefits are much more difficult to evaluate than IT investment costs. And there are several reasons for this.

In the first place evaluation of IT is made difficult because of the types of benefit that a firm can expect to derive from its application. These benefits range from improved efficiency to enhanced effectiveness. Both these notions of efficiency and effectiveness may take numerous forms and much of the task of evaluation of IT investment involves understanding these phenomena.

Generally speaking benefits are divided into two basic groups, which may be described as tangible benefits[2] and intangible benefits. Although tangible benefits are inclined to be straight-

---

[2] The differences between tangible and intangible benefits will be discussed later in the book but for the meantime it is useful to think of tangible benefits as those that directly affect the organisations bottom line profit. In that case an intangible benefit would be one which does not directly affect the organisation's bottom line profit but which has a more subtle and indirect beneficial impact on the organisation.

forward to evaluate, some benefits are intangible in that they can clearly be seen to, for example, provide better information, or can improve the decision-making capability of an individual. However, this is difficult to measure, and it is even harder to directly link the end benefit to an increase in profitability for the firm.

It is important that IT benefit evaluation be performed as part of the business process which it is supporting. For example, if a firm decides to adopt a new manufacturing strategy based on Just-In-Time (JIT) it will probably, almost certainly, require considerable new investment in IT. To attempt to perform an IT investment evaluation that is not focused on the whole JIT process would clearly be unsatisfactory. When evaluating the IT investment in this process it is important to keep in mind how much of the value added by going JIT could not be achieved without the IT system. It is argued by some specialists in IT evaluation that no attempt should be made to separate, for evaluation purposes, the IT component of a JIT system. The JIT procedures and the computer power supporting it are so integrated that the whole business procedure/process must be evaluated together. Increasingly this is perceived as being the only sensible way to approach such an evaluation problem.

Introducing a new IT infrastructure such as e-mail or an Intranet may, hopefully, produce some easily identifiable benefits. But, it is only over time that the full effects on how people use the IT investment in the organisation can be realised and these can often be unpredictable and unexpected. Infrastructural investments offer some of the most difficult challenges to the evaluation analyst. The acquisition of an office automation system, a database administration facility or a wide area network does not easily lend itself to financial evaluation other than by long-term cost avoidance techniques, which will be discussed later in Chapter 8.

2.5 Summary

The evaluation of IT investment is an increasingly important business activity. This is due to the large sums of money that are now required to successfully implement these systems. Its importance is also due to the fact that evaluation procedures are intrinsically learning events and organisations may improve their performance by the appropriate use of evaluation. However there are several difficult challenges that need to be addressed if IT investment evaluation is to be successfully performed.

3 | Aspects of the IT investment decision process

Much of the knowledge required to make efficient economics decisions cannot be expressed as statistical aggregates but is highly idiosyncratic in nature.

Mary Lacity and Rudy Hirschheim, *Information Systems Outsourcing, Myths, Metaphors and Realities* (1995)

The apparent success of ROI for non-IT projects has led organisations to search for some other single technique which can deal with all IT projects in all circumstances. This quest for the 'one best method' is proving fruitless because of the range of circumstances to which that technique would have to be applied is so wide that no one technique can cope, even though some authors have claimed that the method they espouse provides the answer for all situations.

Barbara Farby, Frank Land and David Targett, *IT Investment - A Study of Methods and Practices* (1993)

3.1 Are IT investment decisions different?

Many organisations have special rules for IT investment decisions, which differ from those adopted for core business investment decisions. Signing limits are frequently different, or the decisions may be restricted to staff in the IT function or department. Some organisations have an IT version, or sub-committee, of the capital approvals committee. An important question that needs to be addressed is how far can these, or other, differences be justified or explained by the characteristics of IT. In other words, are IT investment decisions fundamentally different to other investment decisions.

This chapter considers some characteristics of decisions about IT investment, comparing them with other business investment decisions. The analysis points to problems of understanding and credibility rather than to any fundamental difference between IT and other aspects of business, and the chapter concludes with some suggestions for overcoming these problems.

Some organisations have in the past, taken a strategic decision to encourage more use of IT. In such circumstances, the rigour of a case-by-case appraisal process might be relaxed, or the required rate of return for any particular project could be lower than for other, non-IT, projects.

3.1.1 The strategic potential of IT investment

One such example of this type of strategic thinking occurred in the 1980s when British Telecom (then Post Office Telecommunications) decided that it needed to quickly raise the computer literacy of its staff. The organisation relaxed its normal financial rules and 'seeded' the organisation with a large number of small business computers. The reasoning was that such an investment would raise the computer consciousness of the staff; suggest numbers of new applications and uses and thus bring about long-term improvements.

Pretty much as hoped, staff throughout the organisation worked on different problem areas. In many cases a number of personal computer or small business computer-based solutions were developed independently. The organisation picked the most promising for further, generally professional, development. Such an approach has a number of advantages. It harnesses the creative abilities of large numbers of staff and ensures that staff working in particular problem areas are able, in some small way, to direct IT development. A further spin-off was that the use of PC-based tools such as word processing, spreadsheets and databases became widespread throughout British Telecom and staff and managers became familiar with the concepts and practices of PC-based IT.

While such an approach may have had its successes it can probably only be attempted on such a scale once in any organisation's life. As far as is known, no attempt was ever made by British Telecom to cost the experiment. It relied on the visionary approach of one man, Sir George Jefferson, the then new Chairman. It may be considered doubtful whether any but a nationalised industry generating a large amount of cash could consider such a step. In short, this sort of situation is fairly unusual and certainly not a basis for normal business decisions or practice.

In normal circumstances an organisation only invests if it considers that the return on the capital utilised is sufficient to meet the long-term objectives or needs of the business. In other words the benefit gained is worth the expense. The capital utilised in this way costs the same whatever its intended application, and there are likely to be a number of ways the capital can be spent to gain a similar goal. It should therefore be expected that the same appraisal rules and criteria apply to decisions about IT as they do to any other investment. Except in unusual circumstances, similar to those described above, IT should never be regarded as something good, or bad, in its own right so that it need only achieve some lower rate of return. IT has to take its place in the queue for all too scarce cash resources, and the rules for justifying the expenditure needs to be the same as for any other project.

A more sophisticated argument is that, because the risks inherent in decisions about IT are higher, the expected return on investment (ROI) needs to be higher before an investment can be justified. As described below, decisions about IT do carry substantial risks in that they tend to involve large sums of money and have a high potential to damage the organisation.

This chapter will argue that this combination is not unique to IT, for example, a new product launch is equally risky. But, fundamentally, decision-makers are frequently less comfortable about IT because of their ignorance of all the issues and because they lack faith in the estimates presented to them.

3.2 Must-do IT investments

There will be occasions when an organisation undertakes an investment that gives no return at all or perhaps gives an intangible return that is difficult to measure. Complying with some legal requirements is an example of the first; PR or training might be examples of the second. These cases are discussed in greater detail below.

But there is another side to the issue of investment; do the characteristics of information technology mean that there are, or should be, differences in the way that decisions about IT are arrived at? That is, are there good reasons why there should be different processes for making decisions about IT expenditure?

Some of the characteristics of investment decisions are discussed below. Three examples are considered, core business, prestige projects and IT projects. Obviously there will be certain generalisations, but some underlying characteristics of each example will become apparent.

One class of decision, or of investment justification, will not be discussed in any detail; that is the 'must do' changes. They typically result from legislative changes. For example, organisations had no choice but to change their systems to provide VAT information to Customs & Excise, or to implement the provisions of the statutory sick pay regulations, when these were first introduced. Because the organisation has no choice but to comply there is little point in indulging in a formal justification or worrying about decision criteria. But, even in these cases, there is considerable merit in investigating, and costing, alternatives. If there are realistic alternatives, as there certainly are in the examples above, then the 'must do' solution is the cheapest. The more expensive solutions are all optional. The additional expenditure, over and above that required for the cheapest solution, needs to be justified as though it were an optional project.

3.3   A core business investment decision

Decisions about investment in core business are, by definition, what the organisation's managers know most about. The decision to re-equip the production line is easy to cost, so many machines at so much each, plus installation, a lick of paint and retraining. A certain simplification of the details may perhaps be forgiven. The number of options will probably not be large, the new machines have to fit the existing space, work with the remaining machines and be capable of producing the product.

The benefits will be inherent in the reason for considering the decision. It might be that the old machines are getting too expensive to maintain, having too much down time, or are turning out products of insufficient quality. Or it might be that the organisation is changing its product line and this change is necessary to accommodate the new products. The benefits are thus fairly easy to identify and generally fairly easy to cost.

Similarly, the implications of not proceeding with the project, or not changing the machines, are fairly easy to identify; continuing high maintenance costs, high reject ratio, or the inability to produce the new product. However, this 'do nothing' option is often not fully costed, especially when the alternative is not to undertake some new work. The people putting together the financial case are likely to be departmental managers and have limited accounting, financial or investment appraisal expertise. They will probably be emotionally committed to the project and may be under an implied directive from above. This leads to the observation that many such investment cases are a result of an earlier decision, and do not, in fact, represent a true choice but are a means of exercising management control of capital expenditure that needs to be undertaken because of that earlier decision. The decision to launch a new product is a case in point.

There will also be intangible benefits; the production line workers may prefer newer machines, feel they are participating in technological progress, feel pride in using leading edge technology. And they may feel happier that the organisation has enough faith in them and itself to invest in their future. So their morale, and maybe their productivity, will rise. On the other hand some workers may not like the change; the new machines are likely to be from a different manufacturer, perhaps foreign, and they may feel that ' all change is for the worst' . Some upheaval and retraining is probably inevitable. These attitudes would be a distinct disincentive.

The intangible benefits and disadvantages would not normally be costed. Indeed, in some organisations even to mention them in an investment appraisal case would be to risk the accusation of going soft.

However, the difference between the positive and negative attitude is quite likely to result from the way that management proposes the change. In other words, in any project, managing the way that the subsequent changes to working practice are communicated will be an important part of the implementation process. The difference between doing this well and doing it badly or not at all may well make the difference between a successful implementation and a disaster. Ignoring the value of a change in the workers' attitude in the investment appraisal may be acceptable; but if that leads to the issue being ignored altogether it may sink the project.

The case for investment will be prepared by managers in the department concerned, then pushed up the management chain, each level committing its own personal credibility to the case, until it eventually arrives at the board of directors, or capital approvals committee. It is likely to be considered very much on the merits of the case as presented, and on the financial situation of the organisation. The people making the decision will be well versed in the issues surrounding the decision, or at least believe that they are (or want other members of the committee to believe that they are).

The above case can be summarised in the following way:

♦ There are relatively few options.

♦ The decision-makers are 'at home' relevant issues.

♦ It is comparatively simple to cost and the benefits are relatively obvious.

♦ The cost of not undertaking the expenditure is obvious, though probably not costed.

Any intangible benefits will probably get no more than a passing reference.

3.4 Investment in a prestige project

For most organisations investment in prestige projects is not a regular event. However, the prestige project case has strong parallels with much expenditure that does not have an easily quantifiable return, such as advertising or PR for example. These decisions will generally not require much specialist knowledge. Even though experts will probably be invited to give advice, most managers involved will feel fully qualified to give an opinion, or hold an opinion at variance with the experts.

Consider a fairly new, rapidly expanding organisation, which has its head office in a small building in a back street of a provincial city. It has outgrown this office and is looking for larger accommodation. Having illusions, or perhaps delusions of grandeur it is looking for a building that will become the corporate headquarters of a large conglomerate. It will have a number of alternatives available, from old office blocks just like the present one but bigger, to glass and chrome monstrosities in the science park. Or it could just take over the equally small building next door and join them together. This last alternative is likely to be the cheapest option.

The financial case, or justification, for these alternatives is somewhat more difficult to put together. There will be many possible options, albeit many of the elements will be common and a few large costs will tend to swamp the smaller variables. Not all of the costs will be fully predictable, especially if the proposed new office is some distance from the existing one.

In these circumstances the project will almost certainly show a large negative figure at the end. The costs of moving office are very large. What are the measurable money benefits? Practically none.

The most obvious implication of not moving is that the organisation cannot expand; but this may be stated in a loaded manner, ' organisations either expand or die' .

In this case there are lots of intangible benefits to be considered:

♦ A smart office will impress customers and creditors, so will be a benefit in itself.

♦ A smarter location will improve staff morale, and thus improve productivity and staff retention.

♦ A purpose-built office will improve efficiency.

There is probably some truth in these arguments. But how does the project manager go about costing them, measuring them or controlling them? In the event there will almost certainly be no real attempt made to cost them. Whether they are considered to justify the expenditure will be a rationalisation after the decision is made.

Board members will probably have overseen the case from the start. They will have a fair bit of personal credibility tied up in the issue; indeed the genesis of the project may owe more to their view of the organisation than any real need to expand. The decision will probably eventually hinge on the personal views of one or two influential people, essentially ' the Boss' .

Lest the above be considered an excessively cynical view of the decision making process in organisations, it is only necessary to look to the centre of London. The headquarters buildings of many large organisations are built at vast expense on ruinously expensive plots, and rely on staff spending large parts of their days in useless and tiring commuting. While the expense of the buildings and of attracting high calibre staff to central London is readily admitted, the location is generally justified on the grounds that an organisation of this importance is ' expected' to have a presence in the Capital. This is so even amongst organisations whose main product is communications – whether physical or electronic – failing to take the advice they liberally offer to others.

The spending of large amounts of money on a project which shows a negative Net Present Value (NPV), or whose benefits are not assured, is not unusual. Prestige projects aside, mention has already been made of training and PR. Neither of these types of investment can be unambiguously evaluated in strict financial terms. The launch of a new product is surrounded by uncertain estimates of likely benefits. However, most organisations will have launched new products before and will thus have a track record on which to form a judgement of the realism of the sales estimates. The new product will also probably be related to existing core business; indeed, organisations that launch into totally new fields have a much lower chance of success.

In the case of a negative NPV for an optional project it needs to be assumed, if the organisation is behaving rationally, that the un-costed intangible benefits are considered to generate an adequate return. In these cases the organisation has put an implied or imputed cash value to those intangible benefits.

This case may be summarised in the following way:

♦ There are a large number of options.

♦ The decision-makers are probably driving the project.

♦ It is not straightforward to cost and there are few obvious financial benefits.

♦ The cost of not undertaking the project is not obvious.

♦ The intangible benefits will probably carry the case. The weight given to these benefits will be decided arbitrarily.

A simple observation that flows from some of the comments above which should come as no surprise, but which is frequently overlooked, is that organisations are made up of people. These people do not in general behave as automata, following strictly logical and predictable paths. Emotion, personal preferences and even sheer cussedness play an important part in decision making in many organisations. A consideration of the likely personal views of the individuals is thus important in understanding much company behaviour. The imprecision that dogs much social policy, because people do not always behave exactly as predicted, affects large-scale changes in organisations as well.

3.5 Investments in research and development

Research and development investments, which are sometimes called cornseed investments, are investments in the future of the business. Money spent in this area will help the organisation maintain a competitive advantage in the future. Organisations will frequently spend substantial amounts of funds on cornseed investments with little or no cost justification. Research and development money is normally treated as an investment from which an economically viable proposal is produced; otherwise such monies are treated as an expense.

3.5.1   Investment matrix

It is possible to describe these four types of investments in a 2 x 2 matrix, where the vertical axis is risk and the horizontal axis is profit. This is shown in Figure 3.1. From this diagram it is possible to see that prestige investments are high risk/high profit and that core investments are medium risk/medium profit, etc.

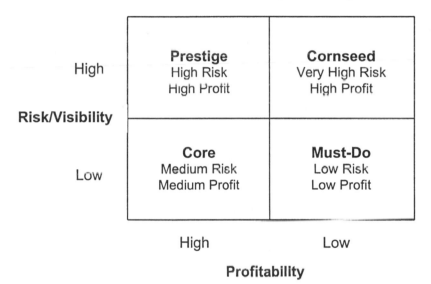

Figure 3.1: Business investment types

It is immediately obvious that the 2 x 2 matrix shown in Figure 3.1 has a strong resemblance to the McFarlan taxonomy of systems, which is shown in Figure 3.2.

When these two diagrams are viewed side by side it can be seen that support systems are actually must-do investments; turn-around systems are corn seed investments; factory systems are the core investments and the strategic systems are prestige investments. This mapping of general investment characteristics on to IT investments can be useful in understanding the nature and possible results of the investment.

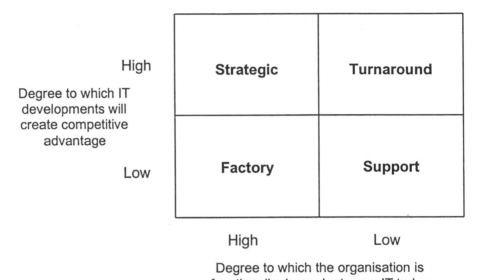

Figure 3.2: The McFarlan grid or matrix

3.6 An IT investment

As expounded earlier, investment decisions about IT generally involve large sums of money. Quite what constitutes 'a large sum' differs from organisation to organisation of course, but a bigger organisation tends to need bigger, more expensive, IT. So to some extent that is self-compensating. Because the decision does involve a lot of money it is generally pushed some way up the company tree. It is a sad fact that most of the men or women in this exalted position are unlikely to have any real knowledge or understanding of IT (some striking exceptions to this generalisation are referred to below).

The characteristics of the decision may include elements of both of the previous examples. The computer or system is likely to be intended to assist the core business, either directly by automating some aspect of the operation, or by improving some back office function. Thus the ostensible purpose of the project may be understood although the details will probably not be. This understanding will not necessarily work in favour of the project, however, as the proposal may well involve changing some long-established working methods.

IT is so all-pervading that examples of its application throughout all parts of an organisation can be expected. However, any decision about the use of IT requires an understanding both of the technology and of the application area. This makes the problems of insufficient understanding all the more severe, especially in a diverse organisation. A senior manager is unlikely to have a good understanding of the basic processes and operations in every part of a reasonably large company. Indeed, he or she may have joined the organisation directly at a senior level and thus have no firsthand knowledge of any of the working departments.

In the days when most IT was used to automate basic processes the benefits were relatively easy to specify and measure; three invoice clerks replaced by a small business computer, for example. However, as more of industry's basic processes are already automated a growing proportion of new IT investment is intended either to marginally improve an existing application or to assist management rather than the shop floor. While the first of these two has strong parallels with the replacement of obsolete equipment of any kind, the second class, helping management, is intended to deliver benefits that will be difficult to pin down with the same precision.

Projects of this kind are often described as intended to informate a business, to distinguish them from those designed to automate. Not only are their benefits more difficult to measure they are also more difficult to describe in advance. However, these benefits will probably be potentially much larger than those delivered by automation projects. Managers used to strictly money-based capital approvals may feel that the benefits claimed for such systems appear wishy-washy or intangible. However, while it may well be difficult to put strict money values to them, these potential benefits are very real, may be very important to the organisation's profitability, and certainly need to be carefully managed.

The third wave of systems is often described as those which transformate (or transform) an organisation. These systems have meant the difference between gentle decline and highly profitable survival for some of the organisations that have mastered them. There is little methodology available to put money values to such benefits, and probably little merit in the attempt. In some senses they are close to the prestige projects described earlier and are likely to stand or fall on the vision of a few senior executives (who are likely to be an exception to the generalisation suggested earlier). While the successes and a few failures are well known, there is no evidence about the organisations, that must surely exist, which decided not to go ahead with a system that had the potential to transform its business, because they could not see the point, or did not dare risk the investment.

Thus there is a spread of potential benefits, ranging from reasonably straightforward cost based, to those based on little more than the vision of a few senior executives. (This is not to imply that senior executives have less faith or vision; but it is only the view of the decision maker that is relevant in this regard.)

An element of prestige will probably also be involved. As IT is still relatively recent, and considered by many to be a good thing in its own right, many organisations will be interested simply in leap-frogging competitors without necessarily fully understanding or considering all the ramifications.

The number of options to be considered will depend on the type of project. The first implementation implies a free choice among a number of suppliers, as well as the option of continuing the current manual process. Subsequent additions or enhancements will be more constrained, but eventually the organisation will reach the point when they could make a break with their existing suppliers and the choice again widens out. In general the number of options is large.

3.6.1 Difficulty in costing

As mentioned before IT investment is difficult to cost accurately. The difficulties of costing software projects are well documented; similar, though less well-researched difficulties exist with large implementations. A naive purchaser will also find that apparently firm and final quotations from hardware suppliers can be surprisingly flexible; a few more pounds will always buy that suddenly vital extra feature. In addition, there will be a low confidence that the cost estimates will prove accurate.

If there are doubts about the costs, the estimates of benefits will be even more problematic. The analyst who devised the system will probably have made these estimates. Because significant benefits are possible from good, well-implemented, systems, and because the analyst will put the best gloss on his own proposals, the estimates may appear unbelievably large. Reactions from the line managers will vary from simple disbelief to alarm about loss of staff and perceived loss of status. More senior managers, including those involved in the investment decision, are likely to view the estimates with considerable scepticism. This is unfortunately well founded as in many, perhaps most, organisations there has been little history of post-investment audits sufficiently detailed or thorough to authoritatively establish what benefits were gained from new systems. And if the benefits were not measured they were probably not managed, nor was any real attempt made to ensure the forecast benefits were achieved, let alone maximised. In such circumstances personal opinion or prejudice has free rein.

The cost of not proceeding may be difficult to ascertain and not well understood by the decision-makers. This will especially be true if the project involves an upgrade to an existing system. Anecdotal stories abound that IT projects or departments are a black hole for money, always wanting to buy the latest gizmo. No matter how much growth there has been recently there may be a suspicion that the project is really nothing more than an admission that the original implementation was under-specified. Where there is ignorance, suspicion is not far behind.

3.6.2 Intangible benefits

Significant intangible benefits will be possible and some will be quoted in the project justification:

♦ Customer perception will improve if front office staff are seen to be using modern technology, or demonstrate the benefits of that technology by having instant access to the organisation's information about the customer.

♦ A mention in trade journals or general press because of a large new system is good publicity.

♦ Giving management access to better, more immediate, information will improve decision-making.

Equally, large disadvantages are likely if the system or implementation is not all that it should be. Also, intangible benefits are unlikely to be well understood and will often not be costed. The putting of financial values to such intangible benefits is not easy, and is discussed elsewhere in this book.

A summary of the above shows the following characteristics of IT decisions:

♦ There are a large number of options.

♦ The decision-makers will probably not understand the details of the project, though they may have an understanding of the process to be automated.

♦ Not straightforward to cost, low confidence in the estimates.

♦ Relatively difficult to estimate benefits. Low confidence in those estimates based on past experience.

♦ Cost of not undertaking the project not understood or accepted.

♦ Intangible benefits will not be quantified, though they may be an important part of the justification.

3.6.3 Making the decision

There is a range of types of decision regarding investment in IT. At one extreme the decision is little more than a question of when it suits the organisation to replace an obsolete part of the production machinery. At the other extreme, an organisation may be considering spending significant amounts of money with little in the way of hard financial justification. Such decisions are taken in other instances by many organisations with equally little hard evidence. A mistaken advertising campaign can be stopped. Poor training will probably not cost more than the wasted courses. A bad choice of new office is unlikely to significantly affect costs or productivity.

However, a bad decision about a large new computer system will affect the organisation at least until a replacement can be installed, which may be a long time, and which the organisation may not be able to afford. In this time there may be significant deleterious effects on costs, productivity and customer service. These effects may be enough to destroy the organisation. A mistaken decision not to go ahead with a system may also destroy an organisation. Simply refusing to consider big IT projects is definitely not a way of playing it safe. Thus decisions about major computer systems carry a high risk, as well as a high price tag. Probably only decisions about major product launches have as much potential for good or bad in most organisations.

In conclusion, it appears that decisions about IT investment have similarities with many other sorts of decisions taken by organisations. Although they are not unique there are certain differences, which result partly from the characteristics of IT and partly from the way management perceives it. The main points are:

♦ IT is high risk, high cost, but capable of delivering substantial benefits so cannot be ignored.

♦ Expenditure on IT will probably constitute a significant proportion of an organisation's capital expenditure.

♦ The rapid pace of change of the technology, and its wide use, make it difficult for managers to be sufficiently conversant with all aspects of the decision.

♦ In most organisations there is no trusted track record in reliable estimates, or subsequent measurements, of costs and benefits.

The overriding impression is of senior managers who, ignorant and distrustful of IT, attempt to make a decision based on inadequate and unreliable information, but at the same time are subjected to a steady diet of propaganda telling them of the enormous benefits competitors have realised from modern computer systems.

Should the decisions, then, be left to the computer professionals, who at least understand the technical issues?

3.7   A way forward

The following are some suggestions as to how the IT investment decision process may be improved.

3.7.1   Getting together

Decisions about IT investments cannot and should not be left solely to IT professionals any more than decisions about product launches should be left to the factory managers. Of course, detailed technical points about the way the machines and systems run are best left to experts but any decisions about large sums of money, or affecting the organisation's core processes, needs to involve the general management of the organisation.

The problems of managers' ignorance and inadequate information need to be tackled. Much research into this question shows that the greatest benefits are achieved by organisations that have an agreed and thought through IT strategy – a result that seems obvious.

It also seems obvious that once such a strategy has been developed it should be adhered to. So the organisation needs a mechanism for developing a strategy and a mechanism for ensuring that all proposed investments are within that strategy. Both the IT professionals and the general management of the organisation need to work at this issue.

The IT professionals are clearly a valuable source of expertise within the organisation. But too many prefer to stick to their chosen speciality rather than (as is common for many managers in large organisations), being prepared to spend time gaining experience in other, core business units. There are risks to the individual in gaining such exposure, and problems, largely related to pay and grading, for the organisation. The benefit is primarily a manager with a more rounded outlook who is likely to be more committed to the organisation.

Similarly, information technology is now too all-pervasive in any modern organisation for an operational manager to be able to justify almost total ignorance of it. He or she has to be familiar with the major issues and problems in order to understand fully the workings of the department.

It is not within the scope of this discussion to describe how an organisation can develop managers with an understanding of both core business and IT. However, on the assumption that the managers concerned are willing to learn and to try, a powerful way of focusing attention and teaching both operational and IT managers some of the key issues is to ask them to co-operatively develop an IT strategy, and to police it. This is a task that is too often left to the IT professionals alone and then rubber-stamped by the board.

The development of a strategy for the use of modern information technology within an organisation needs to be based on a thorough understanding of a number of factors:

♦ The organisation's overall business strategy.

♦ The organisation's position in its marketplace, including an analysis of the facilities available to the competition and of the service expected by the customers. (Taking into account the concept that successful organisations seek to pleasantly surprise their customers with new, more efficient, levels of service, not just grudgingly follow expectations).

♦ The organisation's financial situation. A well thought through strategy that would bankrupt the Bank of England is no help to anyone.

♦ The organisation's current level of IT expertise. As everyone needs to learn to walk before they run, it may be appropriate to introduce a cheap, simple, system for a few years before proceeding to a state of the art system.

♦ An analysis of current IT trends and standards.

A strategy based on these points cannot be completed by either IT professionals or operational managers working in isolation. Development of such a strategy can only be undertaken by the two working together and having a great deal of understanding of each other's specialism. To have any real chance of success the strategy needs to have the visible commitment of senior management. Probably the simplest way of ensuring this is to involve such managers in the original process. And the strategy needs to be regularly reviewed; which implies a mechanism to keep a group of senior managers thinking about current trends in the IT world in general and in their own organisation in particular.

Many organisations seem to regard the, admittedly large, investment of senior management time and effort such advice implies as somehow wasted on a narrow specialism. Such criticism can perhaps best be answered by reference to the amount of money many organisations spend on IT, and on the vulnerability of most organisations to bad decisions in this respect as well as to the enormous potential for those who get their IT investment policy right.

Once a strategy has been established, all investment decisions for information technology can be tested against it. Typically this would not be an onerous job as few cases will be submitted which breach published company policy. A pre-review by the IT group would be appropriate before cases reached the capital approvals committee.

It can be seen that the development of an IT strategy is only possible if senior managers and the IT professionals get together and learn from each other. Maybe it is not so surprising that organisations that have developed such a strategy succeed.

3.7.2 Improving information flow

The other side of the problem described above is that the information about costs and benefits of computer systems is unreliable and inadequate.

There is no easy answer to this. It is an issue that requires patient and diligent application over a number of years. Much research has been done into the forecasting of system development costs and timescales. However, most organisations completely neglect the measurement and control of benefits.

Contrary to the beliefs apparent in many large organisations, merely estimating the benefits in the financial case does not guarantee that they will be achieved. Simply assuming their achievement, and cutting departmental headcounts accordingly, while having the satisfying smack of strong leadership or governance, is no answer unless some attempt is made to measure real productivity. Otherwise, it is all too easy for a department to reduce its real level of service in line with the headcount reduction, instead of taking full advantage of the new system.

The measurement of benefits, a subject in its own right, starts well before the system is implemented. It should be monitored for months, or years, after implementation if the organisation is to maximise the return on its investment and ensure that all departments using the system are gaining equal benefit. Such a programme will almost certainly require the establishment of a benefits monitoring group, staffed by operational as well as systems experts.

Only when an organisation has a record of successful implementations, monitored and controlled to the satisfaction of all parties, will the doubt and mistrust described above begin to break down. It is likely to be neither quick, nor an easy process.

3.8   Summary

To be more effective in measuring and managing IT benefits it is necessary for organisations to change their attitudes towards IT investments in several different ways. IT investments should not be seen as being materially different to other investments. Decisions about IT share many characteristics with core business decisions but often involve high risks and large sums of capital. Traditionally, top management have tried to 'ignore' IT decisions by delegating them to specialist management. In an era when most organisations' core business and competitive advantage is critically affected by the successful use of IT, and when huge sums of money are involved, this practice is no longer acceptable.

Many organisations do not give sufficient senior management attention to the use of IT, especially for strategic applications. Furthermore, many organisations do not educate their IT managers in core business issues, and this sometimes causes them to be business illiterate. As a result senior managers do not sufficiently understand the issues inherent in IT capital appraisal, and IT staff feel insufficient commitment to achieving benefits in core business areas. In fact there is frequently fuzziness as to the responsibility for achieving IT benefits.

Most organisations have little history of monitoring or managing the achievement of benefits from previous use of IT. They consequently have little faith in estimates of benefits included in the appraisals. Both the ignorance and the lack of a trusted track record of benefits monitoring needs be tackled in order to improve the chances of picking IT 'winners'.

4 Issues and techniques for IT evaluation

Although there are no certainties about the overall impact of IT on business economics, there are numerous large-scale examples of IT investment with little or no associated process change. The most prevalent use of computers by individuals in business is word processing – hardly a process innovation ...

..If nothing changes about the way work is done and the role of IT is simply to automate an existing process, economic benefits are likely to be minimal.

Thomas Davenport, *Process Innovation: Reengineering Work through Information Technology* (1993)

4.1 A concept of value

The objective of this chapter is to discuss methodologies by which it will be possible to evaluate the benefits derived from the application of IT investment. In achieving this, it will be necessary to consider *inter alia*, how it is possible to convert the benefits generated by systems based on IT investment into measurable values, as well as how it will be possible to place specific values on less tangible forms of benefits.

Before such an exercise can be contemplated, it is essential to establish a framework in which the value of systems may be assessed. *The Shorter Oxford English Dictionary* states that:

Value is the amount of some commodity, medium of exchange, etc., which is considered to be an equivalent for something else; a fair or adequate equivalent or return.

In business terms, a rough and ready definition of value is generally accepted to be the amount of money that changes hands when a willing buyer trades a good or service with a willing seller. Paul Strassmann expresses this succinctly by stating 'A computer is worth only what it can fetch at an auction' (Strassmann 1990). Although this quick definition is frequently used, it does not offer much insight into the often complex nature of associating a value with a business asset.

Not all goods or services have to be traded or auctioned in order to establish their value. Fixed assets in balance sheets are regularly evaluated without any intention of selling them. Sometimes these fixed assets are revalued in terms of what they would sell for, other times fixed asset evaluation is based on what they earn for the business.

Of course, for physical assets it is generally recognised that the balance sheet value of a business asset is in no way related to its earning capability. It is the earning capability of the organisation's information systems that are addressed in this chapter. Therefore, although the value of an information system could be seen at least in one sense as the amount an organisation would be prepared to pay for the system, in actual fact the value to the organisation represents not so much the purchase price, but rather an amount the organisation believes it earns from the use of the system.

4.2 Value as a function of context and perception

Both context and perception determine value. This is well illustrated by considering how the prices of listed shares behave on stock markets. A share in the public listed company Zoomtec in 1999 cost about 450. After a bid for Zoomtec had been made by Expantec, the same share commanded a price of approximately 700. No change had occurred inside of Zoomtec, nor to the market in which it functioned, yet its value had profoundly changed. The context in which the shares then traded, i.e. of an imminent potential takeover, was quite different, and the market therefore perceived these equities to have a much higher value. Another example is the way in which the oil price has behaved during the 1990s. On 2 August 1990 the cost of a barrel of oil on the Rotterdam spot market was about $16. Within a few weeks, and without any interruption to the oil supply, nor any material increase in demand, the oil price had increased to over $30 per barrel. In this way the oil price has increased and decreased through the 1990s.

On a less dramatic note, the value of the assets in a organisation's balance sheet is entirely dependent on the management view or perception of whether the organisation will remain a going concern, and the expected economic life of the individual items owned by the company. Again, the numbers associated with the individual assets are entirely a function of context and perception.

Changes in value may also occur without any change to context, and thus be entirely a result of a change in perception. There are many examples of this, the most important of which is perhaps the work undertaken by the advertising industry. Advertisers, especially those who concentrate on luxury goods, spend the greater part of their time and efforts trying to enhance the value of the goods or services offered by their clients by raising and maintaining the market's perception of these organisations and their products or services.

Translating this into the information systems arena means that identical organisations with identical systems generating identical benefits (if such a situation could actually exist), may well have entirely different views of the values of their systems. The yardstick used to measure the value of a system is without doubt an elastic device, but then so are all yardsticks used to measure business performance. In fact, the precision and robustness of business measuring technology is most frequently overstated and this applies no less to the efforts in measuring the performance in information systems.

4.3 Measuring business performance

Before embarking on the discussion of how IT effectiveness may be measured and the role of cost benefit analysis in this process, it is appropriate to consider some of the general issues related to the matter of assessing business performance.

There is a very deep need in Western industrial culture to regularly measure business performance. There are several reasons for this, including the need to enhance performance as well as ensure growth. Both performance and growth enhancement are required to meet stakeholding expectations or increased salaries, wages, profits, dividends, etc. Although these business performance measurements take a large variety of forms and are therefore difficult to describe in generalities, it may be said that business performance assessment frequently focuses on the issues of liquidity, activity, profitability and future potential. In assessing these dimensions, standard ratios are produced such as NP%, GP%, Stockturn, ROI, ROE, Administration Costs/Turnover, Asset Turnover, Capital Intensity, etc. The number and type of ratios used varies enormously from organisation to organisation, and reflects the nature of the industry and size of organisation as well as management culture or style.[1] Organisations regularly change their performance measurement indices or ratios as they attempt to perfect the measures they use. The more useful measures are kept and the less useful discarded.

4.3.1 What constitutes good performance?

The question of what constitutes good performance is one that is asked regularly. For example, is a net profit (NP) of 10% good. Is an ROI of 20% satisfactory or is a stockturn of 5 poor.

---

[1] Although performance ratios have been used by almost all companies, the management of Harold Geenen at ITT is often cited as being an example of one of the most ratio-intensive management styles ever known.

Of course this question of good performance cannot be answered in isolation. To be able to assess performance it is necessary to know in what industry the organisation is functioning, the size of the organisation, the history of the organisation and, especially, the approach and the goals of management. For example, an ROI of 15% might be exceptionally good for an organisation in the iron and steel market, and absolutely terrible for an organisation in the electronics industry. A large organisation in a highly concentrated industry might require a net profit of 10%, whereas a small organisation may be quite content with a net profit of 5%. However, perhaps the most important issue with regard to the question of good performance is the expectation of management. If management has set an ROI of 10% as one of its objectives, then good performance is the realisation of this target, i.e. an ROI of 10% or better. Poor performance is then an ROI of less than 10% (all other things being equal).

4.3.2 Ratios

A common approach to the use of these ratios is to consider them over a period of time in order to establish a trend. Thus, if over the past 5 years the ROI has been steadily increasing then it is probably true to say that performance has been improving, although it may not yet be at a stage where it could be considered good. In using this longitudinal approach to ratio analysis, it is necessary to be aware of possible changes in accounting practices which can affect the basis of the way the ratios are calculated, and thus produce apparent movements in the ratios without there being any substantive change in business circumstances. Also, if a measure such as ROI is used and if the organisation is not continually replacing its assets, especially its fixed assets, routine depreciation policy may generate increasing ROI percentages without any improvement occurring.

4.3.3 Inflation

Another difficulty that needs to be addressed when using financial ratios is the deterioration caused to the value of money by inflation. Inflation plays havoc with the generally accepted accounting system. It can cause profits to be overstated and assets to be undervalued in the organisation's accounts. As a result of inflation, ratios may become significantly distorted and reflect a seriously untrue picture.

4.3.4 An art and not a science

It is most important to stress that the measurement of business performance is not a science but rather an art. Two different financial analysts may take diametrically opposed views of the health of a business, and these opinions may be based on the same data set. In the final analysis only future performance can be the arbiter.

4.4 When is performance measured

As a general rule, there are certain circumstances in which performance is either not measured or is measured with less care and attention. These circumstances include, but are not limited to:

♦ Where the amount of funds involved is not substantial;

♦ Where the performance or value is taken for granted;

♦ Where the organisation classifies the activity in terms of an ongoing expense rather than as a capital investment.

Funds spent on the finance division, other than for DP or IT purposes are generally not analysed too closely. This is because the sums are relatively low, the need is commonly agreed, and the accounting treatment does not usually require the amount to be capitalised. Exactly the same argument applies to the personnel division. In the manufacturing environment the size of the investment is typically much bigger and the expenditure is treated as capital. This leads to a more analytical approach being taken.

Although the size of marketing spend is considerable, as it is usually regarded as a necessary expenditure, the concern about the measurement of its effectiveness is not always expressed in an interest for detailed metrics. The time span of marketing effort being relatively short, it is treated as an ongoing expense. Also, because of the closeness of marketing to the survival of the business itself, expenditure may not be questioned in the amount of detail that might otherwise be the case. R&D expenditure is frequently treated similarly.

4.4.1 Why IT investment is heavily scrutinised

The IT investment qualifies for detailed analytical scrutiny for several reasons:

♦ The amounts of money are frequently quite substantial;

♦ Because many IT investments are not always perceived as being close to the revenue or profit-making aspects of the business;

♦ Because there is not always agreement as to the IT investment need, value or performance;

♦ Much of IT expenditure, especially on hardware, has traditionally been capitalised;

♦ Because there has been growing dissatisfaction at the performance of IT functions.

To these five dimensions should be added the question of risk. IT projects have traditionally been seen as high risk. This is due to the fact that there have been a number of IT failures, many of which have involved large amounts of funds and have received quite a lot of visibility. In addition top management frequently has little or no understanding of the IT function and therefore considers all IT activity to carry the highest risk profile.

All these factors have led to management requiring a detailed and analytical approach to the assessment and evaluation of IT investment. It is frequently argued by IT professionals that top management are too rigorous in their demands of estimates and projections. It is said that other functions are not hindered in the same way as the IT department.

4.5   The assessment of IT effectiveness

The assessment or evaluation of IT, and especially IT effectiveness, is a difficult task that needs to be undertaken with considerable care. In addition, attention should be paid to the reasons why the assessment is being undertaken, as the approach to the evaluation depends on the purpose for which it will be used. In practice an important consideration is the individual who commissions the IT effectiveness study.

If an accountant is asking the question of effectiveness, then the answer is probably required in terms of ROI, the formula for which is described in Appendix C. The calculated ROI number on its own is generally regarded as being of little value. This statistic becomes much more valuable when the IT ROI is compared to either the organisation's cost of capital or perhaps to the ROI for the organisation's total assets. A standard such as an industry average would also be considered very useful in this respect.

If the question of effectiveness is being asked by the operating management, the focus of the question is probably directed at the issue of whether the organisation is getting the most from the IT investment. This question cannot be answered by simple reference to an ROI measure, as the investment may be showing quite an acceptable ROI, but may not yet be realising its full potential. Here, what can be achieved needs to be known and the performance of the system to this standard is the essence of the answer to the question. What can be achieved can only be ascertained by comparison to some other installation, either in another department or in another organisation.

If the board of directors is asking the question of effectiveness, then the focus is probably on the issue of whether the computers are enhancing the general performance of the business as a whole. This sort of question is often couched in strategic terms such as: are the systems contributing to the organisation's ability to realise its corporate strategy? This means that a much more general position needs to be considered as it is possible for a computer to enhance departmental effectiveness at the expense of the overall corporate strategy.

4.5.1   How well is the ISD doing?

Some organisations feel the need to ask how well their ISD is doing in order to assure themselves that their IT budget is being well spent. There is, however, no simple answer to this question. Some organisations are content with establishing whether their objectives are being met. This is relatively easy, especially if business objectives and key performance indicators were specified in the original specification of requirements.

However, other organisations want a more absolute evaluation. There are basically only two ways of approaching this type of evaluation. In the first place the organisation can compare themselves to their competitors. Organisations may often obtain a significant amount of information about the way competitors are using IT and they can obtain a rough idea of how much such IT activity costs. The organisation may interview clients and also the clients of competitors to establish their relative performance. This type of evaluation is, at the end of the day, even more subjective than most.

The second approach to answering the question of how well the ISD is doing is to compare current performance with historic performance, which requires the existence of a database of detailed measurements of performance and IT expenditure. This is the most satisfactory way of answering the question. Unfortunately, not many organisations have the required statistical history to be able to perform this type of analysis.

4.6   Purpose of the IT investment

The purpose of the investment is most critical to the process of defining the approach to its evaluation and to its performance measurement. As mentioned in the previous section, IT investment that is used to improve efficiency requires efficiency measuring techniques such as work-study or cost benefit analysis. IT investment which has been implemented to enhance management effectiveness requires value added analysis, value chain assessment, etc. IT investment for business advantage or business transformation requires measuring techniques such as strategic analysis, relative competitive performance, etc. The table in Figure 4.1 suggests how different investment types may be treated.

Investment purpose	Investment type	Evaluate/measure
Business survival	Must do	Continue/discontinue business
Improving efficiency	Vital/core	Cost benefit
Improving effectiveness	Critical/core	Business analysis
Competitive leap	Strategic/prestige	Strategic analysis
Infrastructure	Architecture/must do/corn seed	Very broad terms

Figure 4.1: Investment purposes, types and evaluation techniques

4.7   Matching the assessment effort to strategy

It is important to focus assessment efforts, especially when dealing with systems that have the potential to generate a competitive advantage. Specifically, strategic IT investment may be seen as having an impact on the organisation's ability to function as a low cost leader or as a differentiator.

4.7.1   A strategy of differentiation

If the organisation's strategy is one of differentiation then the following are the issues on which the IT's performance should be measured:

♦ Does IT lead to adding information to the product?

♦ Does the IT application make it easier for the clients to order, buy and obtain delivery of the goods or service?

♦ Are there fewer errors in processing the business?

♦ Have the after sales service aspects of the business been enhanced?

♦ A strategy of cost leadership.

If the strategy is one of low cost leadership then the following are the issues on which the IT's performance should be measured.

♦ Will the IT application result in direct cost reductions?

♦ Will there be labour reductions?

♦ Will the time to market improve?

♦ Will there be greater utilisation of equipment?

♦ Will Just-In-Time manufacturing be possible?

The matching of benefits to systems purpose is really a key aspect to understanding and managing IT benefits.

4.8   Different approaches to measurement

There are two generic approaches to measurement. These approaches are common to all forms of measurement, whether the measurement relates to speed, obesity, water flow, and beauty contests, weighing potatoes or assessing information systems. Measurement may be based on:

♦ Physical counting.

♦ Assessment by ordering, ranking or scoring.

Whether the contents of a tanker, the weight of a boxer or the speed of a jet plane are being measured, units are being counted. When it is difficult or impossible to count, the assessment is made by ordering, ranking or scoring.

Both of these fundamental approaches are used as the basis of a variety of techniques such as cost benefit analysis or strategic match analysis. These are discussed in detail in Section 4.10.

A first approach to measurement of IT effectiveness is to compare the system's objectives to the actual achievements of the system. For such an exercise to work the system's objectives needs to have clearly been stated with key performance indicators (KPI) having been specified. Objectives without KPI are of little value, as objectives that are set without attention as to how the business will know if they are achieved, are frequently too vague to be meaningful. Figure 4.2 shows some satisfactory and some poor objectives. The definition of the objectives and the KPIs should be clearly laid out in the system specification. Unfortunately this is not always done.

Also, even when the objectives and the KPIs have been properly defined, it is not always possible to measure the actual impact of an information technology application, simply because the effects may be indirect, or rendered invisible by surrounding noise in the system.

4.9 Intangible benefits

Where it is hard to directly observe the effect of the IT, the following methodology can be used to help assess the nature of the benefits of the system.

Satisfactory objectives	Poor objectives
To reduce inventories by 5% by value and 10% by volume within the next 180 days	To improve profitability
	To reduce errors
To increase the organisation's ROI by 1% by the end of the financial year	To improve staff morale
	To enhance cash flow
To reduce the amount invested in debtors so that the debtors' days decline from 80 to 68	To obtain a competitive advantage
To improve staff acceptance of the new IT systems as reflected by the attitudes expressed in regular satisfaction surveys	
To deliver detailed proposals of typeset quality to clients within 48 hours of being given leave to present such documents	

Figure 4.2: Examples of satisfactory and poor systems objectives

Steps involved in measuring intangible benefits:

1 Conceptualise the chain of cause-and-effect events that may result from the introduction of the system.

2 Identify how it will be possible to establish the changes that are likely to occur as a result of the introduction of the information system. Here the focus is on the direction of the changes, i.e. will the inventories rise or fall? Will more phone calls be taken, etc.

3 Consider how the size of the change may be measured.

4 Where the effect of the system is clear, the analyst may proceed with the next three steps.

5 Measure the size of the change.

6 Put a monetary value on the changes that have been observed. Use techniques such as payback, ROI, NPV, IRR, etc., to assess whether the information system investment will produce an adequate return to justify proceeding.

This six-step methodology is a useful framework for approaching IT evaluation studies, even where it is hard to identify benefits. The following is an example of how the method is used.

A new billing system as an example of the conceptual approach:

1 A new billing system will reduce errors, get out invoices in less time, etc., by checking prices, discounts and business terms. Month-end statement runs will be two days instead of 10.

2 Changes:

- fewer customer queries
- fewer journal entries
- less reconciliations
- more cash.

3 Measurements:

- keep a register of queries
- count journal adjustments
- record time on reconciliations.

4 Check interest paid on overdraft, and interest earned on cash available.

5 Time released multiplied by the salary paid, or where overdraft is eliminated, interest not paid.

6 Use standard calculations.

The above six-step approach to measuring IT benefits is susceptible to a number of problems of which the following three are the most frequently encountered.

Noise

Noise refers to the fact that the effect of the IT investment may be masked by other events in the environment. Thus, although the inventory levels should have risen or fallen due to the new system, circumstances in the economy produced an effect that overwhelmed the benefits of the system.

Fluctuations in the short term

Sometimes IT benefits are hidden behind short-term fluctuations due to seasonal changes in demand, cost or prices. To make sure that such fluctuations do not obscure the presence of IT benefits, measurements need to be taken at regular intervals over a period of time.

Lies, damn lies and statistics

All measurement techniques are based on assumptions and these assumptions may often be manipulated to show the required results.

4.10 Specific methodologies

There are several different methodologies available to assess the performance of IT. The following are a few of the most commonly used:

1 Strategic match analysis and evaluation.

2 Value chain assessment (organisation and industry).

3 Relative competitive performance.

4 Proportion of management vision achieved.

5 Work-study assessment.

6 Economic assessment – I/O analysis.

7 Financial cost benefit analysis.

8 User attitudes.

9   User utility assessment.

10 Value added analysis.

11 Return on management.

12 Multi-objective, multi-criteria methods.

4.10.1   Strategic match analysis and evaluation

This is a ranking or scoring technique that required the entire primary IT systems to be assessed in terms of whether or not they support the organisation's generic corporate strategy. The two main generic strategies are differentiation and cost reduction. If a system helps improve customer service it generally helps the organisation differentiate itself in the market, while if it helps to reduce costs it is generally supportive of a cost reduction strategy.

Figure 4.3 shows a list of the more important applications in a large organisation and this list may be used to assist in the categorisation of the systems.

Function	Low cost	Differentiation
Product design & development	Product engineering systems	R&D databases
	Project control systems	Professional workstations
	CAD	Electronic mail
		CAD
		Custom engineering systems
		Integrated systems to manufacturing
Operations	Process engineering systems	CAM for flexibility
	Process control systems	Quality assurance systems
	Labour control systems	Systems to suppliers
	Inventory management systems	Quality monitoring systems for suppliers
	Procurement systems	
	CAM	
	Systems to suppliers	

Function	Low cost	Differentiation
Marketing	Streamlined distribution systems Centralised control systems Economic modelling systems Telemarketing	Sophisticated marketing systems Market databases IT display & promotion Competition analysis Modelling High service level distribution systems
Sales	Sales control systems Advertising monitor systems Systems to consolidate sales function Strict incentive monitoring system	Differential pricing Office–field communications Sales support Dealer support Systems to customers
Administration	Cost control systems Quantitative planning and budgeting systems Office automation for staff reduction	Office automation for integration of functions Environmental scanning & non-quantitative planning systems

Figure 4.3 Key business applications

Weights can be associated with the more important systems, and a score be given on the basis of the degree to which these systems have been implemented and are achieving their objectives.

Figure 4.4 shows a strategic match evaluation form used with simple unweighted ratings of 1 to 10, where 1 represents low impact systems and 10 represents high impact systems.

Such an evaluation technique is useful if applied each year so that the organisation can obtain a feel for the direction in which the IT function is progressing.

Function	Low cost possibilities	Actual systems	Rating
Product design & development	Project control systems	Project control systems	6
Operations	Process control systems	Process control systems	3
	CAM	CAM	7
Marketing	Telemarketing	Telemarketing	5
Sales	Sales control systems	Systems to consolidate sales function	4
	Systems to consolidate sales function		
Administration	Cost control systems	Cost control systems	8
	Office automation for staff reduction	Office automation for staff reduction	4

Figure 4.4 Completed evaluation form

4.10.2   Value chain assessment (organisation and industry)

This is another scoring or ranking system. In this case the Michael Porter value-added chain is used as the basic checklist to which the organisation's application systems are compared. This process may be conducted in terms of the organisation's internal value activities as well as the industry value activities. For a thorough analysis, both approaches should be used. In a similar way to the strategic match analysis, evaluation weights may be associated with the more important systems and scores may be given on the basis of the degree to which these systems have been implemented and are achieving their objectives.

4.10.3   Relative competitive performance

Some organisations assess their performance by comparing themselves to their competition. This requires monitoring their competitors' acquisition of IT, the way they use it to achieve their corporate strategy as well as being able to estimate their costs. These are quite difficult processes and frequently rely on very subjective evaluations involving ranking and scoring.

4.10.4 Proportion of management vision achieved

This is another ranking and scoring technique that has a high degree of subjectivity. Managers are asked to assess the current systems in terms of what their original plans were. When a large number of managers are involved a questionnaire or survey approach may be used. Despite being subjective, this approach can be applied in a relatively objective way by conducting regular assessments on a six or twelve-monthly basis.

4.10.5 Work study assessment

The work-study approach to IT benefit evaluation requires regular reviews of how the work in the department is being performed. During these reviews the volume of work is carefully recorded as well as the time required to perform all the necessary tasks. Work-study assessment can be relatively objective particularly if work-study professionals conduct it. The results of a work-study appraisal may be used as input to subsequent cost benefit analysis.

4.10.6 Economic assessment

An economic assessment is a theoretical approach to IT benefit evaluation. It requires the development of a model expressed in mathematical terms in which the relationship of input and outputs are expressed. Although applying rigorous mathematical terms this method also relies on subjective views of the nature of the relationships between the input and output variables.

4.10.7 Financial cost benefit analysis

There are a number of different approaches to financial cost benefit analysis. Some are described in detail in Chapter 7.

4.10.8 User attitudes

User attitudes may be used to assess how IT is performing within the organisation. Here a survey method is used to extract attitudes towards the importance of IT to individual users, as well as how the ISD is performing in its delivery of IT. This issue is fully explored in Chapters 9 and 10.

4.10.9 User utility assessment

It may be argued that systems that are heavily used are more successful than those that are not. By establishing the frequency of use of a system it is believed that it is possible to assess its value to the organisation. This technique involves counting the amount of activity sustained by the system, measured in terms of its input, processing and output. However, excellent systems have been known to fail for trivial reasons, while poor systems have survived for years and therefore this approach leaves many questions unanswered.

4.10.10 Value-added analysis

Using this technique the value of the system rather than its cost is firstly assessed. Once the value or benefit has been agreed then a cost is calculated. The system is then developed on a prototyping basis at a relatively low cost. Once this has been completed an assessment is made to decide whether the benefits derived have justified the cost. If the decision is that the investment is justified then the organisation proceeds to the next stage in the IT applications development.

4.10.11 Return on management

Return on management is a concept proposed by Paul Strassmann initially in his book *Information Payoff* (Strassmann, 1985) and again in *The Business Value of Computers* (Strassmann, 1990). The return on management (ROM) method is a valued added approach that isolates the management added value and then divides this by the management cost.

When expressed as a formula:

$$\text{Management value added} = \frac{\text{ROM}}{\text{Management cost}}$$

Management value-added is the residue after every contribution to an organisation's inputs is paid. If management value-added is greater than management cost then management efforts are productive in the sense that outputs exceed inputs.

This approach attributes surplus value to management rather than capital and as such, it is a departure from classical economics. It is based on the philosophical notion that in contemporary society, the scarcest resource is not capital, raw materials nor technology, but rather management. In Strassmann's view 'good' management makes all the difference between success and failure and ROM recognises this fact.

The method used for calculating management value added could be demonstrated by considering Figure 4.5.

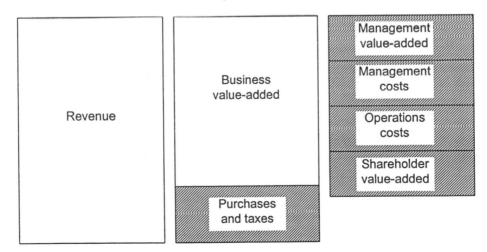

Figure 4.5: Calculating management value added

Revenue is described as being composed of purchases and taxes and business value added. In turn the business value-added consists of:

1 Shareholders' value added;

2 Operations costs;

3 Management costs;

4 Management value added.

The calculation procedure is an exhaust method. First the purchases and taxes are subtracted from the revenue to derive the business value added. The business value added is then decomposed by first, subtracting the shareholders value added, which is the dividend, then, second, subtracting the operations costs, which are all the direct and overhead costs. At this stage only management cost and management value added remain in the figure. When management costs are subtracted only the management value added remains.

Strassmann claims that the ROM method is a superior measure because it combines both financial statement and balance sheet entries, it is self-indexing, it isolates the productivity of management, and it makes possible diagnostic evaluations.

4.10.12 Multi-objective multi-criteria methods

Multi-objective multi-criteria methods are subjective methods for appraising the value of different outcomes in terms of the decision-makers own preferences. It assumes that the value of a project or IT investment may be determined or measured in terms other than money. Therefore, preferences are used instead of ROI, etc.

The philosophy behind multi-objective multi-criteria methods is that different stakeholders may have different ideas about the value of different aspects of an IT investment and that these may not be strictly comparable in money terms. This technique allows different views and values to be investigated and assists in exposing potential conflicts at the decision-making stage.

Multi-objective multi-criteria methods are most useful when strategic choices have to be made between quite different alternatives.

4.11 Classification of methodologies

Each of these methodologies leads to the development of a measure or metric that allows the IT to be evaluated. Sometimes the metric is compared to a corporate or industry standard or sometimes relative metrics are compared, for competing systems. However, in most cases a single measure is not sufficient to make an evaluation. Two or three metrics will usually be required but six or seven measures should be avoided. These methodologies may be categorised as primarily objective or subjective in nature. However, even in the more objectively oriented approaches the calculation of the metric will almost invariably be based on subjective criteria and any suggestion that the method is totally objective should be resisted. Figure 4.6 categorises these measures in terms of their relative subjectivity/objectivity.

Classification	Evaluation Approach
Partially Objective	Cost benefit analysis
	Economic analysis
	System usage
	Quality assurance
	Relative competitive performance
	Work study assessment
Fully Subjective	User attitudes
	Management vision
	Value chain assessment
	Strategic match analysis

Figure 4.6: Classification of evaluation approaches

The key to using these metrics is to attempt to maintain as high a level of consistency between the evaluations of different systems.

Before directly addressing any of these techniques themselves there are several philosophical questions or issues that need to be raised including asking to what extent costs and benefits are a question of definition.

♦ What assumptions underlie the cost and benefit calculations? What goes into the investment? Most commentators would agree that the hardware cost should be included, but there is considerable disagreement as to the amortisation policy for the hardware. Some organisations capitalise their software, while others insist that it needs to be treated as an expense. With some systems, training can represent a substantial proportion of the total costs and this is seldom capitalised. Should it perhaps not be treated as an investment cost? Few organisations bother to attempt to account for staff time, especially management time, while this is known to frequently represent a sizeable element in the development cost of many systems.

♦ It is not always clear what costs should be attributed to a system. Direct costs are relatively easy to identify, although those associated with end-user computing may be difficult to identify. However, overheads or corporate burden often represent a major issue that is not easily resolved. Should the information systems department carry part of the cost of the international headquarters and the chairman's Rolls Royce? In addition the notion of being able to state the cost of a system implies a final date that can be fixed in time. Systems typically do not behave like this as they generally evolve and, therefore, do not lend themselves easily to a cut-off date.

♦ What benefit streams have been identified and for how long? How far into the future can the continued viability of the system be assumed to last? Does the organisation have a rigidly controlled policy on investment horizons?

♦ How are future benefit streams adjusted for inflation? What measure of inflation has been used? Are different estimates of inflation being used for different factors of production?

♦ In the case of international organisations, how are multi-currency situations to be handled and how are future exchange rates accommodated?

Hardly any of these questions can be answered by simple objective facts. Each one is loaded with opinion, subjectivity and value judgements. Therefore the problem of producing sound, objective, unbiased IT evaluations is considerable.

All approaches to IT benefit assessment have significant conceptual or practical flaws. This does not mean that they cannot be or should not be used, but practitioners should be aware of their limitations.

Strategic analysis and evaluation

1 Highly subjective

2 Issues not well understood

3 All but top management may be unaware of strategy

Value chain assessment

1 Very subjective

2 Difficult to obtain hard data

3 Not well understood by management

Relative competitive performance

1 Information available may be sketchy

2 Difficult to compare benefits of different systems

3 Uncertainty about competitors' plans

Proportion of management vision achieved

1   No hard data

2   Virtually no objectivity in this approach to assessment

3   Not always easy to get top management to admit to failure

Work-study assessment

1   Objectivity may be relatively superficial

2   Changes in work patterns may drastically alter the assessment

3   Most managers are not familiar with these techniques

Economic assessment – I/O analysis

1   Requires an understanding of economic analysis

2   Relatively abstract

3   Attempts to avoid detailed quantification of monetary terms

4   Most managers are not familiar with these techniques

Cost benefit analysis based on financial accounting

1   Subject to manipulation

2   Accounting requires a sound infrastructure, which many organisations do not have

3   Financial accounting cannot extend beyond simple monetary terms and thus many issues of value are omitted

4   Has a long-established acceptance in business

Quality assurance assessment

1   A very technical approach

2   Not many practitioners available

3   Has only a low relevance to operating managers

4   Users may not tell the truth or may simply exaggerate

5 Users may have vested interests in presenting a particular viewpoint

6 Corporate culture may colour users' views and the interpretation of the outcome

Value added analysis

1 Very practical approach

2 Keeps costs under control

3 Encourages prototyping

Return on management

1 A major break with classical economics

2 Not easy to operationalise

3 Useful to stimulate re-thinking

Multi-objective multi-criteria methods

1 An unquantifiable method

2 Not useful as a post-implementation tool

3 Useful to stimulate debate

4.12 Choice of evaluation methodology

There is in fact a bewildering choice of evaluation methodologies available to management. Each methodology is designed to assess the organisation' s IT effectiveness in a different way. The critical skill is to be able to select the methodology most appropriate for the organisation' s particular circumstances.

4.13 Summary

There is a wide range of IT evaluation or assessment techniques available. Each approach has some strengths and weaknesses. In order to choose one that is appropriate, it is necessary to focus on the objective of the assessment and what decisions the evaluator intends to make with the results of the assessment. It is essential to always bear in mind that all measurement techniques, by their very nature, have some element of subjectivity built in, and where possible, allowances should be made for this.

5 | Identification of IT costs

Analysts have tended to define assets too narrowly, identifying only those that can be measured, such as plant and equipment. Yet the intangible assets, such as a particular technology, accumulated consumer information, brand names, reputation, and corporate culture, are invaluable to the firm's competitive power. In fact, these invisible assets are often the only real source of competitive edge that can be sustained over time.

Hiroyuki Itami, *Mobilizing Invisible Assets*, cited in R.G. Grant *Contemporary Strategy Analysis* (1995)

5.1 Introduction

Although the costs of an IT investment are often perceived to be easier to estimate than its benefits, this is rarely actually the case. The costs associated with IT projects appear more tangible in nature because, the assumptions and dependencies on which they are based are often *not* fully acknowledged, or are poorly understood by management. The tendency to underestimate costs it is considered widespread practice during the investment decision-making process to account for the upper estimates for costs and the lower estimates for benefits (Hogbin and Thomas 1994).

However, even if this is actually the case it appears *not* to be solving the problem of IT projects running over budget and resulting in failure, as much of the problem lies in management *not* 'fully' understanding IT cost portfolios. There might also be political and organisational reasons for understating the cost implications of an IT investment, such as the need to gain support for, and acceptance of, the project from management and the stakeholders of technology. In a recessionary climate, a search for cost-justification, quick returns and, indeed applying

IT for cost reduction purposes would seem to be paramount, thus pressurising proponents of IT into understating costs.

Farbey *et al.* (1993) have reported the increasing actions of project champions; project leaders who are totally committed towards the 'success' of the IT investment, and who often ignore the 'full' cost implications of their IT investment. In doing so, they include optimistic estimates of benefits and savings even though this management practice may have severe implications on the organisation, for example in the case of a Enterprise Resource Planning (ERP) system, which typically has high running costs. In this instance, the failure to identify the 'full' cost implications, when combined with the use of over-optimistic savings and benefits, may result in several extra years of use to achieve expected financial returns. The impact on the organisation is a reduction in productivity and competitiveness due to the prolonged use of outdated technology.

Hochstrasser (1992) points out that most companies tend to underestimate the total cost of their IT projects, with between 30–50% of costs occurring outside the official IT budget. In one large manufacturing company studied by Willcocks and Lester (1993), IS department user and training costs were 29% of total project costs but, hidden in other departmental, often non-IS related budgets. Ezingeard and Race (1996) offer further empirical evidence by suggesting that many *manufacturing* companies, to their detriment, 'fail' to account for the 'full' complement of IT related costs. Similarly, Hogbin and Thomas (1994) report the use of a contingency factor, with between 10–25% of the project cost being added to the IT projects' budget, and a further 10–15% being added to include underestimated project management costs.

5.2 The costing process

Initial cost estimates that contribute towards determining the level of IT investment required are often governed by the performance characteristics set during the system requirements planning stage. However, such estimates of system costs are often restricted to system architecture and include:

♦ Hardware and software performance required to process tasks;

♦ Data volumes of transactions;

♦ The development work content needed to provide a given set of functions;

♦ Shared processing facilities, for example, terminals, peripherals and networks;

♦ Functions that are extra to a given user's immediate requirement, for example, mandatory security facilities;

♦ System design factors that might protect performance in the long-term but which have short-term development costs;

♦ Ongoing operating expenses;

♦ The balance of development costs against eventual maintenance costs;

♦ Weakest links in the network topography;

♦ Network architecture and associated hubs, routers and gateways;

♦ File-server facilities and in particular dedicated servers; and

♦ Network security such as firewalls.

In addition to architecture and infrastructure costs, there is the issue of whether project costs should include indirect cost factors and more importantly, *how* such costs should be identified and accounted. In the instance of a new system, which can use available processing power, the investment cost may be calculated as a marginal cost of the processing power needed to run the extra application. This marginal cost may be acceptable for one new system but could lead to an understatement of the total costs, for the entire system. It is particularly the case, where the full processing costs include operating and management expenses. Once the initial cost estimates of a proposed IT system have been decided and the system justified, a process of recording the cost implications, and allocating these cost factors to departmental budget often begins. This process is known as 'charge-out' and is where the project costs are offset against the benefits achievable. This management process has evolved from where IT costs were once all in a centralised IT department.

Today many IT costs are often incurred and accounted for at departmental level, with each department buying their own hardware and software, and sending people on training courses from their own budget. Hence, without some structured mechanism of allocating cost implications at a departmental level, it would appear to be extremely difficult to keep track of exactly *how* much expenditure is IT related. Clearly, charge-out is not an easy process or a management panacea, and should be seen as just one of the many techniques available in the management 'toolbag' alongside IT planning processes, project benefits appraisal, management performance measures and cost identification and control.

5.3 Acknowledging cost portfolios

As hardware costs continue to fall in price, IS-related human and organisational costs are set to rise. Indeed, Strassmannn (1990, 1997) concluded that at the US Department of Defense, for every $1 spent on IT and associated equipment, a further $7 needed to be spent on 'softer' human and organisational issues.

Human and organisational costs can be as much as three to four times as high as 'direct' project costs. Invariably however, these costs are rarely 'fully' budgeted for in IT/IS investment proposals, which may partially explain the phenomenon of 'cost-creep', which occurs over the course of most IS. Clearly there is a need to support project management and IT/IS evaluation with a cost framework. As technology penetrates new frontiers, its implications are increasingly acknowledged as being far-reaching. In doing so, it not only impacts on the user, but also on the supply chain. As a result, companies may knowingly or unknowingly be forced to bear some of the costs associated with its customers and suppliers IT/IS infrastructure.

5.4 Direct cost portfolio

'Direct' IT costs are those that can be attributed to the implementation and operation of new technology. Figure 5.1 provides a summary of common direct costs associated with IT projects.

Classification of direct project costs	Direct IT/IS costs
Environmental operating costs	Uninterruptible power supply
Hardware costs	File server Dumb terminals Backup tape streamer Network printer
Software costs	Key vendor software module Relational database software Additional networking software
Installation and configuration costs	Consultancy support (partially grant funded) Network wiring, junctions and connectors Installation hardware 'In-house' customising time Re-engineering business processes to suit software
Overheads	Running costs: electricity; insurance premium rises Consumables: Toner cartridges; disks; and paper
Training costs	Database software course
Maintenance costs	Yearly service contract (hardware) Database user group fees

Table 5.1: Taxonomy of direct IT project costs

Although these costs often go beyond the initial user specification of the system, it is the focus made by management on these aspects, which often dictate the project's budget, and ultimate justification (Irani *et al.* 1998). 'Direct' project costs are often underestimated and go beyond the obvious hardware, software and installation costs. These costs may also include unexpected additional hardware accessories, such as increases in processing power, memory and storage devices. Installation and configuration costs are also classified as direct costs, and typically include consultancy support, installation engineers and networking hardware/software.

5.5 Indirect human cost portfolio

It is increasingly recognised that the 'indirect' costs associated with the adoption of IT are more significant than the 'direct' costs. However, it is the illusive nature of these costs that make their identification and control difficult and cumbersome. As a result, their magnitude and impact is often not discussed during IT decision making. 'Indirect' costs can largely be divided into human and organisational factors, with one of the largest 'indirect' human cost being that of management time. This is the time that is specifically spent on integrating new systems into current work practices. However, the result of newly adopted technologies may force management to spend time revising, approving and subsequently amending their IT-related strategies. A significant amount of resource will also be used to investigate the potential of the IT, and in experimenting with new information flows and modified reporting structures.

There is a further 'indirect' human cost that is often overlooked, which is that of system support and troubleshooting. Indeed, many organisations are now finding it quicker and more efficient to employ their own technicians to provide this service. This appears to be the preferred option, over the reliance on software vendors, who initially try to solve the problems re-

motely, and when unable to, then make personal visits that add
to the cost of the system. Clearly, system support costs are substantial, with Wheatley (1997) reporting the results of a recent
survey that found a third of respondent companies could not
estimate the cost of supporting IT, in relation to the technologies' original purchase price. The vast majority of those
companies that did venture an estimate, thought the cost to be a
small fraction of the original cost of acquisition.

However, a quarter of companies thought that IT support costs
to be less than 20% of their original purchase price, with only
4% prepared to concede that such costs might exceed the origi
nal purchase price. In fact, according to the survey, typical
lifetime support costs are at least 400% of the original purchase
price, which draws on estimates from industry analysts.

Although, it does appear that vendors are starting to perceive
the cost of ownership as the new 'competitive frontier', which
can offer vendors a sales advantage over others. Another 'indirect' cost may result from employees developing new skills,
and therefore increasing their flexibility/overall contribution
towards the organisation. These employees may then request
revised pay scales. Clearly, such 'indirect' costs associated with
employee pay and rewards, together with the cost implications
of increases in staff turnover need capturing, and bringing into
the IT decision-making arena. For example, in one such case, a
number of employees were sent on an expensive skills-based
training course to familiarise themselves with a new ERP system, only to be poached by a competitor months later. The
motivation for the poaching was the need to save significant
training costs whilst offering its new recruits a marginal salary
rise as a 'carrot'.

Figure 5.2 provides a summary of the indirect human costs associated with the adoption of IT.

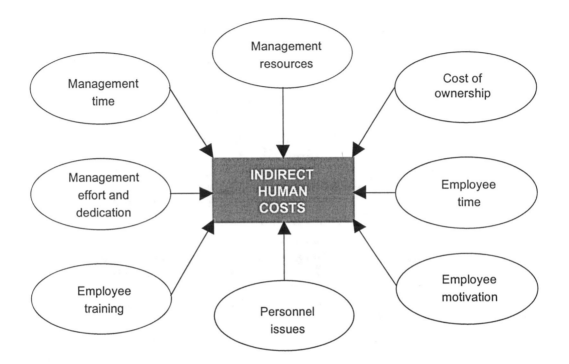

Figure 5.2: Taxonomy of indirect human costs

5.6 Indirect organisational cost portfolio

'Indirect' costs are not simply restricted to human factors but encompass organisational issues as well. Organisational costs are caused by the transformation from old to new work practices, based on the impact of the new system. At first, a temporary loss in productivity may be experienced, as all employees go through a learning curve, while adapting to new systems, procedures and guidelines. This also involves employees being trained and training others.

Additional organisational costs may also be experienced once the basic functions of the system are in place. These costs are associated with management's attempts to capitalise on the wider potential of the system; at an enterprise/strategic level.

Further costs include management's attempt to integrate information flows and increase its availability. An example of these costs in a manufacturing environment could be the development of an electronic data interchange (EDI) link between a customer and suppliers' ERP production schedule. This additional technology links an organisation to its customers and suppliers. The 'openness' in communication allows a customer to view its supplier's capacity before raising a purchase order, therefore preventing unrealistic delivery demands on the supplier. Alternatively, it may allow a supplier to view stock/buffer records to determine whether a delivery is needed. Hence, the implementation of ERP may result in the adoption of a new 'knock-on' technology, together with its associated cost factors. Any additional 'knock-on' costs; direct and indirect, together with efficiency saving, will need to be taken into account, during the justification of the information system. This is essential, to allow for the complete functionality and potential of the new system to be achieved. Furthermore, the adoption of EPR and any 'knock-on technology' are likely to result in the redesign of organisational functions, processes and reporting structures.

Companies with extensive IT infrastructures in place, tend to change their corporate shape, by reducing the number of management levels. This is often achieved by redefining the role of many management functions, through increasing their flexibility and overall contribution to the organisation. The costs of organisational restructuring, or business process re-engineering are considered to be expensive, particularly if isolated groups within the company resist change, and are unwilling to make the transition. These costs therefore need acknowledging and building into a justification costing structure. Figure 5.3 provides a summary of the indirect organisational costs associated with the adoption of IT.

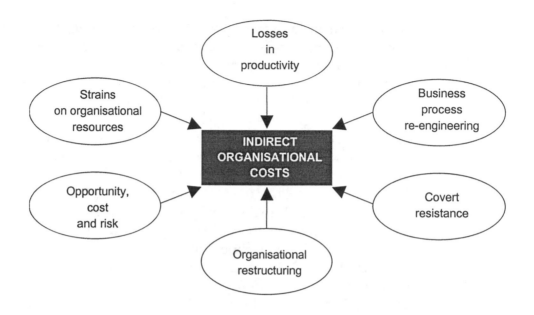

Figure 5.3: Taxonomy of Indirect organisational costs

5.7 Summary

This chapter has identified some of the direct and indirect cost factors associated with IT projects, with examples being drawn from the literature. The identification and acknowledgement of these cost implications during an IT deployment could avoid some of the difficulties encountered when using traditional approaches to investment justification. Furthermore, their identification will give companies a better insight into the actual implications and successes of their manufacturing IT investments. However, the lack of widespread use of non-traditional appraisal techniques; analytical and integrated approaches, as mechanisms for partially addressing some of the 'softer' indirect costs identified in this chapter, would suggest their application being restricted due to their complicated and subjective nature, and more importantly perhaps, their lack of applicability in manufacturing environments.

6 | IT cost control

Building an information system, ..an online, distributed, integrated customer service system ..is generally not an exercise in 'rationality'. It is a statement of war or at the very least a threat to all interests that are in any way involved with customer service.

K. Laudon, *A General Model for Understanding the Relationship between Information Technology and Organisation* (1989)

Expenditures on IT capital were less effective than any other type of expenditure considered. The reason is that firms focus too much on how technology is used instead of what it is used for.

D. Schnitt, *Re-engineering the Organisation using Information Technology* (1993)

6.1 Introduction

The effective control of information technology costs is a very difficult issue to manage. As mentioned in a previous chapter, vast amounts of funds are annually spent on IT by both private and public organisations and it is, in many cases, not entirely clear, whether or not these sums are well invested.

According to research conducted in various parts of the world one of the most frequently cited challenges facing IT managers today is cost containment and this issue is one which offers many difficulties in bringing under control. Nonetheless it has begun to draw an increasing amount of interest from senior management who have insisted that overall IT costs be managed in a more effective way. This had led to researchers and consultants becoming increasingly interested in how IT costs are incurred, how they are planned, monitored, managed and controlled. However, there is still a degree of controversy as to the appropriate management policies to implement in order to ensure that IT costs are kept at a reasonable level.

6.2   An IT or IS department budget

It is useful to look at some typical budgets or cost profiles of IT departments to understand the nature of the cost behaviour of this activity in an organisation.

Figures 6.1 to 6.5 show cost outlines for IT departments under a variety of circumstances relating to growth, inflation, etc. In each case the total cost of the department escalates consistently and in the last case the increase over the ten-year period is very substantial indeed, amounting to a seven-fold increase. These increases in IT costs are regarded by many practitioners as being inevitable due to the very nature of the IT activity within the organisation. There is certainly plenty of evidence that cost increases such as those described here occur regularly.

The main assumptions underpinning the numbers in these IT budgets are that production/operations costs are a base amount of 100 units of currency. A unit of currency could be one thousand pounds for a small organisation or one hundred thousand pounds for a medium organisation and a million pounds for a big organisation. The total cost of maintenance of hardware, software and telecommunications is 38%. On new applications the organisation will spend a constant amount of 25 units of currency per annum throughout the ten-year period.

There are a number of important points that arise out of the projections shown in these figures. Figure 6.1 shows that even without any business growth the organisation's IT expenditure doubles in ten years. With only a modest business growth of 5% the IT bill triples, whereas with some growth in business and application requirements and a small rate of inflation the IT expenditure increases seven-fold.[1]

Scenario one – No business growth										
	1	2	3	4	5	6	7	8	9	10
New applications	25	25	25	25	25	25	25	25	25	25
Maintenance	38	42	47	52	56	61	66	70	75	80
Production/operations	100	113	125	138	150	163	175	188	200	213
Total IS expenditure	**163**	**180**	**197**	**214**	**231**	**248**	**266**	**283**	**300**	**317**
Additional cash each year		17	17	17	17	17	17	17	17	17
Assumptions										
New systems completed PA	50%									

Figure 6.1: ISD cost scenario over a ten-year period – No business growth

Scenario two – 5% business growth										
	1	2	3	4	5	6	7	8	9	10
New applications	25	25	25	25	25	25	25	25	25	25
Maintenance	38	44	51	58	66	74	82	91	100	110
Production/operations	100	118	136	155	175	197	219	242	267	293
Total IS expenditure	**163**	**187**	**212**	**238**	**266**	**295**	**326**	**358**	**392**	**428**
Additional cash each year		24	25	27	28	29	31	32	34	36
Assumptions										
Business growth	5%									
New systems completed PA	50%									

Figure 6.2: ISD cost scenario over a ten-year period – 5% business growth

Scenario three – 10% Business Growth										
	1	2	3	4	5	6	7	8	9	10
New applications	25	25	25	25	25	25	25	25	25	25
Maintenance	38	46	55	65	77	89	103	118	134	152
Production/operations	100	123	147	174	204	237	274	313	357	406
Total IS expenditure	**163**	**193**	**227**	**265**	**306**	**351**	**401**	**456**	**516**	**583**
Additional cash each year		31	34	37	41	45	50	55	60	66
Assumptions										
Business growth	10%									
New systems completed PA	50%									

Figure 6.3: ISD cost scenario over a ten-year period – 10% business growth

---

[1] Totals may sometimes appear not to accurate due to spreadsheet rounding.

Scenario four – 10% business growth and 5% inflation										
	1	2	3	4	5	6	7	8	9	10
New applications	25	25	25	25	25	25	25	25	25	25
Maintenance	38	48	61	75	91	111	133	158	188	222
Production/operations	100	129	162	200	244	295	354	422	500	591
Total IS expenditure	**163**	**202**	**247**	**300**	**360**	**431**	**511**	**605**	**713**	**837**
Additional cash each year		39	45	53	61	70	81	93	108	125
Assumptions										
Business growth		10%								
New systems completed PA		50%								
Inflation		5%								

Figure 6.4: ISD cost scenario over a ten-year period – 10% business growth and 5% inflation

Scenario five - 10 % business growth, 5% inflation and 10% new application growth										
	1	2	3	4	5	6	7	8	9	10
New applications	25	28	30	33	37	40	44	49	54	59
Maintenance	38	48	61	77	95	117	143	174	210	254
Production/operations	100	129	163	204	253	312	381	464	561	676
Total IS expenditure	**163**	**204**	**254**	**314**	**385**	**469**	**568**	**686**	**825**	**988**
Additional cash each year		42	50	60	71	84	100	118	139	164
Assumptions										
Business growth		10%								
New systems completed PA		50%								
Inflation		5%								
Growth in new applications		10%								

Figure 6.5: ISD cost scenario over a ten-year period – 10% business growth, 5% inflation and 10% application growth

A significant implication of the cash hunger of IT is the fact that the discretionary portion of the IT budget dramatically reduces over time. This financial pressure invariably results in shrinking of development expenditure. Figure 6.6 directly addresses the phenomenon of the shrinking development expenditure by showing how IT budget is often reallocated to accommodate growing production/operation and maintenance costs.

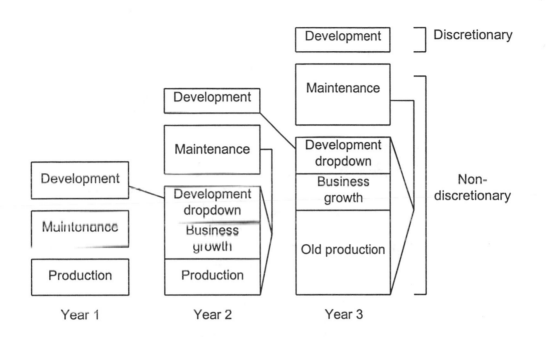

Figure 6.6: The phenomenon of increasing maintenance and of shrinking development expenditure.

The situations illustrated in the above figures, which may be described as the traditional approach to information systems planning and management, needs a radical review if information technology is to be used effectively in organisations today.

6.3 Assumptions underpinning IS management

There are several fundamental assumptions underlying modern information management, which directly stem from the conditions prevalent in the early years of the computer age. These include the fact that information systems are thought to be difficult, expensive and unreliable. These perceptions can be seen as a major contributor to IBM's early success, when many organisations bought from 'Big Blue' because of the fear of purchasing a system from the seven dwarves (the smaller computer manufacturers of the time), who it was suggested could not ultimately deliver effective working systems. Thus the maxim *no one ever got fired for buying from IBM* came to be extensively believed – which could be translated into *inexpensive systems don't work*. Of course IBM has changed since those days and is now largely cost-competitive, but the old belief in the necessity of having to have expensive IT solutions still lingers in some quarters.

Another assumption underpinning the use of IT was that big or large scale is beautiful. Thus organisations wanted to build up their information systems departments. Bigger machines, more staff, etc. meant *economies of scale*. Thus vendors were able, year after year, to sell more equipment on the basis of better price performance, as there was an underlying assumption of an insatiable corporate appetite for IT and especially for raw computing power. This has undoubtedly resulted in overselling in a number of cases and thus the IT budgets being bigger than necessary. Fortunately because IT professionals are more knowledgeable and because the market is more competitive there are far fewer incidents of overselling.

There was also the assumption that every organisation large enough and capable enough should *have its own information technology establishment*. Bureaux, it was generally believed, were with few exceptions such as payrolls and share registers, only suitable for the smaller organisation. To do-it-yourself was firmly believed to be the best approach.

Today these assumptions are no longer valid and IT cost management requires that these ideas be reassessed from first principles.

6.4 Situational audit

The first step in IT cost management is to perform an IT utilisation audit. This means that three basic questions should be asked and answered.

1   What is the organisation actually doing with its IT?

2   Why is the organisation doing these things?

3   How is the organisation utilising the components of its IT resources?

The first question will have an answer such as sales order processing, financial budgeting and reporting, materials requirements planning, etc. The work required here is a relatively simple matter of an information systems inventory.

The second question will typically have an answer such as to support the sales fulfilment process, to ensure financial order, to provide periodic assessment of the performance of the organisation and to improve the organisation's ability to deliver the appropriate type, quality and quantity of goods. Answering this question is not a matter of a simple inventory, as each information system needs to be related back to the organisation's objectives, strategy, and critical success factors and then to business processes. This question in fact should trigger a process evaluation or information systems alignment study, which requires a considerable amount of discussion and debate involving top management. Information systems that do not have a direct link to the organisation's objectives, strategy and critical success factors are by definition suspect and should be strongly considered for discontinuity. This could be the trigger for a cost reduction exercise.

The third question will be answered by a description of the hardware and software platforms in use. The work in answering this question is similar to that described in Chapter 11 on value for money (VFM) studies.

6.5   Future requirements – a strategic information systems plan

Knowing the present situation in terms of the organisation's IT is not enough. What is then required is to establish what the future needs of the organisation are likely to be.

This is established by asking the following three questions:

1 What next does the organisation want to do with its IT?

2 Why does it want to do this?

3 How does the organisation want to implement these plans?

This is basically answered by a strategic information systems plan which is a lengthy and complex process but which will result in a clear understanding of what is required, what is currently in place and the gap between the two. A strategic information systems plan will also spell out what must be done to ensure that the organisation achieves its IT objectives. The question is now how to implement such a plan in the most cost-effective way.

6.6   Methods for cost improvement

There are basically three macro-strategies available for information systems cost reduction. These are:

1 Systems may be wholly or in part outsourced

2 Systems may be wholly or in part downsized or rightsized

3 IT may be harvested.

Outsourcing is a strategy that is relatively easy to implement, but it is often difficult to manage. When projects that have been outsourced are going well then outsourcing is a most beneficial arrangement, but when they run into difficulty outsourcing has horrendous implications for the organisation. Outsourcing reduces costs by having an organisation, whose core competence is IT, manage all or part of the organisation's information systems requirements. The outsourcer can frequently deliver the systems cheaper because of greater expertise and because of economies of scale. It is important to control an organisation's outsourcing activities by means of formal contracts and it is not a trivial matter to ensure that such contracts are well drawn up. Therefore there is some risk in using outsourcers. Also it is frequently argued that organisations should never outsource strategic applications. As some organisation regard much of their IT to be strategic it may be difficult for them to take advantage of this approach to cost curtailment.

Downsizing or rightsizing, which usually involves replacing mainframes with mid-range machines or even networks of personal computers, is not as easy as has been claimed. The industry has hyped this issue far beyond it current capability and therefore there are many perils associated with this activity. In addition although there have been some remarkable successes, many organisations who have downsized claim that they have not actually reduced their costs.

IT harvesting refers to cutting back on development, postponing upgrades, reducing service, keeping old equipment beyond the usual period in order to reduce the organisation's costs. Harvesting may be seen in terms of the strategic matrix, shown in Figure 6.7.

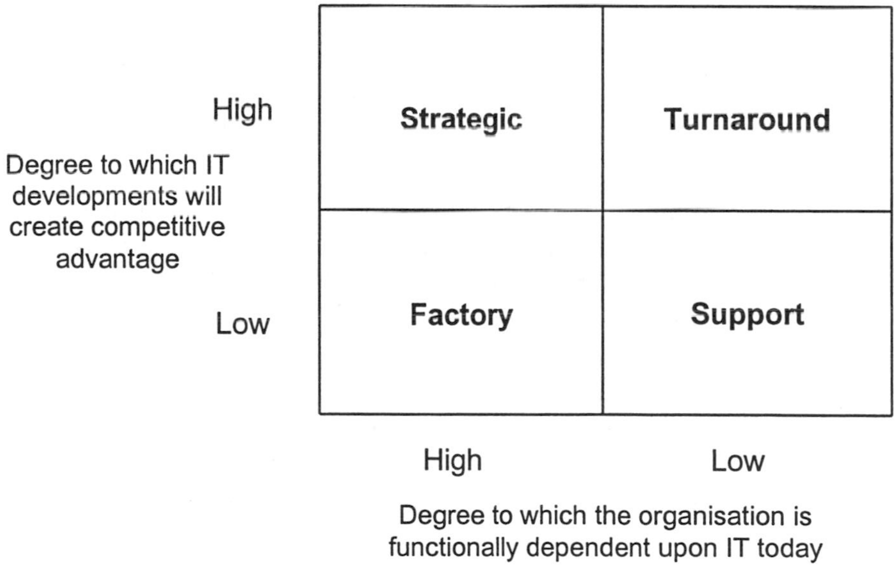

	High	**Strategic**	**Turnaround**
Degree to which IT developments will create competitive advantage			
	Low	**Factory**	**Support**

	High	Low

Degree to which the organisation is functionally dependent upon IT today

Figure 6.7: The strategic grid or matrix

Harvesting represents the discontinuance of activities in the turnaround quadrant, movement of systems away from the strategic and the turnaround quadrants towards the factory and the support quadrants. In fact in several cases of harvesting, even the factory quadrant has pressure on it as systems are pushed back to the support position.

As a short-term strategy harvesting can be very effective in making the organisation show better financial results. However its long-term effect may be problematical if not downright disastrous because at some point in the future all the cost cutting will have to be reversed and a more balanced regime of expenditure and investment reintroduced.

6.7   The commercialisation of the IT department

A more effective strategy, which transcends cost control but which ensures sensible IT expenditure, is the commercialisation of the IS department. This involves, not necessarily looking for the low-cost solution but making sure that costs and benefits are matched. What is being referred to here is not a simple matter of cost benefit analysis but rather a new approach to IT investment. Commercialisation means underpinning IT investment with business considerations that directly relate to material benefits and which directly or indirectly improve the organisation's profits. However commercialisation does not mean that management should not be sensitive to costs. On the contrary, costs are the central issue here. In some cases where a commercialisation approach has been followed, organisations have attempted to sell the time of their IT staff and processing power at a price that will make a contribution to their overall costs. This has meant that the IS department has become a profit or investment centre and have been given the authorisation to in-source work from other organisations wishing to outsource. Although this approach may be effective in reducing the overall IT cost profile, it needs to be managed quite carefully. There is a danger that the IS department's priorities may become confused and it may lose its sense of direction and purpose, or simply acquire another, less appropriate sense of direction and purpose.

Other issues to be considered are micro cost reducing strategies, which include using off-the-shelf packages, CASE tools, etc., and matching services to what users are prepared to spend. These are actually a subset of the greater picture described above.

6.8 Summary

There is no easy answer to IT cost control. Outsourcing, downsizing and harvesting are relatively quick solutions, which may or may not produce the desired results. The longer-term approach of commercialisation requires much more care and attention to management of the organisation as well as of the technology.

7 | IT business case accounting

We are merely reminding ourselves that human decision affecting the future, whether personal or political or economic, cannot depend on strict mathematical expectations, since the basis for making such calculations does not exist; and that it is our innate urge to activity which makes the wheels go round, our rational selves choosing between the alternatives as best we are able, calculating where we can, but often falling back for our motive or whim or sentiment or chance.

John Maynard Keynes, *The General Theory of Employment, Interest and Money* (1936)

There are three kinds of lies: lies, damned lies and statistics.

Benjamin Disraeli, cited in: *Mark Twain, Autobiography* (1959)

7.1 Introduction

Having decided the direction of the organisation's IT investment at a business level it is then necessary to perform some detailed analysis of the financial impact that the proposed investment is likely to have on the organisation. This involves business case accounting or cost benefit analysis.

The techniques used for this type of analysis include capital investment appraisal, which involve the calculation of financial ratios such as the payback, the return on investment (ROI), the net present value (NPV) and the internal rate of return (IRR).

7.2 Concepts required for business case accounting

There are many different financial concepts and issues involved in business case accounting. It is essential that all these elements be addressed in the financial analysis. In Chapter 5, the concept of IT costs was discussed and therefore does not require much further definition. However, there are a number of different financial notions that need to be considered when preparing an IT business case.

These financial notions include:

♦ Hidden costs

♦ Opportunity costs

♦ Marginal costs

♦ Time value of money

♦ Discounted cash flow

♦ Interest rate or hurdle rate or cost of capital

♦ Horizon or economic life

♦ Terminal value.

7.2.1 Hidden costs

A hidden cost is a not so obvious cost of IT that may appear in another department or function, but is there as a result of computerisation. Operations and maintenance costs are sometimes considered to be hidden, and these can amount to as much as 2.5 times the development and installation costs over the first four years of the life of an IT project. As the impact of IT has become better understood there is much more understanding of IT costs, and thus less scope for costs to be hidden.

7.2.2 Opportunity costs

The opportunity cost of an investment or project is the amount the organisation could earn if the sum invested was used in another way. Thus the opportunity cost of a computer system might be the amount that could be earned if the funds were invested in the core business, or if the funds were placed in an appropriate bank account.

7.2.3   Marginal costs

Cost benefit analysis is traditionally performed on a marginal cost and revenue basis. This means that numbers are based on the variable cost associated with the new IT investment and excludes the general overhead. When it comes to benefits evaluation the same rule applies and thus only new, or extra benefits are included. The marginal costing approach prevents double counting of either the cost or the improvements.

7.2.4   Time value of money

The concept of the time value of money refers to the fact that money today is worth more to the organisation than money tomorrow. It is on the notion of the time value of money that discounted cash flow is based and this is one of the most important methods for the evaluation of any investment proposal.

7.2.5   Discounted cash flow

Discounted cash flow is the way that the concept of the time value of money is operationalised. Cash flow is discounted by calculating its present value, which requires the sum to be reduced by a rate of interest equivalent to the organisation's investment opportunity rate. This discounting is done for each year that it takes to obtain or to make the payment.

7.2.6   Interest rate or hurdle rate or cost of capital

The interest rate, hurdle rate or cost of capital are three different terms for the rate of interest that is used in the discounted cash flow calculation. Whatever name is used for this interest rate, the number used needs to represent the rate at which the organisation can earn on the funds under its control. Thus this is also sometimes referred to as the required rate of return.

7.2.7   Horizon or economic life

The horizon or economic life of the investment is the period for which it is believed that the investment will be effective and thus for which it will earn an economic return.

7.2.8   Terminal value

The terminal value of an investment is the amount for which the investment could be sold at the end of its economic life.

7.3   Pattern of costs

As mentioned in Chapter 5 it is interesting to note that the distribution of costs when implementing new IT systems has changed dramatically over the past 30 years. Organisational costs have increased from about 20% to 50% of the total cost of implementation. This is clearly shown in Figure 7.1.

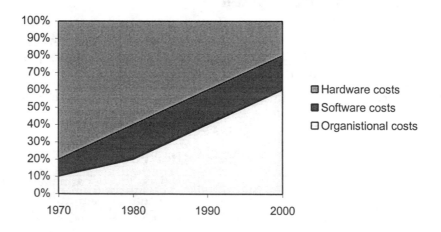

Figure 7.1: Increase in organisational costs incurred during IT implementation

Of course the trend shown in Figure 7.1 is likely to continue for quite some time. The change in the proportion of cost is due both to the decline in hardware cost but also due to the absolute rise in organisational cost. Organisational costs have escalated dramatically because of the much more comprehensive types of systems that are now being implemented by organisations. The more comprehensive the IT investment the more organisational expense will be required.

The figures included in the cost estimates of a system should be based on the ownership costs over a projected five-year system life. Systems lasting longer than this period will in some senses produce a bonus for the organisation. Systems that do not remain in place for five years could produce negative results, but this does not mean that the investment should not be undertaken.

7.4   Sources of cost estimates

Obtaining reliable cost estimates has always been difficult and this has contributed the on-going problems with IT project budgets.

There are various sources of cost estimates. These include obtaining quotations from the different contributors to the project. These could include suppliers, contractors, consultants, outsourcers, etc. The cost of these resources can often be negotiated on a fixed fee basis, which may then be reliably used in the business case accounting exercise.

Another source of costs is estimations of the development work required by the system's in-house team. This will include an analysis of the problem, the creation of a project specification and the amount of time required to develop or write code for the system. There are also the in-house costs of training the staff. The commissioning cost may also be incurred internally. This type of cost estimation is subject to considerable error and some organisations cope with this by comparing the proposed project with previous similar developments. This is, of course, a form of internal benchmarking and can drawn on corporate best practice if this has been recorded. Many of the organisational costs shown in Figure 7.1 fall into this category and these are not easy to estimate. The idea of benchmarking can then be taken outside the organisation where estimations of costs can be gathered by looking at similar projects.

Whichever approach is taken to cost, estimates have to be produced with considerable care, as they are always prone to error. A provision for contingency for cost escalation is often used as a way of coping with this. Another approach to the uncertainty of costs is the use of risk or stochastic analysis, which is discussed in Chapter 8.

7.5   Business case accounting in practice

Cost benefit analysis can be defined as the process of comparing the various costs of acquiring and implementing an information system with the benefits the organisation derives from the use of the system. In general cost benefit analysis should be performed on a marginal-costing basis. This means that only additional costs incurred by the new system should be included. Likewise only marginal benefits, i.e. new or additional benefits, should be compared to the costs.

It is sometimes suggested that only benefits are difficult to estimate. However, as many IT projects over-run their cost, this is clearly not the case. Considerable care must be given to cost estimation, especially where software development is concerned. Also on-going costs should be carefully scrutinised.

Different approaches to benefit analysis are required for automate, informate and transformate investments. The following are among the most important.

7.6   Cost displacement

Cost displacement considers the cost of the investment and compares this to the other costs the system has saved. This is typically used in the more traditional data processing environments where computers are used to replace clerical workers or even sometimes blue-collar workers. Cost displacement is not really appropriate for situations where the IT system is intended to add value rather than reduce costs. A cost displacement justification is a classic automate situation, although it may also have informate implications. Figure 7.2 shows an example of cost displacement analysis of an investment for one year.

Using IT to automate jobs 1 year Cost displacement	All costs in 000s	
	Year 0	Year 1
Set up costs		
Hardware – PCs, LANs and other peripherals	125	
Software – spreadsheet, word processing, database, etc.	98	
Training	75	
Installation and testing	52	
Total	**350**	
Monthly on-going costs		
Staffing, including support		28
Maintenance and upgrades		20
General		8
Total		**56**
Monthly benefits		
Reduction in clerical salaries		42
Reduction in supervisory salaries		8
Reduction in other staff costs		13
Office space released		5
Other office expenses saved		3
Total		**71**
Improvement per month		15
Annual net benefit		180
Annual ROI		51%
Simple payback		2 Years

Figure 7.2: The cost displacement approach – 1 year

It should be noted that the costs and benefits are marginal costs and benefits and therefore will not necessarily display the relationship described in Figure 7.1 The cost displacement approach is an ex-ante analysis of what the organisation hopes to achieve with the proposed IT investment. It is nothing more than a statement of intent. To ensure that these intentions are carried out, a list of details about the system and the environment in which it will function must also be supplied. It is sometimes preferable to perform this type of analysis over a number of years and Figures 7.3 and 7.4 show the cost displacement approach for three and five years.

Using IT to automate jobs 3 years Cost displacement	All costs in 000s			
	Year 0	Year 1	Year 2	Year 3
Set up costs				
Hardware – PCs, LANs and other peripherals	125			
Software – spreadsheet, word processing, database, etc.	98			
Training	75			
Installation and testing	52			
Total	**350**			
Monthly on-going costs				
Staffing, including support		28	29	31
Maintenance and upgrades		20	21	22
General		8	8	9
Total		**56**	**59**	**62**
Monthly benefits				
Reduction in clerical salaries		42	44	46
Reduction in supervisory salaries		8	8	9
Reduction in other staff costs		13	14	14
Office space released		5	5	6
Other office expenses saved		3	3	3
Total		**71**	**75**	**78**
Improvement per month		15	16	17
Annual net benefit	−350	180	189	198
Simple annual ROI		51%	54%	57%
Simple payback		2	Years	
Cost of capital	20%			
Discounted annual net benefit	−350	150	131	115
Discounted payback		3	Years	
Net present value		46.09		
Internal rate of return		28%		
Profitability index		1.13		

Figure 7.3: The cost displacement approach – 3 years

Using IT to automate jobs 5 Years Cost displacement	All costs in 000's					
	Year 0	Year 1	Year 2	Year 3	Year 4	Year 5
Set up costs						
Hardware – PCs, LANs and other peripherals	125					
Software – spreadsheet, word processing, database, etc.	98					
Training	75					
Installation and testing	52					
Total	**350**					
Monthly on-going costs						
Staffing, including support		28	29	31	32	34
Maintenance and upgrades		20	21	22	23	24
General		8	8	9	9	10
Total		**56**	**59**	**62**	**65**	**68**
Monthly benefits						
Reduction in clerical salaries		42	44	46	49	51
Reduction in supervisory salaries		8	8	9	9	10
Reduction in other staff costs		13	14	14	15	16
Office space released		5	5	6	6	6
Other office expenses saved		3	3	3	3	4
Total		**71**	**75**	**78**	**82**	**86**
Net improvement per month		15	16	17	17	18
Annual net benefit	–350	180	189	198	208	219
Simple annual ROI		51%	54%	57%	60%	63%
Simple payback		2	Years			
Cost of capital	20%					
Discounted annual net benefit	–350	150	131	115	100	88
Discounted payback		3	Years			
Net present value		235				
Internal rate of return		47%				
Profitability Index		1.67				

Figure 7.4: Cost displacement over five years

There is considerable debate as to whether IT investments should be planned on a three, five or even seven-year horizon. Some organisations use a three-year period for personal computers, a five-year period for mid-range systems and a six or seven-year period for mainframes. However, a growing number of practitioners believe that three to five years is the maximum period for which IT should be planned. This, however, does produce problems for some large-scale systems that can take three years to develop. Obviously in such cases a longer time horizon would need to be used.

7.7 Cost avoidance

Figure 7.5 is an example of cost avoidance analysis for five-year investment.

Using IT to automate jobs 5 Years Cost avoidance	Year 0	All costs in 000's				
		Year 1	Year 2	Year 3	Year 4	Year 5
Set up costs						
Hardware	345					
Software	299					
Training	345					
Installation and testing	179					
Total	**1168**					
Monthly on-going costs						
Staffing, including support		55	58	61	64	67
Maintenance and upgrades		78	82	86	90	95
General		44	46	49	51	53
Total		**177**	**186**	**195**	**205**	**215**
Monthly benefits						
Staff not required		120	126	132	139	146
Other costs avoided		85	89	94	98	103
Total		**205**	**215**	**226**	**237**	**249**
Improvement per month		28	29	31	32	34
Annual net benefit		336	353	370	389	408
Annual ROI		29%	30%	32%	33%	35%
Simple payback		3	Years			
Cost of capital	20%					
Discounted annual net benefit	−1168	280	245	214	188	164
Net present value		(484.05)				
Internal rate of return		-2%				
Profitability Index		0.59				

Figure 7.5: The cost avoidance approach

A cost avoidance analysis is similar to cost displacement, except that no cost has been removed from the system because the introduction of the IS has prevented cost from being incurred. Cost avoidance, like cost displacement is typically used in the more traditional data processing environments and is generally less relevant to more modern IT applications. Thus, cost avoidance is most appropriate in automate systems.

7.8 Decision analysis

Decision analysis attempts to evaluate the benefits that can be derived from better information, which is assumed to lead to better decisions. In turn, better decisions are believed to lead to better performance. As it is hard to define good information, let alone good decisions, cost benefit analysis performed using this method is difficult.

Decision analysis is a classic informate situation and requires a financial value to be associated with information. In some cases, it is relatively easy to measure the effect of information, although there will frequently be considerable noise in the environment that can obscure the effects of the system. The key to decision analysis is to perform rigorous business analysis of the situation before the introduction of the proposed technology. The types of business relationships at work and their effects on each other must be understood. Also how the proposed IS will disrupt these business relationships, hopefully in a positive way, needs to be explained. A model of how information is used in the organisation to make decisions and how these decisions impact upon actions, which in turn affect performance is useful when conducting decision analysis. Such a model is shown in Figure 7.6.

Figure 7.7 shows an example of decision analysis. This case relies on understanding how the organisation's credit control works, how the cash flow functions, and how investment availability impacts sales.

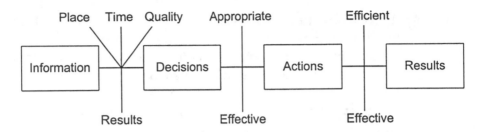

Figure 7.6: Decision analysis model

Using IT to improve performance through more information						
5 Years						
Decision analysis	*Year 0*	*Year 1*	*Year 2*	*Year 3*	*Year 4*	*Year 5*
Set up costs						
Hardware	555					
Software	450					
Initial training	250					
Commissioning	150					
Installation and testing	300					
Total	**1705**					
Monthly on-going costs						
Staffing, including support		292	307	322	338	355
On-going training		50	53	55	58	61
Maintenance and upgrades		95	100	105	110	115
General		120	126	132	139	146
Total		**557**	**585**	**614**	**645**	**677**
Monthly benefits						
Reduction in bad debts		25	25	25	25	25
Interest earned by faster receipts		50	53	55	58	61
Reduction in obsolete inventories		120	126	132	139	146
Increased sales – better availability		430	452	474	498	523
Total		**625**	**655**	**687**	**720**	**754**
Improvement per month		68	70	72	75	77
Annual net benefit	−1705	816	842	869	897	927
Annual ROI		48%	49%	51%	53%	54%
Simple payback		2	Years			
Cost of capital	20%					
Discounted annual net benefit		680	585	503	433	373
Net present value		2573				
Internal rate of return		41%				
Profitability index		2				

Figure 7.7: An example of decision analysis

7.9 Impact or time release analysis

Impact analysis attempts to quantify the effect IT can have on the physical performance of employees. Impact analysis may have elements of automate, informate and even transformate, depending on the exact circumstances involved. Figure 7.8 shows an example of impact analysis.

Using IT to improve salespersons' productivity *Investment costs for 10 systems*	All costs in 000s
PCs, cellular modems and peripherals	125
Software	23
Training	30
Installation and testing	60
Total initial cost	**238**
Monthly On-Going Costs	
Staffing, including support	10
Communications costs	2
Maintenance	5
General	3
Amortisation	6
Total monthly costs	**26**
Monthly benefit analysis	
Average no. of sales calls per day	6
Average value of sales per call	1.70
Reduction in average sales call time from 35 to 15 minutes	20
Reduction in time for daily form filling from 60 to 10 minutes	50
Total time release in minutes (50+(6 x 20))	**170**
Average travel time required between sales calls	25
Average increase in sales calls is therefore	3
Monthly revenue analysis	
Resulting additional revenue (3 x 1.5)	5.10
Profit margin %	4.00%
Daily profit improvement from 10 systems	0.20
Profit improvement per salesperson (22 days per month)	4.49
Annual profit improvement	539
Annual operating cost of system	312
Annual net benefit	227
ROI	95%
Payback	1 Year

Figure 7.8: An example of impact analysis

The primary benefit of time release is that staff can do other work, and when this leads to acquiring extra sales it can contribute to transforming the business.

7.10 How to put a financial estimate to an intangible benefit

A typical intangible IT benefit is the ability of management to perform what-if analysis on financial plans and budgets. More information of this type is clearly advantageous and valuable to management, but it is difficult to associate a particular financial value with this type of benefit.

There are two and only two ways of evaluating intangible benefits. The first approach is by negotiation and the second approach is by imputation.

The first step in evaluating this type of benefit is to ask the managers who are using a facility to place a value on it. For example, ' would you pay £10 for this report' ? If the answer is yes, then the next question might be ' would you pay £10,000 for this report?' If the answer is no, then a binary search can be conducted to find the value of the facility to the user between these two numbers. A binary search refers to a computer algorithm, which in this context would involve adding the first suggested amount, i.e. £10 to the second suggested amount, i.e. £10,000 and then dividing the sum by two. The resulting number of £5005 would then be suggested to the manager as the value of the facility. If this number is rejected because it is still considered to be high, the £5005 will be added to the £10 and again divided by two. This would result in an offer of £2507. If, however, the £5005 were considered to be too low then it would be added to the £10,000 and the resulting £15,005 divided by two. In this case the resulting offer would be £7502. The binary reduction process continues until an amount is accepted. The value so derived may be considered as the size of the intangible benefit. Of course, this approach produces a subjective evaluation of the benefit. However, it does result in an actual value as opposed to a simple comfort statement, and the number can be used in a cost benefit analysis calculation to see if the investment makes sense. This approach might be considered to be semi-hard or semi-soft analysis and is sometimes referred to as benefit negotiation.

7.11 Transformate analysis

The type of analysis used to assess a transformate opportunity is the same as that analysis employed for any strategic investment. Strategic investments often involve many considerations that are particularly difficult to quantify. Issues such as competitive advantage, market share, and new product development are just a few examples. Strategic investments are frequently considered so important that a full ex-ante cost justification cannot be undertaken, or if it is, the results of the analysis are simply ignored. Statements such as ' it' s too important to ignore' or ' the cost of not doing it will be crippling' are frequently heard in association with strategic investments. Therefore, strategic investment appraisal studies will often contain more words than numbers. The descriptive part of the proposal will contain words such as those shown in Figure 7.9.

1	This investment represents an attractive opportunity for the organisation to penetrate a new and profitable market
2	The demand in the new market is likely to increase at a compound rate of 25% p.a. for the rest of the decade.
3	The new production facility will substantially reduce our costs so we will be able to undercut our nearest competitors.
4	Client service will improve substantially.

Figure 7.9: Strategic considerations

Good practice, however, requires some numeric analysis to be performed. As transformate or strategic investments will have a longer time implication than efficiency or effectiveness investments, the simple ROI and payback methods are not adequate.

The time value of money-based techniques such as discounted cash flow need to be used.

7.12 Ex-post investment evaluation

This is the most difficult aspect of cost benefit analysis and the choice of evaluation technique depends on the type of ex-ante analysis being used. An example of cost displacement ex-post evaluation may be seen in Figure 7.10.

Using IT to improve performance through more information	All costs in 000s				
Transformation project - 4 Years	Year 0	Year 1	Year 2	Year 3	Year 4
Set up costs					
Hardware	990				
Software	876				
Re-organisation costs	700				
Initial training	450				
Commissioning	555				
Total initial costs	**3571**				
Annual on-going IT costs of project					
Staff	340				
Maintenance	172				
General	38				
Amortisation	900				
Total on-going costs	**1450**				
Annual Benefits					
Additional sales		2700	3510	4563	5932
Cost of sale		2750	2819	2889	2961
Net profit		−50	691	1674	2970
Tax		0	207	502	891
After tax profit		−50	484	1172	2079
Amortisation		900	900	900	900
Net cash flow	−3571	850	1384	2072	2979
Cost of capital	15%				
Tax rate	30%				
Economic life of the project	4				
Net present value	1280				
Internal rate of return	28%				
Profitability index	1.36				

Figure 7.10: A cost benefit analysis for a transformate proposal

Cost displacement cases might allow actual data to be captured from the accounting system and these figures can then be used for evaluation. The relevant actual data will be the difference between the old-recorded values and the new-recorded values.

7.13 Processes for business case accounting or financial analysis

Traditional cost benefit analysis is undertaken using discounted cash flow techniques involving estimates of the investment amount, the annual benefits and the cost of capital. All these variables are difficult to estimate. However, the cost of the organisation's capital is frequently considered the most difficult variable to determine. The rate of interest the organisation pays on its debt, or an arbitrarily chosen hurdle or discount rate is sometimes used as a surrogate for the cost of capital.

IT systems evaluation can be undertaken in several different ways using a variety of measures and at least two different processes. The two processes discussed here are the *deterministic* approach using single-point estimates for the input values and generating a single estimate for the result, and the *stochastic* approach which uses ranges as input and generates a range of results. The stochastic method is sometimes referred to as *simulation* or *risk analysis* and is discussed in Chapter 8.

Deterministic analysis assumes a certain world where the exact value of input variables can be known. Once the values of these inputs are entered, a unique result, determined by the logic of the algorithm and the precise data, is calculated. Because ex-ante investment analysis exclusively uses estimates of future values for the investment amount in the form of the on-going costs and the benefits, it is frequently said that as soon as the single point values are determined, the input and output will be wrong.

7.14 Deterministic analysis

Figure 7.11 is the input form of a deterministic model for capital investment appraisal in a spreadsheet. All the data are single point estimates.

Capital investment appraisal system A deterministic model	Cash-out	Cash-in			
IT investment – cash out	350,000				
Net IT benefits: Year 1		60,000			
Year 2		95,000			
Year 3		120,000			
Year 4		180,000			
Year 5		200,000			
Fixed cost of capital or interest rate	20.00%				
	Y1	Y2	Y3	Y4	Y5
Inflation adjusted interest rates	25%	29%	30%	35%	40%

Figure 7.11: Input form for a deterministic model

The use of inflation-adjusted cash flow techniques requires that all figures used actually represent cash dispensed or received by the organisation. Therefore, profit figures that include non-cash items such as depreciation or reserves should not be included. Figure 7.12 is an investment report based on the input in Figure 7.11, which shows a number of different investment measures including payback, NPV, PI, IRR, etc.

An important feature of this spreadsheet model is the use of variable costs of capital or interest rates. These interest rates can be used to reflect either anticipated rates of inflation, or more generally, to account for an increasing risk profile. The further into the future the estimated benefit the greater the degree of uncertainty or risk, and therefore the higher the discount or interest rate associated with the investment. The high interest rate has the effect of reducing the future value of the benefit.

Investment reports on IT System				
Payback in years and months	3	years	5	months
Rate of return (%)	37.43%			
NPV at a fixed discount rate (FDR)	2,598			
Profitability index (PI) – FDR	1.01			
Internal rate of return (IRR)	20.28%			
Varlable Discount Rates				
NPV at variable discount rates (VDR)	−71,754			
PI – VDR	0.79			
Discounted payback FDR in years and months	4	years	11	months

Figure 7.12: Results produced by the deterministic model

The results in Figure 7.12 are, of course, highly dependent upon the assumptions made concerning the cost of capital, the investment amount and the annual cash flows. As these future estimates are always uncertain it is useful to perform what-if analysis on these assumptions. The table in Figure 7.13 is sometimes referred to as a what-if table and is built into the functionality of most if not all spreadsheets. It indicates the way in which the NPV and the PI varies in relationship to the cost of capital.

FDR	NPV	PI
10%	120,342	1.34
12%	92,597	1.26
14%	67,176	1.19
16%	43,839	1.13
18%	22,375	1.06
20%	2,598	1.01
22%	−15,656	0.96
24%	−32,533	0.91
26%	−48,162	0.86
28%	−62658	0.82
30%	−76124	0.78

Figure 7.13: Effect of changing fixed cost of capital on the NPV and PI

The table in Figure 7.14 shows the combined effect of differing investment amounts and different fixed costs of capital on the NPV of the project.

FDR	Investment amount				
2,598	200,000	250,000	300,000	350,000	400,000
10%	270,342	220,342	170,342	120,342	70,342
12%	242,597	192,597	142,597	92,597	42,597
14%	217,176	167,176	117,176	67,176	17,176
16%	193,839	143,839	93,839	43,839	−6,161
18%	172,375	122,375	72,375	22,375	−27,625
20%	152,598	102,598	52,598	2,598	−47,402
22%	134,344	84,344	34,344	−15,656	−65,656
24%	117,467	67,467	17,467	−32,533	−82,533
26%	101,838	51,838	1,838	−48,162	−98,162
28%	87,342	37,342	−12,658	−62,658	−112,658
30%	73,876	23,876	−26,124	−76,124	−126,124

Figure 7.14: Effect of varying the fixed cost of capital and the investment amount on the NPV

Looking at this table it can be seen for example that with an investment of 300,000 and a cost of capital of 22% the resulting NPV will be 34,344.

The use of the what-if tables can provide considerable insight as to how the project outcome can vary if the input factors change.

7.15 Summary

There are a number of different approaches to business case accounting or cost benefit analysis that range from single point estimate techniques to rather sophisticated risk or stochastic analysis. In developing an IT investment business case it is important to choose the appropriate level of sophistication and not to spend an excessive amount of time on the financial numbers.

In some cases, where the amounts are small, it may not be necessary to perform any business case accounting or cost benefit analysis at all.

Business case accounting is only at best a part of the IT investment business case and as such needs to be seen as a supporting tool to the main justification of the IT investment proposal.

8 | Risk analysis

The computer press is littered with examples of information technology fiascos or near disasters. An example is the computer aided dispatch system introduced into the London Ambulance Service in 1992. The £1.5 million system was bought into full use at 07:00 hours on 26 October and almost immediately began to 'lose' ambulances. During that and the next day less than 20% of ambulances reached their destinations within 15 minutes of being summoned, a very poor performance when compared with the 65% arriving within 15 minutes the previous May and the target set by the Government of 95%. The service reverted to semi-computerized methods during the afternoon of 27 October and then right back to manual methods on 4 November when the system locked up altogether and could not be re-booted successfully (South West Thames Regional Health Authority, 1993)

Joyce Fortune and Geoff Peters, *Learning from Failure: The Systems Approach* (1995)

8.1 Introduction

Risk analysis, attempts to accommodate the inherent variability in the input estimates and produces a result that more closely reflects the level of uncertainty frequently experienced in the real world.

In situations where uncertainty is small, deterministic models can provide suitable solutions. However, it is more likely that uncertainty in the input variables, evidenced by their variability, is likely to relatively high and therefore this uncertainty will have to be taken into consideration.

Specifying a probability distribution for each of the input variables – such as investment, cash flows, and cost of capital – can capture this uncertainty. There are many candidate probability distributions that can be usefully employed for this purpose.

Some of the more useful distributions are likely to be the uniform, the triangular and the beta.

Operationalisation of the above uses the Monte Carlo method. This involves generating a range[1] of outcomes for the input variables, e.g. investment, described by some specified probability distribution, and then evaluating the behaviour of an associated output variable, e.g. internal rate of return. The Monte Carlo method can also be used to establish how robust and sensitive the outcomes are with respect to the assumptions concerning the input variable(s).

For more on the properties of a number of probability distributions, and guidance on how to generate random samples from these distributions, see Johnson and Kotz (1970) and Gonin and Money (1989). Also within all major spreadsheets there is a facility to create these types of distributions.

---

[1] Peter Drucker in describing the use of ranges in accounting has recalled the following anecdote 'When I started work in 1927 with a very old and prosperous cotton exporter in Hamburg, most businesses did not have double entry book-keeping. It was introduced at the organisation by the chief book-keeper. The boss never accepted it. He said: "If I want to know where we stand, I stay behind on Saturday and count the petty cash. That's real. The rest is allocations." He had a point. When I went to London to work for a small investment bank. I was taught by my boss, who was a very old shrewd banker, always to begin with cash flow. He argued it was the only thing that even the smartest accountant couldn't fudge. Proper accounting on these lines only came in after the Second World War, with the flow of funds statement. The next step could be a comparable statement of the investment flow and productivity of knowledge. I've toyed with that, but I didn't work it up. I'm not saying I could. There are problems in putting numerical value on it. I think it would be the first statement to use ranges, not precise figures. I believe that if accounting hadn't been invented 700 years ago – if we had waited until the 18th century – most of our accounts would show ranges. We now know how to handle plus-or-minus probabilities. The accountant's figure for receivables is basically a mid-point between guesses.' (Drucker, *Financial Times*, 10 April 1999)

The risk of an investment is the potential of input/output variables to fluctuate from their original estimates. As in the vast majority of cases, input/output variables do fluctuate, and risk analysis accommodates this by allowing ranges, rather than single point estimates, to be used. It is generally much easier to confidently state that an investment will be between 200,000 and 300,000 than it will be 250,000.

There are a variety of techniques available to assist management and other risk assessors in evaluating the extent and the size of the risk inherent in a particular investment. There are at least three generic approaches to identifying and assessing risk. These are:

♦ Group brainstorming

♦ Expert judgement

♦ Assumption analysis.

Group brainstorming uses group interaction to identify the variables that carry the most exposure to variability. Once the variables have been identified, the group then attempts to quantify the limits of the variability as well as the probability associated with the range of possible inputs and outputs. Brainstorming groups may meet several times before the estimates of the variables are finalised.

Expert judgement uses experienced individuals who are aware of the factors causing the investment potential to vary. This is the quickest and easiest way of identifying risk, but considerable care must be given to choosing the expert.

Assumption analysis requires the detailed questioning of each assumption. This analysis requires each assumption to be modified in such a way that those circumstances that are disadvantageous to the investment will be evaluated. The effects of the changes in assumptions are then used as part of the range of variable specification.

A useful tool in assessing different types of risk is the influence diagram. An influence diagram is a perceptual map showing concepts or issues to illustrate how different aspects of a proposed investment may interact with each other, causing variability in the input/output estimates.

8.1.1 Influence diagrams

An influence diagram allows all the related concepts and issues to be mapped showing the interconnections between them. Such conceptual mapping can be used to quickly identify areas of high variability, which are those with a high number of interconnections. This technique is especially useful for facilitating creative thinking in the search for the identification and quantification of risk. Figure 8.1 shows an influence diagram illustrating nine possible factors that directly or indirectly affect sales volumes.

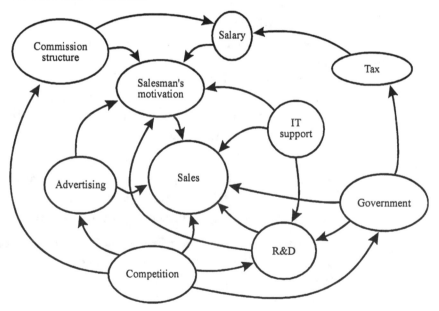

Figure 8.1: An influence diagram

However, after the conceptual map has been developed it is then necessary to debate the size of the potential fluctuations in the variables. Bringing together a group of experienced managers and discussing the likely value of each factor can achieve this. At the conclusion of such a debate, maximum and minimum values should be established for sales, costs, prices, assets, cash flows, etc.

8.2 Using spreadsheets for risk analysis

The spreadsheet is a useful tool for performing financial risk analysis for IS development projects. Figure 8.2 shows the results of a capital investment appraisal model. This is the same model that was used in Chapter 7 to illustrate deterministic business case accounting.

	A	B	C	D	E	F	G
1	Capital Investment Appraisal System						
2	A deterministic model						
3		Cash-Out	Cash-In	Net Cash Movement each year			
4	IT Investment - Cash Out	350,000			-350000		
5	Net IT Benefits	Year 1	66106		66106		
6		Year 2	99902		99902		
7		Year 3	120901		120901		
8		Year 4	194590		194590		
9		Year 5	249671		249671		
10	Fixed Cost of Capital or Interest Rate	25%					
11							
12			Y1	Y2	Y3	Y4	Y5
13	Forecast inflation rates		22.00%	30.00%	37.00%	40.00%	42.00%
14							
15	Investment Reports on IT System						
16	Payback in years & months		3	years	4	months	
17	Rate of return(%)		41.78%				
18	N P V Fixed Discount Rate (FDR)		-9760				
19	Profitability Index FDR (PI)		0.97				
20	Internal Rate of Return (IRR)		23.91%				
21	Variable Discount Rates						
22	N P V Variable Discount Rates (VDR)		-55414				
23	Profitability Index VDR (PI)		0.84				
24	Discounted Payback FDR in years and months		5	years	1	months	

Figure 8.2: A capital investment appraisal spreadsheet model

The model in Figure 8.2 has been developed using deterministic logic. This means that single-point estimates have been made for all the input values from which the output is calculated.

Risk management, by its very nature, suggests that the single-point estimate approach that is normally used in evaluating information system investments is not adequate. The single-point estimate, or deterministic approach, assumes that all cost and benefit estimates are known with certainty. Clearly this is seldom ever the case in reality. When risk management is being applied this lack of accuracy is admitted and cost estimates and revenue estimates are expressed, not as single points but as ranges of values (Nugus 1997).

Figure 8.3 considers an investment for which the actual amount to be invested, the precise benefits to be derived and the interest rates are not known. However it is known that the investment amount will be between £350,000 and £400,000. Similarly the IT benefits for years 1 to 5 have also been entered into the spreadsheet as ranges, for example in year 1 the minimum benefit is estimated at £65,000 and the maximum value of the benefit is stated at £75,000. Similarly, the exact rate of interest is not known, but it is estimated at between 20% and 30% per annum.

By recalculating the spreadsheet thousands or even tens of thousands of times using values between the specified maximum and minimum, different outcomes will be obtained. Due to the uncertainty of exactly what the actual costs and benefits will be it is important to recalculate the model a large number of times. By so doing, a large number of different combinations of costs and benefits are selected. It is then by analysing the large number of different outcomes that an understanding of the probable results of the investment can be seen (Nugus 1997).

	A	B	C	D	E	F	G	H	I	J	K	L	M
1	Input form for Risk Analysis												
2				Minimum	Maximum								
3	IT Investment - Cash Out			350000	400000								
4													
5	Net IT Benefits	Year 1		65000	75000								
6		Year 2		100000	110000								
7		Year 3		125000	135000								
8		Year 4		185000	205000								
9		Year 5		205000	255000								
10													
11	Fixed Cost of Capital			20.00%	30.00%								
12													
13	Inflation adjusted cost of capital			Y1 Min	Y1 Max	Y2 Min	Y2 Max	Y3 Min	Y3 Max	Y4 Min	Y4 Max	Y5 Min	Y5 Max
14				20%	25%	30%	35%	35%	40%	40%	45%	45%	50%
15													
16													
17	Select variable to report				NPV (FDR)								
18	with an X in the appropriate box			X	IRR								
19					NPV (VDR)								
20													
21				N.B. You must mark ONLY ONE box with an upper case X									

Figure 8.3: Risk analysis input form

Figure 8.4 is a results scenario for the internal rate of return using the input data in Figure 8.3 and Figure 8.5 shows the results graphically.

Summary statistics for	IRR
Mean	0.204
Standard deviation	0.016
Range	0.078
Minimum	0.163
Maximum	0.241
No. of recalculations	2000

Figure 8.4: Summary results for risk analysis on IRR

The data used in Figure 8.3 to produce the results in Figures 8.4 and 8.5 would be regarded as being of relatively low risk.[2] The reason for this is that the most likely outcome is a return of 20% with a standard deviation of 1.6%.

---

[2] This view of risk is of course contingent upon the rate being at least as big as the organisation's standard hurdle rate.

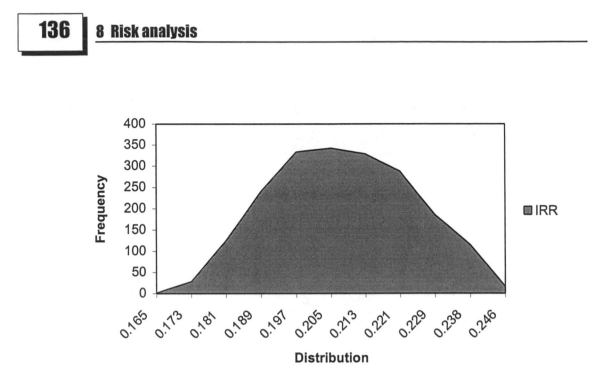

Figure 8.5: Graphical representation of risk analysis results for IRR

This means that even if all the most unfavourable estimates occur, i.e. maximum investment costs, lowest benefits and highest cost of capital, the investment is still expected to produce an IRR of 16%. On the positive side, if the investment is kept low and the highest benefits are achieved, then the investment could produce a return as high as 24%.

A different set of input data can of course produce quite a different scenario. Figure 8.6 shows a different set of data and Figures 8.7 and 8.8 show the result of the risk analysis using the NPV as the outcome variable.

	A	B	C	D	E	F	G	H	I	J	K	L	M
1	Input form for Risk Analysis												
2				Minimum	Maximum								
3	IT Investment - Cash Out			450000	600000								
4													
5	Net IT Benefits	Year 1		60000	80000								
6		Year 2		85000	115000								
7		Year 3		120000	140000								
8		Year 4		170000	210000								
9		Year 5		200000	260000								
10													
11	Fixed Cost of Capital			15.00%	40.00%								
12													
13	Inflation adjusted cost of capital			Y1 Min	Y1 Max	Y2 Min	Y2 Max	Y3 Min	Y3 Max	Y4 Min	Y4 Max	Y5 Min	Y5 Max
14				20%	25%	30%	35%	35%	40%	40%	45%	45%	50%
15													
16													
17	Select variable to report			X	NPV (FDR)								
18	with an X in the appropriate box				IRR								
19					NPV (VDR)								
20													
21			N.B. You must mark ONLY ONE box with an upper case X										
22													

Figure 8.6: Different set of input data

Summary statistics for	NPV (FDR)
Mean	−197,123
Standard deviation	74,201
Range	364,181
Minimum	−359,200
Maximum	4,981
No. of recalculations	2,000

Figure 8.7: Summary results of risk analysis on NPV

The example used to produce the results shown in Figures 8.7 and 8.8 would be regarded as a relatively high risk. The most likely outcome of this investment is an NPV of around −197,000, which of course is unsatisfactory and would suggest that it is inappropriate to proceed with the investment under these terms. In fact the worst scenario is an NPV of. −359,200. However, it is possible, with a favourable discount rate and good annual net benefits, for this investment to return a positive NPV of 4,981. This variability is the risk.

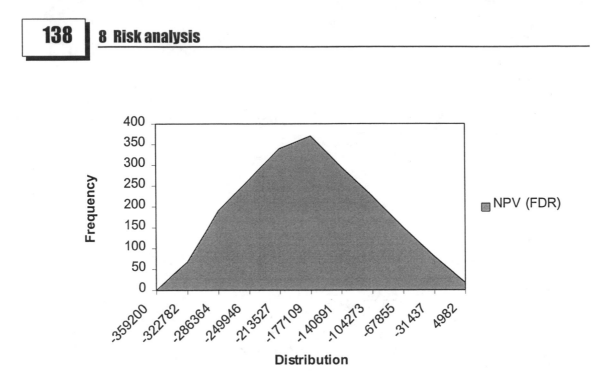

Figure 8.8: Graphical representation of risk analysis results on NPV

8.3 Worked examples

The following is a worked example financial risk analysis in the IS risk management process. It describes an organisation where there is a considerable degree of uncertainty about both the costs and the benefits that will be derived from the IS investment.

Continental Products Limited were considering the acquisition of a new information system. After considerable discussion the IS staff produced the following cost estimates for hardware, software and commissioning.

1 The hardware cost will be between 400K and 900K.

2 The software costs are estimated at between 350K and 500K.

3 The commissioning costs will be between 200K and 300K.

It was thought that there was an equal probability that the actual costs would be anywhere between the highest and the lowest estimates. Thus the probability distribution is said to be uniform or rectangular. A similar set of assumptions was employed to establish the ongoing costs and the benefits to be derived from the information system.

The four columns in Figure 8.9 reflect the possible values for the three cost variables. The *lowest* and the *highest* columns are self-explanatory. The *average-ML* (where ML is the *Most Likely*) column is the mid-point between the Lowest and Highest values. The *risk data* column is calculated with the spreadsheet RAND() function and generates a random number between the lowest and highest values.

Capital investment appraisal for Continental Products Ltd				
Costs in 000s	Lowest	Highest	Average-M L	Risk data
Hardware	400	900	650	706
Software	350	500	425	406
Commissioning	200	300	250	238
Total	950	1700	1325	1350

Figure 8.9: Cost estimates using the deterministic and stochastic measures

The operations director at Continental was especially concerned about how long it would take for the benefits to appear. It was at his insistence the stakeholders agreed that there would be no benefits in the first year and that there might not be any benefits even in the second year. The stakeholders debated the benefits issue for several days before finally agreeing to the following estimates of benefits:

1 In the first year after implementation the organisation believes that there is little likelihood of the benefit exceeding the ongoing costs. Thus, the net benefit is estimated at zero.

2 For the second year the system is expected to produce up to 100K of benefits, although there are some members of staff who believe that the system will only produce net positive benefits in the third year.

3 In year 3 the benefits will be between 450K and 650K and in year 4 they will be between 850K and 100K.

4 In year 5 the benefits are to be fixed at 1500K.

5 The organisation's cost of capital is at present 25% and it is believed that over the next five years it will fluctuate between 20% and 30%.

6 The stakeholders were not able to agree on the economic life of the project. Everyone agreed that the system would still be operational in five years' time, but certain members believed that an IT investment should be fully amortised in no more than three years. Other stakeholders suggested that a seven-year approach should be taken, as there was little likelihood of any real benefits in the first or second year.

7 The stakeholders agreed that the NPV should be the primary measure by which the investment will be judged. However, they all unanimously wanted to know what the IRR and also the discounted payback would be.

Figure 8.10 has been created in a similar way to Figure 8.9, but reflects the possible values for the benefits over the five years and Figure 8.11 shows the estimated cost of capital.

Benefits in 000s	Lowest	Highest	Average-M L	Risk data
Year 1	0	0	0	0
Year 2	100	100	100	100
Year 3	450	650	550	467
Year 4	850	1100	975	923
Year 5	1500	1500	1500	1500

Figure 8.10: Five year benefit estimates using deterministic and stochastic measures

Cost of capital	Lowest	Highest	Average-M L	Risk data
	20%	30%	25%	27%

Figure 8.11: Cost of capital estimates using deterministic and stochastic measures

The capital investment appraisal analysis in Figure 8.12 shows four sets of calculations.

Capital investment appraisal for Continental Products Ltd						
Scenario 1						
Cash flows	YR0	YR1	YR2	YR3	YR4	YR5
(Most likely)	−1325	0	100	550	975	1500
Cum. cash flow	−1325	−1325	−1225	−675	300	1800
Year number	0	1	2	3	4	5
NPV	−88					
IRR	23%					
Payback in year	4					
Scenario 2	YR0	YR1	YR2	YR3	YR4	YR5
(Worst scenario)	−1700	0	100	450	850	1500
Cum. cash flow	−1700	−1700	−1600	−1150	−300	1200
Year number	0	1	2	3	4	5
NPV	−4,259					
IRR	13%					
Payback	>5 years					
Scenario 3	YR0	YR1	YR2	YR3	YR4	YR5
(Best scenario)	−950	0	100	650	1100	1500
Cum. cash flow	−950	−950	−850	−200	900	2400
Year number	0	1	2	3	4	5
NPV	628					
IRR	36%					
Payback in year	4					
Scenario 4	YR0	YR1	YR2	YR3	YR4	YR5
(Risk analysis)	−1350	0	100	467	923	1500
Cum. cash flow	−1350	−1350	−1250	−783	139	1639
Year number	0	1	2	3	4	5
NPV	−31.86					
IRR	21%					
Payback in year	4					

Figure 8.12: Estimates of the performance of the investment using most likely, best and worst projections as well as risk analysis

Scenario 1 in Figure 8.12 represents the possible outcome if the average or most likely numbers are achieved. In terms of the NPV these calculations show a result that does not earn an adequate return to justify proceeding with the investment. One way of interpreting this is that the cost of capital the organisation needs to earn is higher than the IRR that it appears the investment can generate.

Scenario 2 represents the possible outcome if the worst numbers are achieved, i.e. the highest cost and the lowest benefits and the highest cost of capital. In terms of the NPV these calculations show a very poor result, which clearly does not earn an adequate return to justify proceeding with the investment.

Scenario 3 represents the possible outcome if the best numbers are achieved, i.e. the lowest cost and the highest benefits and the lowest cost of capital. In terms of the NPV these calculations show a good result, which does earn an adequate return to justify proceeding with the investment.

Scenario 4 is a risk analysis, showing the possible outcome using randomly generated numbers between the best and worst case scenarios. In terms of the NPV these calculations show a good result, which does earn an adequate return to justify proceeding with the investment. This data can be used to perform a simulation based on 5000 reiterations; the summary statistics for which are shown in Figure 8.13.

Summary statistics for	NPV
Mean	−82
Standard error	3
Median	−86
Standard deviation	199
Sample variance	39,580
Range	1,099
Minimum	−620
Maximum	479
Sum	−408,897
Count	5,000

Figure 8.13: The statistical results of the risk simulation

The result of this analysis is likely to be regarded as unsatisfactory as the most likely outcome is an NPV of −82. This can be clearly seen in the graph in Figure 8.14.

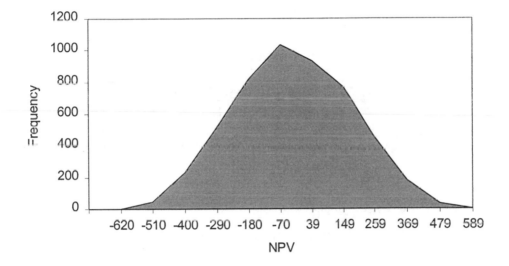

Figure 8.14: The graphical results of the risk simulation

8.3.1 Re-examining the input assumptions

At this stage, from a risk management perspective the task is to return to the original estimates and to attempt to question each of the values. The aim is to see if there is a way of reducing the costs and increasing the benefits in absolute terms, as well as looking for opportunities to reduce the potential variability in the estimates.

After further discussion with the stakeholders, the IS staff produced the following revised cost estimates for hardware, software and commissioning. It is believed that it will be possible to reduce the investment cost without materially affecting the benefit stream that is being left with the original estimated numbers. Thus the following estimates are now relevant for the investment:

1 The hardware cost will now be between 250K and 500K.

2 The software costs are now estimated at between 150K and 250K.

3 The commissioning costs will be unchanged between 200K and 300K.

These revised cost estimates are shown in Figure 8.15.

Capital investment appraisal for Continental Products Ltd				
Costs in 000s	Lowest	Highest	Average-M L	Risk data
Hardware	250	500	375	352
Software	150	250	200	152
Commissioning	200	300	250	216
Total	600	1050	825	720

Figure 8.15: The revised range of cost estimates

Using these assumptions the capital investment appraisal analysis can be performed again, where the NPV, the IRR and the payback are all recalculated. As can be seen from Figure 8.16 the IS investment opportunity now looks for more attractive.

It is important to note that the estimates of cost and benefit should not be lightly changed. If the stakeholders cannot find a reasonable cause for expecting to be able to reduce the cost, or increase the benefit, or reduce the variability in these estimates, then they should not be changed. Producing better figures for the sake of the financial analysis is simply a method of self-delusion.

The most likely, the best scenario and the risk analysis scenario all show improvement. However Scenario 2, which is the worst-case scenario, still shows a potential loss or negative NPV. Thus the IS project manager needs to pay careful attention to not operating near the parameters described by these circumstances. In general if any of the three positive scenarios can be achieved then the project will have been worthwhile.

Capital investment appraisal for Continental Products Ltd						
Scenario 1						
Cash flows	YR0	YR1	YR2	YR3	YR4	YR5
(Most likely)	–825	0	100	550	975	1500
Cum. cash flow	–825	–825	–725	–175	800	2300
Year number	0	1	2	3	4	5
NPV	411					
IRR	38%					
Payback in year	4					
Scenario 2	YR0	YR1	YR2	YR3	YR4	YR5
(Worst scenario)	–1050	0	100	450	850	1500
Cum. cash flow	–1050	–1050	–950	–500	350	1850
Year number	0	1	2	3	4	5
NPV	–2,026					
IRR	27%					
Payback	>5 years					
Scenario 3	YR0	YR1	YR2	YR3	YR4	YR5
(Best scenario)	–600	0	100	650	1100	1500
Cum. cash flow	–600	–600	–500	150	1250	2750
Year number	0	1	2	3	4	5
NPV	978					
IRR	53%					
Payback in year	3					
Scenario 4	YR0	YR1	YR2	YR3	YR4	YR5
(Risk analysis)	–729	0	100	506	944	1500
Cum. cash flow	–728	–728	–628	–122	821	2321
Year number	0	1	2	3	4	5
NPV	625					
IRR	41%					
Payback in year	3					

Figure 8.16: The revised range of investment statistics

Running the simulation again using the revised data produces the summary statistics in Figure 8.17, which further illustrates the improved projection for the IS investment, as does the graph displayed in Figure 8.18.

Summary statistics for	NPV
Mean	420
Standard error	2
Median	419
Standard deviation	148
Sample variance	22,019
Range	887
Minimum	−12
Maximum	876
Sum	2,101,617
Count	5000

Figure 8.17: The statistical results of the risk simulation using the revised data

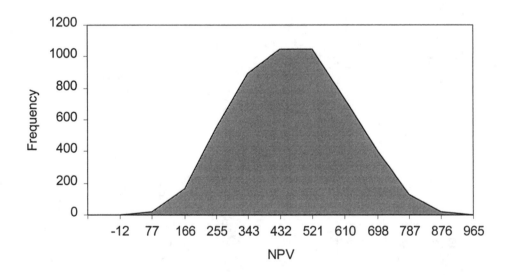

Figure 8.18: Graphical results of the risk simulation using the revised data

In addition to the estimates of the returns that will be achieved looking better in the second set of calculations, these figures also show a significant reduction in the risk profile faced by the IS development. This reduction in risk can be seen by looking at the relative range of numbers across the X-axis of the graphs in Figures 8.14 and 8.18, as well as sometimes by observing the relative shapes of the curves. In this respect the rule is that the narrower the curve the lower the risk. In addition the standard deviation, which is regarded as an important measure of risk, is 199 and 148 in the two cases. Thus the second set of projections show lower risk.

8.4 Financial risk review process

The process of stating assumptions and examining their financial implications by using stochastic type analysis as described in this chapter is very important for the better understanding of the costs and the benefits associated with an IS investment. However it is important to remember the words of Wittgenstein (1980) who said, 'Nothing is so difficult as not deceiving oneself'.

The numbers are only as good as the intentions and actions they represent, and a project with a great business case can fail just as quickly as one without any cost benefit analysis at all.

8.5 Summary

In the past it was difficult and expensive to perform sophisticated financial risk analysis whereas today it is inexpensive and relatively easy. Furthermore, historically there was very little understanding of how to use the output from financial risk analysis. Today there is a much greater awareness of how to uses the result of this type of thinking.

Thus in some respects this question could now be considered to be obsolete or at least on the verge of obsolescence.

But on the other hand, there are many who would argue that information technology is so clearly a basic requirement for business that it is unnecessary to perform regular cost benefit analysis at all, never mind sophisticated financial risk analysis. Such an argument implies that IS are as essential to the organisation as an adequate telephone system.

Yet again, investment in IS developments still does not represent trivial amounts of money to most organisations and, therefore, should not be compared to telephones. In reality, unless some planning and estimating is done, management will never know how it is performing. And, therefore, even though the estimation and/or prediction of IS performance is imperfect, it is essential to perform these calculations to obtain some sort of indication of what might be expected. However, whatever method or metric is chosen it must be realised that it is likely to be no more than a subjective assessment with a low level of objectivity.

As a tool to aid the understanding of the project and its costs and benefits as well as a means of supporting IS project risk management the use of financial risk analysis is certainly a most useful device and it is simple enough that it should be used extensively. There are excellent software products available on the market today that will produce risk analysis. These are easy to use and inexpensive to purchase.

9 | Evaluation of the IT function

> Only two of the thirteen companies that participated in the study agree that their IS departments are critical to corporate success. The remaining eleven companies all see their IS department as a necessary, but burdensome, cost pit.

> Mary Lacity and Rudy Hirschheim, *Information Systems Outsourcing, Myths, Metaphors and Realities* (1995)

> Exploiting the informated environment means opening the information base of the organization to members at every level, assuring that each has the knowledge, skills and authority to engage with the information productively.

> Shoshana Zuboff, *The Emperor's New Workplace* (1995)

9.1 A holistic approach to IT function evaluation

The IT function of an organisation is involved in the development, implementation and maintenance of numerous systems. These systems aim to meet needs at all levels within the organisation. In evaluating the success or effectiveness of the IT department it is normally necessary to evaluate the performance of the individual systems, and then use the aggregate of the performances on the individual systems as an overall measure of the success or effectiveness of the IT department. Especially in organisations where there is a high degree of decentralisation of the IT function, the evaluation is not focused so much on the IT department but rather on the users of the information systems.

For the organisation's IT function to be managed successfully, management will need to have appropriate instruments whereby it can measure the effectiveness of IT within the organisation. In fact, recent surveys reveal that general management consider measurement of IT effectiveness a key issue. Unfortunately, there is little agreement on how to measure effectiveness.

The measurement problem is exacerbated by the many ways in which effectiveness may be viewed. For example, an IT department can be considered effective when it:

♦ Is meeting its objectives;

♦ Operates within its budgets;

♦ Delivers on time;

♦ Is a major catalyst in directing the firm's use of IT;

♦ Ensures that the firm is using IT competitively;

♦ Has a clearly understood role in the organisation;

♦ Is generally perceived to be an ally;

♦ Is at least as internally efficient as the industry average;

♦ Can deliver systems for no greater cost than they can be purchased in the open market;

♦ Is perceived by top management to be value for money and users believe that IT is being deployed in a way which supports their pursuit of excellence;

There is, however, one thing on which there is agreement, success is not necessarily reflected in the level of investment in IT.

Despite the obvious difficulty in measuring the effectiveness of the IT function, the fact that it is competing for resources with other functions, such as marketing, finance, production and so on, means it is essential that there are credible ways not only of identifying the benefits of the IT function, both 'hard' and 'soft', but also a means of measuring them.

9.2 Goal-centred vs systems' resources

There are basically two general views with respect to measuring IT effectiveness. These are the goal-centred view and the systems' resource view (Hamilton and Chervany 1981 (a) and (b)). In the goal-centred view we focus on the outcomes of the IT function. We determine the task objectives of the system and then establish the criteria for measuring whether these objectives have been achieved. In the systems' resource view we focus on the process or functional aspects of the system. In this case effectiveness is measured against such things as user job satisfaction, communication between IT staff and users, and quality of service.

Where the firm's task objectives or system resources are relatively obvious, and where intangible benefits play a relatively small role, direct physical measurements may be used to assess the effectiveness of the system. However, where complex situations are involved, simple techniques are no longer appropriate and perceptions become a critical part of the process for measuring the overall effectiveness of an information system.

In this chapter some significant contributions to the problem of measuring the effectiveness of management information systems (MIS) are reviewed. User information satisfaction (UIS) is recognised as an important indicator (surrogate) of MIS effectiveness. It is on this approach to the measurement problem that we now concentrate, and in particular on perceptual measures of UIS. This involves incorporating user feelings, beliefs, opinions and attitudes towards IT into the evaluation procedure.

In the context of IS effectiveness, it is generally believed that if users declare themselves to be satisfied with the system then the system may be said to be effective. Clearly, such satisfaction measurement is at best an indirect and relative measure, which must be used with considerable care. In some organisations users could be happy with inadequate systems. However, trends are the most important aspect.

9.3 Tangible vs intangible benefits

Thirty or so years ago the evaluation of the IT function was relatively straightforward. At this time computers were used to automate well-understood, well-structured office systems, thereby increasing efficiency through cost savings. These systems were used to perform time consuming accounting, stock control and wages tasks by operational staff. Traditional cost benefit and work-study methods for calculating the effectiveness of the IT function were adequate. The techniques used to perform cost benefit analysis included *cut-off period, payback period, discounted cash flow (DCF)* and *return on investment (ROI).*

Since then, new technology, particularly the advent of the microcomputer, has resulted in information technologies having progressed from the basic cost reduction and control type applications to the provision of decision support at the strategic level (Money *et al.* 1988). The influence of new technologies is, therefore, increasingly being felt at top management level.

This upward penetration of new information technologies raises issues that previously did not exist. In evaluating IS effectiveness we have to consider both the MIS and the environment within which it operates. Thus, broader organisation-wide issues have to be considered, and this includes behavioural aspects. A consequence is that there is a certain 'invisibility' associated with the contributions of the information systems to the effectiveness of the organisation as a whole. This invisibility is usually expressed by reference to intangible benefits. The traditional cost benefit approaches to evaluating effectiveness are now generally regarded as inadequate, especially when a holistic view of the firm is required.

More recent approaches account for the intangible benefits that tend to be overlooked by traditional cost benefit analysis (see

Chapter 7). These approaches incorporate user perceptions on a number of criteria relating to IS, into an overall measure of satisfaction with it. These include perceptions on numerous variables related to such things as input procedures, output procedures, computer processing capabilities, speed of response, quality of service, IS staff quality, availability of training, quality of documentation, and organisational factors such as top management involvement and user participation. These issues considered holistically, represent a framework that may be used to measure effectiveness.

9.4   User information satisfaction (UIS)

User satisfaction is generally considered to result from a comparison of user expectations (or needs) of the IS with the perceived performance (or capability) of the IS on a number of different facets of the IS. This is considered to be a holistic approach to systems effectiveness as it addresses the whole IS function rather than individual systems.

More specifically, overall attitude to the IS function can be considered to be influenced by the size and direction of the discrepancies (or gaps) between expectations and performance. A positive (negative) gap results when perceived performance exceeds (is below) expectation. A large 'positive' gap can be interpreted as indicating that IS resources are being wasted, whereas a large 'negative' gap indicates a need for improved performance.

A variant to the above approach is to use the correlation between expectations and performance scores as a measure of 'fit'. The correlations provide a means for assessing the overall effectiveness of the IS function, where high positive correlations can be taken to imply 'consensus' of views.

Of the many published papers on UIS two will be discussed in more detail below, namely, the Miller and Doyle (1987), and the Kim (1990) papers. Both these studies propose conceptual models to explain UIS, thereby adding credence to the instruments developed from them. These models have their roots in the theory of organisational and consumer behaviour. This is easy to comprehend if one accepts that the IS function impacts on the whole organisation and is aimed at satisfying the user (i.e. customer) who can be both internal as well as external to the organisation.

9.5   A gap approach to measurement

9.5.1   The Kim model

A feature of Kim's model is that UIS is considered to be influenced not only by post-implementation experience with the IS but also by pre-implementation expectations of the IS. The latter is captured through the user's initial expectations of the IS.

In this approach, UIS is measured by the discrepancy between the user's perception score of the IS performance and the user's expectation score of the IS. Further, the model describes how UIS is influenced by the discrepancies that arise during the developmental and service delivery processes. The developmental stage comprises two sub-stages, namely, the determination of the IS requirements and the design and installation of the IS. These various stages give rise to three gaps that influence the UIS. These gaps may in turn be influenced by various organisational factors. Examples include: user participation in defining the IS requirements; top management support which may take the form of increased investment in IS, thereby influencing the gap between the design specifications and the quality of the IS installed; and the extent of user training which is likely to impact on the gap between the actual quality of the IS installed and what the user perceives the quality to be through use of the system. There may also be other organisational factors which directly impact on the IS, rather than indirectly through the gaps. The Kim model is represented diagrammatically in Figure 9.1.

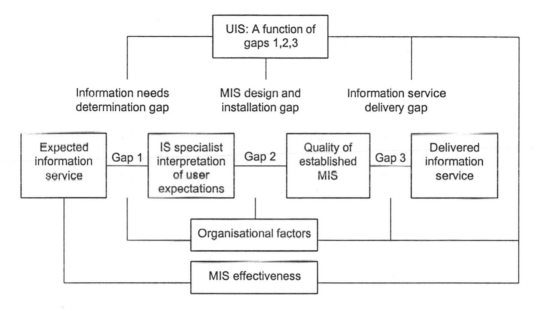

Figure 9.1: A UIS model

Interpretation of the gaps

Gap 1 This is the discrepancy between the users' expectations of the IS and the systems designers' interpretations of these expectations.

Gap 2 This is the discrepancy between the IS specialist's interpretation of the users' needs and the quality of what is actually installed for the user.

Gap 3 This is the discrepancy between the quality of what is actually installed and what the user experiences when interacting with the MIS.

Incorporation of organisation factors

The model postulates that the three gaps can be affected by organisational factors. For example, Gap 1 could be influenced in a positive way by encouraging user participation in the design stage. This involves determining the information requirements desired from the MIS. On the other hand, top management support for MIS, exhibited through, say, the provision of enough resources, should be positively correlated with Gap 2. Finally the provision of proper training should be positively correlated with Gap 3.

Formulating and fitting the model

UIS is measured as the discrepancy between user expectations and the perceptions of the MIS. Furthermore, the model assumes that overall UIS can be explained by Gaps 1 to 3 and also organisational factors. More formally:

$$UIS = f(Gap1, Gap2, Gap3, Organisational\ Factors)$$

To operationalise the model, it will be necessary in the first instance to develop instruments to measure the three gaps. This should be possible by applying the methodologies used by researchers when modelling consumer satisfaction with quality of service, where consumer satisfaction is expressed as a function of a number of gaps (Parasuraman *et al.* 1985, 1988; Brown and Swartz, 1989). The approach most used to conceptualise and determine the dimensions for the evaluation of IS effectiveness is the multivariate statistical analysis technique of factor analysis (see section 9.6). Once these instruments are available it should be possible, through the use of correlation and regression analysis, to determine which organisational factors affect these gaps. Also, the extent and nature of the influence of the gaps and the identified organisational factors on overall UIS can be determined through the use of such statistical methods.

9.5.2 The Miller-Doyle approach

Of the many instruments proposed for measuring, through perception, user satisfaction with information systems, the one due to Miller and Doyle is described here (Miller and Doyle, 1987). It is, in spirit, similar to the conceptual model described above.

The instrument has been extensively used in many different firms, in many different sectors, and the results provide convincing evidence of the instrument's reliability and validity.

Description of the instrument

The instrument is designed to measure the perceived effectiveness of the overall IS function and involves the use of a questionnaire. The questionnaire comprises five parts, A to E.

Part A consists of 34 questions which measure the extent to which certain facets of the IS are perceived to be important in ensuring the organisation's IS will be effective and successful. The attitudes are rated on a semantic differential scale of 1 (irrelevant) to 7 (very critical). Part B consists of four questions on the future needs for IS; Part C consists of the same 34 questions as Part A but in this case the respondent is asked to rate the 34 questions with respect to the actual performance achieved within their organisation. Again a seven-point scale is used but in this case the levels of perceived importance go from 1 (very poor) to 7 (excellent); Part D consists of four questions relating to the organisation's performance in developing new systems; Part E consists of four questions which capture certain demographic data. There is also a question which asks for a rating of the organisation's overall IS performance on a scale of 1 (complete failure) to 7 (very successful).

The importance ratings in Parts A and B capture perceptions on the business needs, while the performance ratings in Parts C and D capture perceptions of the organisation's IS capabilities.

A factor analysis of the 38 performance ratings revealed that there were seven dimensions of user satisfaction underlying the responses to these 38 questions. These are:

♦ Functioning of existing transaction/reporting systems

♦ Linkage to strategic processes of the firm

♦ Amount and quality of user involvement

♦ Responsiveness to new systems needs

♦ Ability to respond to end user computing needs

♦ IS staff quality

♦ Reliability of services.

See Appendix F for an abridged list of the original 38 questions. The full questionnaire is given in Miller and Doyle (1987). Also see section 9.10 for a description of the factor analysis method.

Interpreting the results

The mean of the performance responses to each of the 38 questions can be taken as a measure of the perceived performance on each of the 38 facets.

Overall user attitude to the IS function is measured by a composite score derived from the user performance mean ratings on the 38 questions, by calculating their mean value. This gives the user an overall assessment of the organisation's IS capabilities.

The fit between importance and performance ratings can be measured by the square of the correlations between these scales, and/or by the discrepancies (gaps) between these scales. Miller and Doyle recommend the use of correlation as the preferred measure of success of the MIS.

Importance and performance ratings are obtained from both IS specialists and users. This results in six correlation measures of fit. These are shown in Figure 9.2.

These correlations between the 38 items mean importance and mean performance scores provide a quick and reliable method for assessing the overall effectiveness of the IS function. High positive correlations imply a consensus of views. Firms in which the IS function is successful tend to demonstrate high squared correlations for, in particular, measures 1, 3 and 6.

Measure of fit	IS specialist		User		Significance of R^2 implies:
	Imp.	Perf	Imp.	Perf.	
1	X	X			IS staff satisfaction
2	X		X		Agreement on what is important for the business
3	X			X	IS provides capabilities that are highly rated by users
4		X	X		IS staff aware of organisational needs and are meeting these
5		X		X	Agreement on how IS is performing
6			X	X	User satisfaction

Figure 9.2: Measures of fit

Further analysis is possible. The instrument can be used to assess the IS function on each of the seven critical areas for success. Also, an analysis of responses on individual items can provide useful information. For example, a count of item non-responses can identify those items on which respondents can provide an opinion, and those for which they have difficulty in expressing an opinion. The variability in responses, as measured by the standard deviation, can also provide useful information. Should the standard deviation of both the importance and performance ratings be greater for IS specialists than users; this may imply that users are less able to discriminate in their responses to the questionnaire than the specialists. This in turn may suggest a need for education in IS. There are many other possibilities of very basic, but worthwhile, analyses of the responses to this questionnaire.

Use of the approach described does make it possible to quickly obtain a reliable and valid assessment of the IS function and thereby identify those areas where effort is required to improve the chances of success. The questionnaire does appear to offer significant advantages over the traditional approaches of cost benefit and economic analysis.

9.6 A gap model applied to an office automation system

The effectiveness of a computer network system of a business school is investigated. The focus is on users of the system who include academics, secretarial and administration staff, and MBA students.

The study involved the use of a self-completion questionnaire, which is shown in Figure 9.3. The questionnaire comprised four sections. The first section captured background information relating to the individual's position in the Business School, years of work/study experience, years of work experience with a PC, and finally years of work experience with a PC network. This is followed by three parts labelled A, B and C. Parts A and B use the same set of 24 questions, where these questions capture information on various facets of the system.

Part A measures the extent to which the attributes are perceived to be important to the effectiveness of the system. Expectation was measured on a 4-point scale from 1 – irrelevant to 4 – critical.

Part B uses the same items but now the respondent was asked to rate the performance of the Information Systems Department on a 4-point scale from 1 – very poor to 4 – excellent.

Part C involves a general question about the individual's overall satisfaction with the computer network system.

There were 86 questionnaires available for analysis. Of these 76 were completed by the MBA students. The analysis that follows was performed on the MBA responses.

Measurement of IS effectiveness in a business school

The following questionnaire has been designed to help assess the effectiveness of the computer network system used by academics, secretarial and administration staff as well as students in your business school.

The questionnaire is divided into three parts. Parts A and B use the same set of 24 questions. Part C is an open-ended question. Your answers to the questions in Part A refer to the system's attributes that you believe are important to the *effectiveness* of the system. Your answers to the second set of 24 questions in Part B refer to how the information systems department of the business school *perform* in terms of these systems attributes. Finally, in Part C we would welcome any comments that you would like to make concerning your own experience with the computer network and/or with the information systems department. The questionnaire uses a four-point scale.

First set of 24 questions:
    Critical
    Important
    Not important
    Irrelevant

Second set of 24 questions
    Excellent
    Good
    Poor
    Very poor

For example, you might think that ease of access to computer facilities is critical, and therefore your rating in the first set of questions will be:

Irrelevant	Not important	Important	Critical ✓

If you feel that the performance of the information systems department in providing these facilities is good, this will mean you rating in the second set of question will be:

Very poor	Poor	Good ✓	Excellent

The questionnaire should not take more than 15–20 minutes to complete. All information supplied by respondents will be treated with the utmost confidence.

Please supply the following information about your position in the business school:
Are you academic, secretarial/administrative or student? ....
How many years have you been working with a PC? ....
How many years experience have you had working with a computer network? ....

Thank you very much for your assistance in this study. Please return your completed questionnaire to the administrator:

IT Effectiveness Assessment Services

PART A - Importance
Please respond by ticking the option which corresponds to your opinion of the *importance* of the following 24 attributes in ensuring the effectiveness of your system.

1	Ease of access for users to computing facilities.
	Irrelevant _____ Not important _____ Important _____ Critical _____
2	Up-to-dateness of hardware.
	Irrelevant _____ Not important _____ Important _____ Critical _____
3	Up-to-dateness of software.
	Irrelevant _____ Not important _____ Important _____ Critical _____
4	Access to external databases through the system.
	Irrelevant _____ Not important _____ Important _____ Critical _____
5	A low percentage of hardware and software downtime.
	Irrelevant _____ Not important _____ Important _____ Critical _____
6	A high degree of technical competence from systems support staff.
	Irrelevant _____ Not important _____ Important _____ Critical _____
7	User confidence in the systems.
	Irrelevant _____ Not important _____ Important _____ Critical _____
8	The degree of personal control people have over their systems.
	Irrelevant _____ Not important _____ Important _____ Critical _____
9	System's responsiveness to changing user needs.
	Irrelevant _____ Not important _____ Important _____ Critical _____
10	Data security and privacy.
	Irrelevant _____ Not important _____ Important _____ Critical _____
11	System's response time.
	Irrelevant _____ Not important _____ Important _____ Critical _____
12	Extent of user training.
	Irrelevant _____ Not important _____ Important _____ Critical _____

13	Fast response time from support staff to remedy problems.
	Irrelevant_____ Not important _____ Important _____ Critical_____
14	Participation in the planning of system requirements.
	Irrelevant_____ Not important _____ Important _____ Critical_____
15	Flexibility of the system to produce professional reports.
	Irrelevant_____ Not important _____ Important _____ Critical_____
16	Positive attitude from IS staff to users.
	Irrelevant_____ Not important _____ Important _____ Critical_____
17	User's understanding of the systems.
	Irrelevant_____ Not important _____ Important _____ Critical_____
18	Overall cost-effectiveness of the information systems.
	Irrelevant_____ Not important _____ Important _____ Critical_____
19	Ability of the systems to improve my personal productivity.
	Irrelevant_____ Not important _____ Important _____ Critical_____
20	Ability of the systems to enhance the learning experience of students.
	Irrelevant_____ Not important _____ Important _____ Critical_____
21	Standardisation of hardware.
	Irrelevant_____ Not important _____ Important _____ Critical_____
22	Documentation to support training.
	Irrelevant_____ Not important _____ Important _____ Critical_____
23	Help with database development.
	Irrelevant_____ Not important _____ Important _____ Critical_____
24	Ability to conduct computer conferencing with colleagues.
	Irrelevant_____ Not important _____ Important _____ Critical_____

PART B - Actual performance

Please respond by ticking the option which corresponds to your opinion of the actual *performance* of the information systems department in terms of the following 24 attributes.

1	Ease of access for users to computing facilities.
	Very poor _____ Poor _____ Good _____ Excellent _____
2	Up-to-dateness of hardware.
	Very poor _____ Poor _____ Good _____ Excellent _____
3	Up-to-dateness of software.
	Very poor _____ Poor _____ Good _____ Excellent _____
4	Access to external databases through the system.
	Very poor _____ Poor _____ Good _____ Excellent _____
5	A low percentage of hardware and software downtime.
	Very poor _____ Poor _____ Good _____ Excellent _____
6	A high degree of technical competence from systems support staff.
	Very poor _____ Poor _____ Good _____ Excellent _____
7	User confidence in the systems.
	Very poor _____ Poor _____ Good _____ Excellent _____
8	The degree of personal control people have over their systems.
	Very poor _____ Poor _____ Good _____ Excellent _____
9	System's responsiveness to changing user needs.
	Very poor _____ Poor _____ Good _____ Excellent _____
10	Data security and privacy.
	Very poor _____ Poor _____ Good _____ Excellent _____
11	System's response time.
	Very poor _____ Poor _____ Good _____ Excellent _____
12	Extent of user training.
	Very poor _____ Poor _____ Good _____ Excellent _____

13	Fast response time from support staff to remedy problems.
	Very poor _____ Poor _____ Good _____ Excellent _____
14	Participation in the planning of system requirements.
	Very poor _____ Poor _____ Good _____ Excellent _____
15	Flexibility of the system to produce professional reports.
	Very poor _____ Poor _____ Good _____ Excellent _____
16	Positive attitude from IS staff to users.
	Very poor _____ Poor _____ Good _____ Excellent _____
17	User's understanding of the systems.
	Very poor _____ Poor _____ Good _____ Excellent _____
18	Overall cost-effectiveness of the information systems.
	Very poor _____ Poor _____ Good _____ Excellent _____
19	Ability of the systems to improve my personal productivity.
	Very poor _____ Poor _____ Good _____ Excellent _____
20	Ability of the systems to enhance the learning experience of students.
	Very poor _____ Poor _____ Good _____ Excellent _____
21	Standardisation of hardware.
	Very poor _____ Poor _____ Good _____ Excellent _____
22	Documentation to support training.
	Very poor _____ Poor _____ Good _____ Excellent _____
23	Help with database development.
	Very poor _____ Poor _____ Good _____ Excellent _____
24	Ability to conduct computer conferencing with colleagues.
	Very poor _____ Poor _____ Good _____ Excellent _____

PART C – Overall Opinion

Please rate your overall opinion of the computer network system.

Very poor _____ Poor _____ Good _____ Excellent _____

Please supply any further comments you wish concerning the performance of the IT&S Division

_____
_____
_____
_____
_____
_____
_____
_____
_____
_____

Figure 9.3: User satisfaction questionnaire

9.7 Basic results

A basic analysis of the expectation and performance percep-tions was initially performed. Averages and standard deviations for the expectation and performance scores appear in Figure 9.4. Also in Figure 9.4, for each of the questions, are the mean perceptual gap scores, as well as their standard de-viations, where the gap is determined by subtracting the expectation score from the performance score. In the last col-umn of Figure 9.4 are the correlations between the gap scores and the overall satisfaction scores.

Att. No.	Attributes	Expectation			Performance			Perceptual		Gap correlation with satisfaction
		Rank	Mean	SD	Rank	Mean	SD	Gap	SD	
6	High degree of technical competence from support staff	1	3.45	0.60	2	2.82	0.53	−0.63	0.73	0.0232
11	System's response time	2	3.42	0.50	19	2.20	0.83	−1.22	1.05	0.5738***
5	Low percentage of hardware and software downtime	3	3.39	0.54	10	2.49	0.60	−0.90	0.90	0.4307***
1	Ease of access for users to computing facilities	4	3.37	0.65	5	2.75	0.59	−0.62	0.92	0.2154*
13	Fast response from support staff to remedy problems	5	3.34	0.53	11	2.47	0.62	−0.87	0.85	0.0524
3	Up to dateness of software	6	3.33	0.53	1	3.01	0.53	−0.32	0.77	0.3794**
20	Ability of the system to enhance learning experience	7	3.32	0.59	8	2.66	0.64	−0.66	0.81	0.3328**
15	Flexibility of the system to produce professional reports	8	3.22	0.69	17	2.22	0.72	−1.00	1.06	0.2330*
7	User confidence in systems	9	3.20	0.59	11	2.47	0.60	−0.73	0.79	0.3112*
19	Ability of the system to improve personal productivity	10	3.18	0.53	9	2.62	0.59	−0.56	0.81	0.4160***
16	Positive attitude of IS staff to users	11	3.16	0.49	3	2.78	0.62	−0.38	0.77	0.0945
22	Documentation to support training	12	3.11	0.56	22	1.96	0.62	−1.15	0.95	0.3165**
9	Systems responsiveness to changing users needs	13	3.05	0.49	11	2.47	0.64	−0.58	0.77	0.2947*
12	Extent of user training	14	3.04	0.72	20	2.14	0.69	−0.90	0.95	0.0795
2	Up-to-dateness of hardware	15	3.01	0.53	14	2.46	0.72	−0.55	0.89	0.3056**
17	User's understanding of the system	15	3.01	0.62	16	2.36	0.56	−0.65	0.84	0.0563
8	Degree of personal control users have over their systems	17	2.95	0.56	15	2.37	0.65	−0.58	0.90	0.2528*
10	Data security and privacy	18	2.80	0.80	3	2.78	0.45	−0.02	0.89	−0.1314
4	Access to external databases through the system	19	2.78	0.62	18	2.21	0.55	−0.57	0.79	−0.0127
23	Help with database development	20	2.72	0.69	21	2.12	0.65	−0.60	0.90	0.2050*
21	Standardisation of hardware	21	2.63	0.69	6	2.74	0.50	+0.11	0.81	0.0625
14	Participation in planning of system requirements	22	2.47	0.66	22	1.96	0.64	−0.49	0.81	0.0033
18	Cost-effectiveness of IS	23	2.46	0.74	7	2.72	0.51	+0.26	0.96	0.4160***
24	Conduct computer conferencing with colleagues	24	2.11	0.67	24	1.93	0.57	−0.17	0.77	0.3204**

* implies correlation is significant at 5% level, ** implies correlation is significant at 1% level, *** implies correlation is significant at the 0.1% level

Figure 9.4: Basic analysis of perceptions

9.8 Some implications arising from the analysis

1   System's response time is ranked second in terms of expectation but nineteenth on performance.

2   Ability to conduct computer conferencing with colleagues and help with database or model development was ranked low on both expectation and performance.

3   Overall cost effectiveness of information systems, standardisation of hardware, and data security and privacy received relatively low rankings on expectation, but relatively high rankings on performance.

4   The correlation between the ranked expectation and performance item means is 0.39, which is not significant at the 5% level. This implies a lack of consensus between the perceived needs for the system to be effective and the perceived ability of the IT department to meet these needs.

5   The general evaluation of performance across all attributes was poor. Up-to-dateness of software with a mean score of 3.01, being best on performance.

6   The gaps for 15 of the 24 statements about the system are positively and significantly correlated with the overall satisfaction score, and therefore can be considered to be potentially 'good' indicators of user satisfaction. Since the gap is determined by subtracting the expectation score from the performance score, the positive correlation implies that the greater the gap, in a positive sense, the more the user satisfaction.

To visualise the gaps between the expectation and the performance scores, a *snake diagram* may be drawn. The snake diagram shown in Figure 9.5 highlights the score for both the performance and expectation questions on the same axis.

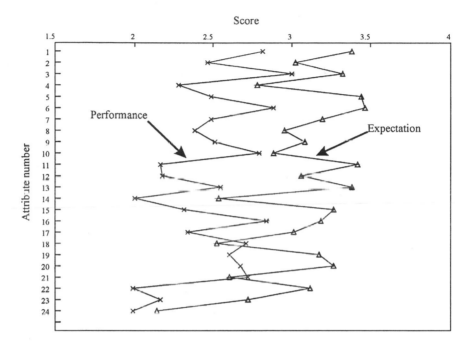

Figure 9.5: A snake diagram

Figure 9.6 is a modified snake showing the two sets of scores as well as a graph of the gaps.

In this figure, the line indicating the zero value is most important. Attributes that display a gap greater than zero, i.e., positive gaps, are those on which the firm is committing more resources than are perhaps required. Attributes that display a negative gap are those where the performance is less than the expectation and therefore in these respects the information systems department is under performing. Where the gap is actually zero, or in other words, no gap, there is an exact match between users' expectations and performance.

From Figure 9.6 it can be seen that in this case only three attributes scored close to a zero gap, whilst the majority show negative gaps.

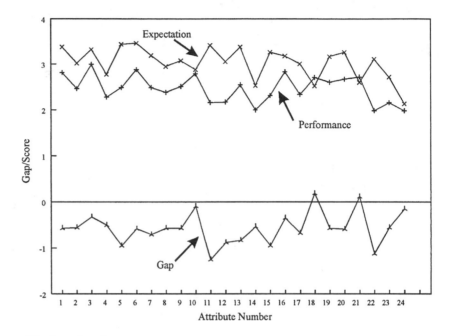

Figure 9.6: A modified snake diagram

9.9 Performance analysis

The next step in the analysis was to perform further evaluation of the performance scores. This involved calculating standard errors for each attribute. The simple average performance scores show only one of the attributes, namely, 'up to dateness of software' performing at an above average score of 3.01. In order to establish whether these attributes could possibly fall into the category 'good', hypothesis testing was performed. This was done by calculating, using the t-distribution, the upper confidence limit of 97.5%. For a sample of this size the upper limit is calculated by adding to the mean performance score for the attribute two standard errors. This corresponds to carrying out a one-tailed t-test on the mean at a 2.5% level of significance. Should the calculated upper limit exceed 3 then the attribute can be considered to be 'good' otherwise 'poor'. This result is displayed in the last two columns of Figure 9.7.

Attributes	Performance Mean	Std Err	Upper Limit Mean + 2SE	Indi-cator
6 High degree of technical competence from support staff	2.82	0.061	2.94	Poor
11 System's response time	2.20	0.096	2.39	Poor
5 Low percentage of hardware and software downtime	2.49	0.069	2.63	Poor
1 Ease of access for users to computing facilities	2.75	0.068	2.89	Poor
13 Fast response from support staff to remedy problems	2.47	0.071	2.61	Poor
3 Up-to-dateness of software	3.01	0.061	3.13	Good
20 Ability of the system to enhance the learning experience of students	2.66	0.074	2.81	Poor
15 Flexibility of the system to produce professional reports	2.22	0.083	2.37	Poor
7 User confidence in systems	2.47	0.069	2.61	Poor
19 Ability of the system to improve personal productivity	2.62	0.067	2.75	Poor
16 Positive attitude of IS staff to users	2.78	0.072	2.92	Poor
22 Documentation to support training	1.96	0.071	2.10	Poor
9 Systems responsiveness to changing users needs	2.47	0.074	2.62	Poor
12 Extent of user training	2.14	0.079	2.30	Poor
2 Up-to-dateness of hardware	2.46	0.083	2.63	Poor
17 User's understanding of the system	2.36	0.064	2.49	Poor
8 Degree of personal control users have over their systems	2.37	0.075	2.52	Poor
10 Data security and privacy	2.78	0.052	2.88	Poor
4 Access to external databases through the system	2.21	0.063	2.34	Poor
23 Help with database development	2.12	0.075	2.27	Poor
21 Standardisation of hardware	2.74	0.057	2.85	Poor
14 Participation in planning of systems requirements	1.96	0.074	2.11	Poor
18 Cost-effectiveness of IS	2.72	0.058	2.84	Poor
24 Conduct computer conferencing with colleagues	1.93	0.066	2.06	Poor

Figure 9.7: Evaluation of performance scores using standard errors

The performance scores can also be analysed graphically. The average performance scores on an attribute by attribute basis, as well as the overall evaluation score ('Please rate your overall opinion of the network system') and the all-data or all-attributes average are displayed graphically in Figure 9.8.

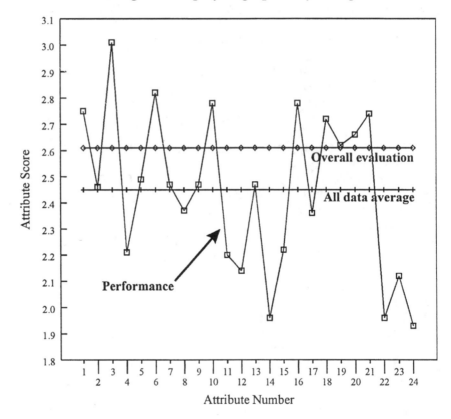

Figure 9.8: Performance analysis

The overall evaluation score is the average result of the question asked in Part C of the questionnaire. The all-data average is the arithmetic mean of all the attribute performance scores for all the questionnaires.

An interesting feature of Figure 9.8 is that the mean overall evaluation score of 2.61 is higher than the all-data average of the performance scores, which is 2.45. In fact the mean overall evaluation is statistically significantly higher at the 5% level.

This gap is very important and suggests that the user community, although scoring the performance of the individual attributes quite poorly, give the service as a whole a significantly higher score.

This might be regarded as a forgiveness factor. It could be that the students although being aware that most aspects of the service were bad still felt that the ISD were doing as well as can be expected considering the level of resourcing and investment going into the system.

9.10 Factor analysis

Factor analysis is a mathematical procedure that can assist the researcher in conceptualising a problem.

According to Kerlinger (1969) it is a method for determining the number and nature of the underlying dimensions (or factors) among large numbers of measures of the concept being evaluated. Factor analysis is a technique used to locate and identify fundamental properties underlying the results of tests or measurements and which cannot be measured directly (a factor is a hypothetical entity that is assumed to underlie the results of the tests). It is therefore a technique that can be used to provide a parsimonious description of a complex multi-faceted intangible concept such as UIS.

Factor analysis is available on many statistical software packages. In this study it was performed using the SPSS/PC+ software package. In using factor analysis there are traditionally four steps to be performed with the computer results which are:

1   Consult the Kaiser-Meyer-Olkin (KMO) measure of sampling adequacy. The rule for the use of this statistic is that if the KMO is less than 0.50 there is no value in proceeding

with the technique. The greater the value of the KMO the more effective the factor analysis is likely to be.

2   Examine the eigen values. Only factors with an eigen value of greater than one are used in the analysis.

3   Study the rotated factor matrix. Examine each factor one at a time, looking for the input variables that influence the factor, which have a loading of 0.5 or more.

4   Attempt to combine the meaning of the variables identified in 3 above into a super-variable that will explain the combined effect of these individual variables, and will become the invisible factor the analysis attempts to isolate.

See Appendix D for a more detailed description of factor analysis.

9.10.1   Factor identification

In order to gain a better understanding of the scores, a factor analysis was performed on both the expectation and performance data. The underlying factors were determined through the principal component procedure of the SPSS/PC software package. Each of the set of expectation statements and performance statements were analysed by using the principal components procedure for extraction of the factors followed by a varimax rotation. The resulting factor matrices are displayed in Figures 9.9 and 9.10. Only those statements with a factor loading of 0.5 or more are listed in the tables.

9.10.2   Expectation scores

Eight factors with eigen values greater than 1 were extracted from the expectation data, accounting for 62.2% of the overall variance. Only the first four of these were interpretable. It could be that perceptions of what is important are not clear in the respondents' minds.

Ease of use emerged as the factor explaining most of the variance. Modernness of the system, system control, and technical competence available, in order of variance explained, were the remaining factors. These factors and the attributes loading on them are given in Figure 9.9. The KMO measure for these scores was 0.543.

Attrib. no.		Factor loading	Gap correlation with satisfaction
Factor 1: Ease of use (14.2% of variance)			
A23	Help with model/database development	0.7466	0.2154*
A16	Positive attitude of information systems staff to users	0.6173	0.0945
A21	Standardisation of hardware	0.6043	0.0625
A22	Documentation to support training	0.5507	0.3165**
Factor 2: Modernness (9.8% of variance)			
A3	Up-to-dateness of software	0.8067	0.3794**
A2	Up-to-dateness of hardware	0.6489	0.3056**
Factor 3: System's control (8.0% of variance)			
A18	Overall cost effectiveness of information systems	0.7746	0.0678
A10	Data security and privacy	0.7092	−0.1314
A14	Participation in the planning of the system requirements	0.6083	0.0033
Factor 4: Technical competence available (6.7% of variance)			
A12	Extent of user training	0.7621	0.0795
A17	User understanding of the system	0.6800	0.0563
A6	A high degree of technical competence	0.5403	0.0232

* implies correlation is significant at 5% level, ** implies correlation is significant at 1% level, *** implies correlation is significant at the 0.1% level

Figure 9.9: Factor analysis of student expectation scores

Only four of the 12 gap scores are significantly correlated with overall satisfaction. This implies that the dimensions identified by the factor analysis of expectation scores are likely to be weak measures of user satisfaction with the system.

Attrib. no.		Factor loading	Gap corre- lation with satisfaction
Factor 1: Effective benefits (28.4% of variance)			
B19	Ability of the system to improve personal productivity	0.8430	0.4160***
B20	Ability of the system to enhance the learning ex- perience of students	0.7003	0.3328**
B11	System response time	0.5745	0.5738***
B7	User confidence in systems	0.5174	0.3112**
B12.	Extent of user training	0.5118	0.0795
Factor 2: Modernness (7.8% of variance)			
B9	System's responsiveness to changing user needs	0.7357	0.2947*
B8	Degree of control users have over their systems	0.6647	0.2528*
B2	Up-to-dateness of hardware	0.6141	0.3056*
B21	Standardisation of hardware	0.6091	0.0625
Factor 3: System access (7.3% of variance)			
B15	Flexibility of the system to produce professional reports	0.7172	0.2330*
B17	Users' understanding of the system	0.6995	0.0563
B22	Documentation to support training	0.5339	0.3165**
B5	A low percentage of hardware and software downtime	0.5115	0.4307***
Factor 4: Quality of service (6.4% of variance)			
B16	Positive attitude of IS staff to users	0.7665	0.0945
B13	Fast response time from support	0.6588	0.0524

* implies correlation is significant at 5% level, ** implies correlation is significant at 1% level, *** implies correlation is significant at the 0.1% level

Figure 9.10: Factor analysis of student perceptions of performance

9.10.3 Performance scores

Four factors with eigen values greater than 1 were extracted from the performance data, accounting for 49.9% of the total variance. Effective benefits realisation emerged as the factor ex- plaining most of the variance. Modernness of the system, system access and, quality of service were the remaining factors. These factors and the statements loading on them are given in Figure 9.10. The KMO for these scores was 0.7439.

Only three of the 13 gap scores relating to statements loading on the first three factors are uncorrelated with the overall satisfaction scores. Thus, the performance factors are potentially 'good' measures of satisfaction with the system. The fourth dimension, namely, perception of the quality of the IS staff, is a weak measure of user satisfaction with the system, since for both statements loading on this factor, the gap scores are uncorrelated with overall user satisfaction.

In contrast to the analysis of the expectation data, the respondents appear to have a much clearer view of the performance of the IT department and thus the performance dimensions are likely to be more reliable measures of user satisfaction than those derived from the expectation data.

9.10.4 Regression analysis: Explanation of overall satisfaction scores

Regression analysis was performed with a view to establishing which variables were important in explaining the overall satisfaction scores. The initial explanatory variable pool consisted of: the summated gap scores for each of the four perceptual performance factors, as well as the two factual variables; years of experience working with a PC; and years of experience working with a PC network. Subsequent theoretical considerations lead to a revision of the pool.

The quality of service factor shown in Figure 9.10 was excluded from the analysis, as the gaps for variables loading on this factor were not correlated with the overall satisfaction scores. Also, for each of the first three factors (effective benefits, modernness and system access), those variables loading on the factor, but not correlating with overall satisfaction, were excluded from the summated gap scores. The exclusion of these variables did not change the interpretation of the factors.

In the first instance, a full regression analysis was performed using the SPSS/PC+ regression program. In this regression, the overall satisfaction scores were regressed on the *summed gap scores* for the *modified* perceptual factors, i.e. effective benefits, modernness and system access, as well as the two factual variables; years of experience working with a PC; and years of experience working with a PC network. The results of this regression are reported in Figure 9.11.

	Correlation with overall opinion	Regression coefficient	Beta weight	Signifi-cance
Gap variables:				
Effective benefits	0.548***	0.1021	0.4597	0.0001
Modernness	0.366**	0.0340	0.1246	0.2389
System access	0.492***	0.0486	0.1797	0.1082
Non-gap variables:				
PC experience	−0.058	−0.0036	−0.0176	0.8751
Network experience	−0.127	−0.0365	−0.1190	0.2874
** Correlation is significant at the 1% level				
*** Correlation is significant at the 0.1% level				
Multiple correlation R_{Full} = 0.6478				
Coefficient of determination R^2_{Full} = 0.4196				
F = 10.12 Significance = 0.0000				

Figure 9.11: Results of full regression analysis

The results of the full regression reveal a significant regression (F=10.2, significance=0.0000) with a multiple correlation R of 0.6478. The multiple correlation R indicates the extent of the correlation between the overall satisfaction scores and all the explanatory variables collectively. The interpretation of the R^2 value of 0.4196 is that the explanatory variables collectively explain 41.96% of the variation in the overall satisfaction scores. The relative impact of each explanatory variable can be inferred from the so-called, beta weights, which are standardised regression coefficients. The beta weights are used in preference to the ordinary regression coefficients, as they are independent of the unit of measurement for the variable itself. In the fitted model, effective benefits with a highly significant beta weight of 0.4597 is the factor that has by far most impact on the overall opinion score. The impact of effective benefits can be considered to have approximately 2.5 times as much impact as system access, which has a beta weight of 0.1797.

It is interesting to note from the second column of Figure 9.11 that while all three gap variables are significantly and positively correlated with overall satisfaction, both the PC and PC network experience variables are not significantly correlated with overall satisfaction. It is of additional interest to note that, although not significant, the correlations in the sample between overall satisfaction and both the PC and PC network experience variables, are negative. It is just possible, therefore, that overall satisfaction can be inversely related to these experience variables, which would imply that the more experienced users are more difficult to satisfy.

The regression model was re-computed using the stepwise regression procedure and the results are presented in Figure 9.12.

	Correlation with overall opinion	Regression coefficient	Beta weight	Signifi- cance
Gap variables:				
Effective benefits	0.598***	0.1089	0.4890	0.0000
Modernness	0.366**	–	–	–
System access	0.492***	0.0586	0.2167	0.1082
Non-gap variables:				
PC experience	–0.058	–	–	–
Network experience	–0.127	–	–	–
** Correlation is significant at the 1% level				
*** Correlation is significant at the 0.1% level				
Multiple correlation R_{Full} = 0.6264				
Coefficient of determination R^2_{Full} = 0.3924				
F = 23.5721 Significance = 0.0000				

Figure 9.12: Results of stepwise regression analysis

The stepwise regression retains only two of the original five variables included in the full regression model. Despite this, the two models are very similar in terms of fit. (R^2_{Full} = 0.4196 versus $R^2_{Stepwise}$ = 0.3924).

The results of the stepwise regression reveal that effective benefits and system access are significant in explaining the overall satisfaction scores. Also, a comparison of the beta weights suggests that effective benefits have about 2.25 times more impact on overall satisfaction than system access. The full regression and stepwise regression beta weights are essentially the same.

9.11 Summary of findings

The gaps on the two perceptual performance factors, namely effective benefits and system access, are significant in assessing overall satisfaction with the network. The gap on effective benefits is approximately twice as important as system access in terms of its impact on overall satisfaction. Previous PC and PC network experience do not impact significantly on overall satisfaction with the network system.

The fitted model in this case only explains about 40% of the variability in the overall satisfaction scores. Thus, there are other factors, not identified in the study, which impact on overall satisfaction. This is turn suggests that the evaluation of an office automation/network system is far more complex, involving more than just the two dimensions identified.

9.12 Analysing qualitative information

In an attempt to find out more precisely the nature of problems with the systems and service the user satisfaction survey usually includes an open ended question inviting the respondent to comment on the effectiveness of their organisation's systems (see Part C of Figure 9.3).

A collation of these comments and criticisms can run into many pages of text, which clearly will pose problems to the analyst. Not only do we wish to extract the key problems but also desire a deeper understanding of the nature of the problems to be brought to the attention of management. The authors have found the application of two well-established methods, namely, that of content analysis and correspondence analysis, to be very successful in facilitating this process.

A description of these techniques together with application follows. The study described was carried out at a business school different from that of section 9.6.

This study was conducted at a UK business school during March and April 1991. Self-completion questionnaires were distributed to users of the system in an attempt to measure user satisfaction with the network, the information system staff, and other information systems services offered. There were six different groups of users.

The questionnaire used was similar to that of Figure 9.3. Of the 220 questionnaires distributed 108 were returned, of which 95 were completed and of these 57 contained comments and criticisms resulting in over 12 pages of text requiring analysis. For a full discussion of the study and a copy of the questionnaire the reader is referred to Remenyi and Money (1993).

9.12.1   Content analysis

Content analysis is a simple but laborious process of examining the transcript or text with the objective of categorising its content. This is achieved by identifying keywords, themes, or some other content category as the unit for analysis, and then counting the number of occurrences of the category. In this study the unit used in the analysis was themes such as printer problems, poor systems access and so on. A more detailed discussion of content analysis can be found in Berelson (1980).

The result of the content analysis for this study is a one-way frequency table in Figure 9.13. This table shows the number of occasions a particular comment or criticism was made.

No.	Comment	Frequency	Abbreviation
1	Unhelpfulness of ISD staff	14	UHS
2	Slow response to requests for assistance	12	SRA
3	Printer problems	12	PRP
4	Outdated equipment	10	OUE
5	Systems not easy to use	10	NEU
6	Incompatibility of hardware and software	9	IHS
7	Poor access to systems	9	PAS
8	Insufficient funding of ISD	6	IFI
9	Lack of standards	6	LOS
10	Poor quality of training available	6	PQT
11	ISD staff priorities are wrong	4	IPW
12	Promises not kept	2	PNK
13	Accounting too complex	2	APC
14	Too many errors in software	2	EIS
15	Poor linkage to accounting system	2	PLA
16	ISD is technically excellent	1	ITE
17	ISD is totally and hopelessly incompetent	1	ITT
18	Some improvements in ISD recently	1	SII
19	ISD service is far better than other b'schools	1	IBO
20	ISD service is far worse than other b'schools	1	IWO

Figure 9.13: Summary of respondents' remarks

The comments in Figure 9.13 have been coded with a three-letter abbreviation, which is used in the following reports and graphs.

The one-way frequency analysis provides no real surprises. However in terms of other similar work conducted by the authors it is worth noting that there is a high number of respondents claiming that the ISD staff are unhelpful. There were relatively few contradictory comments although comments 16 and 17 as well as comments 19 and 20 are very good examples of how different some opinions can be.

The contingency table, or two-way frequency table as it is sometimes called in Figure 9.14 shows the frequency with which the content categories occur by user group.

The frequency table forms the basic input for the correspondence analysis described in the next section.

Abbrevia-tions		User job codes						Frequency
		1	2	3	4	5	6	
1	UHS	7	2	0	5	0	0	14
2	SRA	6	3	0	3	0	0	12
3	PRP	5	5	0	1	0	1	12
4	OUE	3	0	1	2	1	3	10
5	NEU	4	1	0	3	1	1	10
6	IHS	0	4	0	3	2	0	9
7	PAS	2	1	0	2	1	2	8
8	IFI	1	2	2	1	0	0	6
9	LOS	2	2	1	1	0	0	6
10	PQT	2	0	0	3	1	0	6
11	PNK	1	1	0	3	0	0	5
12	IPW	2	1	0	0	0	0	3
13	APC	0	2	0	0	0	0	2
14	TES	0	2	0	0	0	0	2
15	PLA	0	2	0	0	0	0	2
16	ITE	0	0	1	0	0	0	1
17	ITI	1	0	0	0	0	0	1
18	SII	0	0	1	0	0	0	1
19	IBO	0	1	0	0	0	0	1
20	IWO	1	0	0	0	0	0	1

Figure 9.14: Frequency table of user remarks

Although a simple listing of these comments and the criticisms is quite useful on its own, to explore further the information potential of the above content analysis it is necessary to use another technique – correspondence analysis.

9.12.2   Correspondence analysis

Correspondence analysis was developed in France being the brainchild of Benzecri (1969). Popularisation of this technique to the ' English speaking' world can be largely attributed to Greenacre (1984). It is an exploratory data analysis technique that provides a simultaneous graphical representation of the rows and columns of a two-way contingency table thereby possibly helping the analyst to gain an understanding of the nature of the associations among the rows and columns. The display in two dimensions is known as a perceptual map.

According to Greenacre:

Correspondence analysis is a technique for displaying the rows and columns of a data matrix (primarily, a two-way contingency table) as points in dual low-dimensional vector spaces. (Greenacre 1984, p.54)

The only constraint on the cell entries in the contingency table is that they be non-negative. The data matrix actually used was the contingency table, Figure 9.14, showing the occurrence of comments and criticisms offered by different user groups.

In the table the columns represent the job codes for different user groups. Thus 1 is academics, 2 is Sec/Admin, 3 is ISD Staff, 4 is Research Associates, 5 MBA Students and 6 is Executive Course Member. The rows represent the different issues mentioned such as UHS represents unhelpful staff and SRA represents slow response to request for assistance.

The primary output of the correspondence analysis is a map identifying the row and column attributes as points in a space of two or more dimensions. This graphical display or perceptual map represents the relative positions or grouping of the various concepts listed in the contingency table. Those rows (issues), which have similar profiles, are plotted close together, and columns (user groups) with similar profiles are plotted close together. It is the objective of correspondence analysis to present the results in as simple a form as possible.

The decision concerning the number of dimensions that will suffice to represent the contingency table is made on the basis of the amount of variation, or inertia as it is sometimes called, that the retained dimensions explain. There is no hard and fast rule concerning what is a sufficient amount of explained variation.

For this study the first two dimensions accounted for 63% of the inertia. Because of the difficulties in representing three-dimensional space it was decided that two dimensions was sufficient. The resulting perceptual maps show the relative positions of the different concepts and different participating informants.

The axes are purely numerical scales that are produced to show relative distance from the centroid in a graphical way. These axes may be thought of as two artificial variables synthesised from the original data set that give the maximum explanation of the differences and the similarities between the originally observed values. It is up to the analyst using the correspondence analysis to actually attribute meaning to these axes.

From Figure 9.15 it is possible to see that some of the comments and criticisms may be conveniently grouped together. For example, by projecting each of the user remark category points onto the vertical axis and studying the order in which they are positioned on this axis it will be noticed that the issues UHS, SRA, PNK, IHS, PRP and PQT are all below the horizontal axis. All these issues are related to people. The issues OUE, IFI, PAS, LOS and NEU are above the horizontal axis. These issues may be thought of as funding matters.

Issues that are grouped together on the perceptual map are said to be associated or similar. The association of such variables may be thought of as a type of correlation in that the association shows that there exists a relationship between these variables. However, the perceptual map does not indicate the type of relationship. The specification of the nature of the relationship depends on the environment being described by the correspondence analysis.

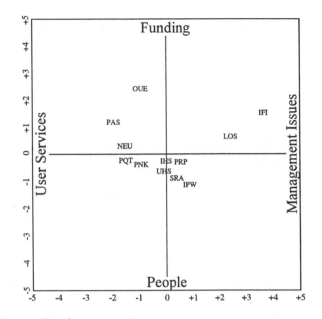

Figure 9.15: Perceptual map showing concepts

The positions or projections of the issues on the horizontal axis suggest that they are lined up with user services such as PAS (poor access to system), NEU (not easy to use), PQT (poor quality training) and OUE (out of date equipment) on the left and the more management related issues such as LOS (lack of standard) and IFI (insufficient funds) on the right.

It is not surprising that the concepts described as service issues, when projected onto the horizontal axis, lie in close proximity to one another. The groups of respondents that fall close to this area on the graph could be described as having a service focus. In fact they constitute a cluster, and the main theme of this cluster is lack of service. Clearly this is the most pressing problem facing the ISD.

In the same way as the issues have been grouped, so the participating respondents may be grouped. Figure 9.16 shows the grouping of the respondents.

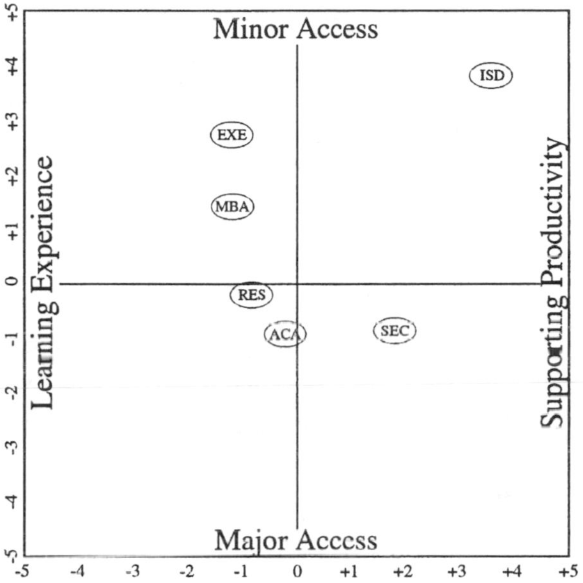

Figure 9.16: Perceptual map showing user groups

The plot for the respondent groupings reveals a horizontal axis with one pole appearing to be 'learning experience' and the other 'supporting productivity'. The vertical axis appears to be a scale from 'major access' to 'minor access'.

It may be seen that five of the groups lie in an arc around the origin of the axes. This shows that although they have different views they also have much in common. However there is one group that lies quite distant from the rest. This is the ISD, and the perceptual map confirms that their views are quite out of line with the rest of the business school.

Finally Figure 9.17 shows the issues and the respondent groups superimposed on the same set of axes. This perceptual map gives a clear indication of which groups have which problems with the system.

The research associates and academics are positioned close to one another and therefore have fairly similar concerns. The main concerns for the research associates appear to be poor quality training, promises not kept, unhelpful staff, equipment not easy to use and incompatible hardware and software. The academics are primarily concerned with issues such as unhelpful staff, promises not kept, slow responses, printer problems and ISD staff priorities are wrong.

The administration/secretarial staff shares with academics concerns with regard to ISD staff priorities being wrong as well as slow response.

The MBA and Open Executive course members have similar profiles with poor access to the system being of most concern to the MBAs and outdated equipment being of major concern to the executives. This is not surprising, as the equipment in the business school is somewhat dated.

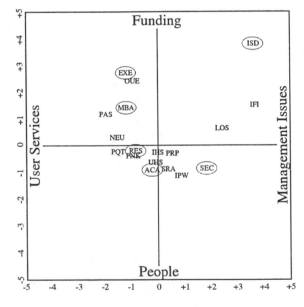

Figure 9.17: Perceptual map showing respondents and user groups on the same axes

As mentioned above, the ISD appear to have views markedly out of line with the five other user groups. Their main concerns are associated with insufficient funds and lack of standards, which are operational and technical issues, normally associated with their work.

From the joint map (rows and columns superimposed) a study of the horizontal axis reveals that the executives, MBAs and research associates are more concerned with user services, while the secretarial and ISD staff are more concerned with management issues. The academic staff are positioned at the centroid, thus apparently concerned equally with user services and management issues.

A study of the vertical axis reveals that the ISD and executives, and to a lesser extent the MBAs, focus more on funding, while the research associates, academics and secretarial staff tend to focus on people issues.

In summary the findings of the correspondence analysis suggests that the problem is a lack of service concerning a group of seven key issues:

1 Unhelpfulness of ISD staff

2 Slow response to requests for assistance

3 Printer problems

4 Outdated equipment

5 Systems not easy to use

6 Incompatibility of hardware and software

7 Poor access to systems.

The correspondence analysis reveals the views of the ISD staff are out of line with the rest of the user community at the business school. Whereas the various user groups are concerned about issues such as Unhelpfulness of ISD staff, Slow response to requests for help, Outdated equipment, Poor printers, etc., the ISD perceive the business school's information systems problems to be lack of funds and lack of standards. This lack of congruence is one of the most important difficulties facing the management of the business school.

9.13 A multiple gap approach to measuring UIS

A multiple gap approach to measuring UIS has been investigated by the authors. This original research is designed to find ways and means of offering assistance to those seeking to obtain a penetrating insight into how systems are viewed at various stages of their production, implementation, and use, and how this has an impact on UIS. Multiple gap analysis is a useful instrument in this respect.

In a study presently in progress at the College, three measures of a system's benefit profiles are being studied. The first measure related to how the system's original architects perceived the potential benefits. The information relating to potential benefits is extracted from the original specification of requirements documentation. Sixteen different benefit types were defined by the firm. These include the system's ability to:

1   Reduce overall costs

2   Displace costs

3   Avoid costs

4   Provide opportunity for revenue growth

5   Provide improved management information

6   Provide improved staff productivity

7   Provide capacity for increased volume

8   Reduce error

9   Provide a competitive advantage

10   Catch up with competition

11   Provide improved management control

12   Provide improved management productivity

13   Provide improved staff morale

14   Provide an improved corporate image

15   Provide improved customer service

16   Provide improved client/supplier relationships.

During the development of the original specification of requirements, the authors of the document were required to state the relevance of each benefit type to the system by rating the benefit on a four-point scale. This is a measure of the importance or need that the firm has for each of the benefit types. A questionnaire used for this data collection is shown in Figure 9.18.

The second measure of benefits was obtained by requesting that the project manager and other members of his or her team, on completion of the system's development, answer the same set of questions relating to the 16 different benefit types. This data provides a second view of the potential benefits by obtaining an opinion as to what extent the project manager believes the system, as it has been developed, can actually achieve the stated benefits. This is a measure of the expectations of the IS professionals who have developed the system. Figure 9.19 shows the questionnaire required for the capture of this data.

Unlike the first questionnaire, which is administered either by the researcher studying the actual specification of requirements, or by discussion with only one informant, i.e. the project manager, the second and third questionnaires can be administered to many users. As a result, when there are multiple users involved, summary statistics have to be calculated.

THE MEASUREMENT OF INFORMATION SYSTEMS BENEFITS

Answer the questions by ticking the option which corresponds to your opinion of the importance of the following types of benefit which may be achieved by the proposed system

1	The system's ability to reduce overall costs.
	Irrelevant _____ Not important _____ Important _____ Critical _____
	If you answered either IMPORTANT or CRITICAL, please give details:
	_____
	_____
2	The system's ability to displace costs.
	Irrelevant _____ Not important _____ Important _____ Critical _____
	If you answered either IMPORTANT or CRITICAL, please give details:
	_____
	_____
3	The system's ability to avoid costs.
	Irrelevant _____ Not important _____ Important _____ Critical _____
	If you answered either IMPORTANT or CRITICAL, please give details:
	_____
	_____
4	The system's ability to provide opportunity for revenue growth.
	Irrelevant _____ Not important _____ Important _____ Critical _____
	If you answered either IMPORTANT or CRITICAL, please give details:
	_____
	_____
5	The system's ability to provide improved management information.
	Irrelevant _____ Not important _____ Important _____ Critical _____
	If you answered either IMPORTANT or CRITICAL, please give details:
	_____
	_____

6	The system's ability to provide improved staff productivity.
	Irrelevant _____ Not important _____ Important _____ Critical _____
	If you answered either IMPORTANT or CRITICAL, please give details:
	_____
	_____
7	The system's ability to provide capacity for increased volume.
	Irrelevant _____ Not important _____ Important _____ Critical _____
	If you answered either IMPORTANT or CRITICAL, please give details:
	_____
	_____
8	The system's ability to reduce error.
	Irrelevant _____ Not important _____ Important _____ Critical _____
	If you answered either IMPORTANT or CRITICAL, please give details:
	_____
	_____
9	The system's ability to provide competitive advantage.
	Irrelevant _____ Not important _____ Important _____ Critical _____
	If you answered either IMPORTANT or CRITICAL, please give details:
	_____
	_____
10	The system's ability to catch up with competition.
	Irrelevant _____ Not important _____ Important _____ Critical _____
	If you answered either IMPORTANT or CRITICAL, please give details:
	_____
	_____
11	The system's ability to provide improved management control.
	Irrelevant _____ Not important _____ Important _____ Critical _____
	If you answered either IMPORTANT or CRITICAL, please give details:
	_____
	_____

12	The system's ability to provide improved management productivity. Irrelevant _____ Not important _____ Important_____Critical _____ If you answered either IMPORTANT or CRITICAL, please give details: _____ _____
13	The system's ability to provide improved staff morale. Irrelevant _____ Not important _____ Important_____Critical _____ If you answered either IMPORTANT or CRITICAL, please give details: _____ _____
14	The system's ability to provide an improved corporate image. Irrelevant _____ Not important _____ Important_____Critical _____ If you answered either IMPORTANT or CRITICAL, please give details: _____ _____
15	The system's ability to provide improved customer service. Irrelevant _____ Not important _____ Important_____Critical _____ If you answered either IMPORTANT or CRITICAL, please give details: _____ _____
16	The system's ability to provide improved client/seller relationships. Irrelevant _____ Not important _____ Important_____Critical _____ If you answered either IMPORTANT or CRITICAL, please give details: _____ _____

Figure 9.18: Questionnaire used in conjunction with the specification of requirements

THE MEASUREMENT OF INFORMATION SYSTEMS BENEFITS

Answer the questions by ticking the option which corresponds to your opinion of the probability that the following benefits will be achieved by the proposed system.

1	The system's ability to reduce overall costs.
	Unlikely_____ Possibly _____ Probably_____ Certainly _____
	If you answered either PROBABLY or CERTAINLY, please give details:
	_____
	_____

2	The system's ability to displace costs.
	Unlikely_____ Possibly _____ Probably_____ Certainly _____
	If you answered either PROBABLY or CERTAINLY, please give details:
	_____
	_____

3	The system's ability to avoid costs.
	Unlikely_____ Possibly _____ Probably_____ Certainly _____
	If you answered either PROBABLY or CERTAINLY, please give details:
	_____
	_____

4	The system's ability to provide opportunity for revenue growth.
	Unlikely_____ Possibly _____ Probably_____ Certainly _____
	If you answered either PROBABLY or CERTAINLY, please give details:
	_____
	_____

5	The system's ability to provide improved management information.
	Unlikely_____ Possibly _____ Probably_____ Certainly _____
	If you answered either PROBABLY or CERTAINLY, please give details:
	_____
	_____

6	The system's ability to provide improved staff productivity.
	Unlikely _____ Possibly _____ Probably _____ Certainly _____
	If you answered either PROBABLY or CERTAINLY, please give details:
	_____
	_____
7	The system's ability to provide capacity for increased volume.
	Unlikely _____ Possibly _____ Probably _____ Certainly _____
	If you answered either PROBABLY or CERTAINLY, please give details:
	_____
	_____
8	The system's ability to reduce error.
	Unlikely _____ Possibly _____ Probably _____ Certainly _____
	If you answered either PROBABLY or CERTAINLY, please give details:
	_____
	_____
9	The system's ability to provide competitive advantage.
	Unlikely _____ Possibly _____ Probably _____ Certainly _____
	If you answered either PROBABLY or CERTAINLY, please give details:
	_____
	_____
10	The system's ability to catch up with competition.
	Unlikely _____ Possibly _____ Probably _____ Certainly _____
	If you answered either PROBABLY or CERTAINLY, please give details:
	_____
	_____
11	The system's ability to provide improved management control.
	Unlikely _____ Possibly _____ Probably _____ Certainly _____
	If you answered either PROBABLY or CERTAINLY, please give details:
	_____
	_____

12	The system's ability to provide improved management productivity. Unlikely_____ Possibly _____ Probably_____ Certainly _____ If you answered either PROBABLY or CERTAINLY, please give details: _____ _____
13	The system's ability to provide improved staff morale. Unlikely_____ Possibly _____ Probably_____ Certainly _____ If you answered either PROBABLY or CERTAINLY, please give details: _____ _____
14	The system's ability to provide an improved corporate image. Unlikely_____ Possibly _____ Probably_____ Certainly _____ If you answered either PROBABLY or CERTAINLY, please give details: _____ _____
15	The system's ability to provide improved customer service. Unlikely_____ Possibly _____ Probably_____ Certainly _____ If you answered either PROBABLY or CERTAINLY, please give details: _____ _____
16	The system's ability to provide improved client/seller relationships. Unlikely_____ Possibly _____ Probably_____ Certainly _____ If you answered either PROBABLY or CERTAINLY, please give details: _____ _____

Figure 9.19: Questionnaire used by systems development project managers

The third measure of benefits was obtained by requesting that the users complete a questionnaire that attempting to collect data on the actual performance of the system. This questionnaire is shown in Figure 9.20.

THE MEASUREMENT OF INFORMATION SYSTEMS BENEFITS

Answer the questions by ticking the option which corresponds to your opinion of the performance of the system.

1	The system's ability to reduce overall costs. Very poor_____ Poor _____ Good_____ Excellent _____ If you answered either GOOD or EXCELLENT, please give details: _____ _____
2	The system's ability to displace costs. Very poor_____ Poor _____ Good_____ Excellent _____ If you answered either GOOD or EXCELLENT, please give details: _____ _____
3	The system's ability to avoid costs. Very poor_____ Poor _____ Good_____ Excellent _____ If you answered either GOOD or EXCELLENT, please give details: _____ _____
4	The system's ability to provide opportunity for revenue growth. Very poor_____ Poor _____ Good_____ Excellent _____ If you answered either GOOD or EXCELLENT, please give details: _____ _____
5	The system's ability to provide improved management information. Very poor_____ Poor _____ Good_____ Excellent _____ If you answered either GOOD or EXCELLENT, please give details: _____ _____

6	The system's ability to provide improved staff productivity.
	Very poor _____ Poor _____ Good _____ Excellent _____
	If you answered either GOOD or EXCELLENT, please give details:
	_____
	_____

7	The system's ability to provide capacity for increased volume.
	Very poor _____ Poor _____ Good _____ Excellent _____
	If you answered either GOOD or EXCELLENT, please give details:
	_____
	_____

8	The system's ability to reduce error.
	Very poor _____ Poor _____ Good _____ Excellent _____
	If you answered either GOOD or EXCELLENT, please give details:
	_____
	_____

9	The system's ability to provide competitive advantage.
	Very poor _____ Poor _____ Good _____ Excellent _____
	If you answered either GOOD or EXCELLENT, please give details:
	_____
	_____

10	The system's ability to catch up with competition.
	Very poor _____ Poor _____ Good _____ Excellent _____
	If you answered either GOOD or EXCELLENT, please give details:
	_____
	_____

11	The system's ability to provide improved management control.
	Very poor _____ Poor _____ Good _____ Excellent _____
	If you answered either GOOD or EXCELLENT, please give details:
	_____
	_____

12	The system's ability to provide improved management productivity. Very poor_____ Poor _____ Good_____ Excellent _____ If you answered either GOOD or EXCELLENT, please give details: _____ _____
13	The system's ability to provide improved staff morale. Very poor_____ Poor _____ Good_____ Excellent _____ If you answered either GOOD or EXCELLENT, please give details: _____ _____
14	The system's ability to provide an improved corporate image. Very poor_____ Poor _____ Good_____ Excellent _____ If you answered either GOOD or EXCELLENT, please give details: _____ _____
15	The system's ability to provide improved customer service. Very poor_____ Poor _____ Good_____ Excellent _____ If you answered either GOOD or EXCELLENT, please give details: _____ _____
16	The system's ability to provide improved client/seller relationships. Very poor_____ Poor _____ Good_____ Excellent _____ If you answered either GOOD or EXCELLENT, please give details: _____ _____

Figure 9.20: Questionnaire used by ultimate users of systems

As there are three data sets collected, described in Figure 9.21, there is a potential for three distinct sets of gaps. The three different data sets collected are shown in Figure 9.22, and Figure 9.23 shows how the relative values from the different

9.23 shows how the relative values from the different question-naires could be presented.

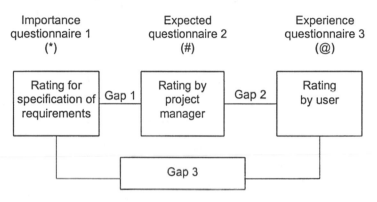

Figure 9.21: Gap analysis concepts

In Figure 9.23 importance scores are indicated by *, while expectation scores are shown as # and experience scores are expressed as @.

Concerning the first gap, GAP₁, if (* – #) > 0 then the systems developers are claiming to have under-achieved in terms of what the original systems architects believed was possible. If however (* – #) < 0 then the systems developers are claiming to have over-achieved in terms of what the original systems architects believed was possible. If (* – #) = 0 then there is a concurrence of opinion between the systems architects and the systems developers.

Concerning the second gap, GAP₂, if (# – @) > 0 then the systems users are claiming that the benefits delivered have under-performed in terms of what the systems development project manager believed was possible. If however (# – @) < 0 then the systems users are claiming that the system has over-performed in terms of what the systems development project manager believed was possible. If (# – @) = 0 then there is a concurrence of opinion between the systems architects and the systems users.

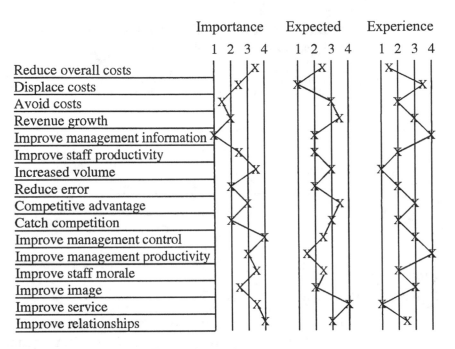

Figure 9.22: Results showing three different data sets

	1	2	3	4
Ability to reduce overall costs	@	#	*	
Ability to displace costs	#	*	@	
Ability to avoid costs	*	@	#	

*   Importance scores
\#   Expectation scores
@   Experience scores

Figure 9.23: Presentation of results

Concerning the third gap, GAP_3, if (* – @) > 0 then the systems users are claiming that the benefits delivered have under-performed in terms of what the original systems architects believed was possible. If however (* – @) < 0 then the systems users are claiming that the systems has over-performed in terms of what the original systems architects believed was possible. If (* – @) = 0 then there is a concurrence of opinion between the systems architects and the systems users.

A positive GAP$_1$, i.e. gaps between the original systems architects and the systems development project manager may be interpreted as an under-achievement in the firm's delivery process. This under-delivery may be attributed to over-enthusiasm or the lack of expected resources, or the fact that the system was not fully understood at the outset. A negative GAP$_1$ may be attributed to the reverse.

A positive GAP$_2$, i.e. gaps between the systems development project manager and the users, may be interpreted as an under-achievement in the firm's systems realisation process. This under-achievement may be attributed to the lack of training, the lack of systems documentation or the fact that the system was not fully understood or to all three such causes. A negative GAP$_2$ may be attributed to the reverse.

A positive GAP$_3$, i.e. gaps between the original systems architects and the systems users may be interpreted as an indication of user dissatisfaction, or as an indication of the lack of effectiveness of the firm's IT. Attributing this to specific causes may be difficult and thus GAP$_1$ and GAP$_2$ may be an invaluable guide in this respect. A negative GAP$_3$ may be attributed to the reverse. This gap analysis may identify complex relationships within the firm between users and systems people.

It is possible for there to be a positive or negative GAP$_3$ while GAP$_1$ and GAP$_2$ have different signs. For example, it is possible that there is general user dissatisfaction with the system as shown by the positive GAP$_3$ and by a positive GAP$_2$ but there may be simultaneously a negative GAP$_1$. Such a situation would indicate a position where there were major misunderstandings between the systems professionals and the users. On the other hand there may be a very positive user view while the architects and the systems development project manager rated the system less favourably. Both these situations suggest the need for extensive training of IS professionals and users.

The same type of analysis conducted on the results of the one gap, as has been described earlier in this chapter, may be performed on the two/three gap approach. Snake diagrams may also be drawn which are invaluable in interpreting the results. Factor analysis may also be used to explore underlying relationships in the data. As may be seen from the questionnaires shown in Figures 9.18 to 9.20 this research calls for descriptive explanations from all three types of informants. These explanations may also provide most valuable insights for management.

This type of study is longitudinal in nature. Therefore it will take at least a year or two between the time the first data set is obtained until final analysis may be conducted. However, the insight this technique can provide will be worth the effort and the wait.

9.14 Using a questionnaire approach to measure IT effectiveness

The following is a step-by-step guide to using a survey approach to the measurement of IT effectiveness.

Obtain authorisation for the measurement exercise

This is best obtained from the highest possible level in the firm and should also have the approval of the IS director.

Establish a focus group

A focus group consists of a number of IS and user executives who define the issues to be included.

Construct the questionnaire

Use information obtained from the focus group to develop the measuring instrument.

Conduct a pilot survey

Produce a questionnaires, and complete on a face-to-face basis with 5 to 10 prospective respondents.

Use feedback from the pilot to refine the questionnaire

The pilot survey will show those areas of the questionnaire that need enhancing and those areas that are extraneous.

Select a sample

Choose an appropriate sample that is representative of the organisation as a whole. It should include users from all levels of the management hierarchy.

Dispatch questionnaires

A fixed date for the return of questionnaires is essential, and respondents should be made aware of this fact.

Collect questionnaires

Depending on the distribution of the sample, the questionnaires can either be collected or returned by the respondents.

Analyse results

Collate and analyse the results. This can be time-consuming, but is essential if valuable information is to be generated.

Present report

The results of the questionnaire should be summarised in a written report, using as little technical jargon as possible.

9.15 Summary

There is a growing trend towards the utilisation of user satisfaction measurements as a surrogate for information systems effectiveness. This is a holistic approach which enables the firm to obtain an overview of the effectiveness of the IS function. Gap analysis is a popular way of conducting these studies and it is not difficult to construct an appropriate questionnaire. However, the analysis of the statistics that these techniques produce is not trivial and requires the assistance of a statistician.

10 | Ranking and scoring

We propose that the real benefits of information technology results from a change in the business.

M. Parker and R. Benson, 'Information Economics: An Introduction'
(1987)

10.1 Introduction

An approach that an organisation may wish to undertake in assessing the potential of an IT system is to perform an overview evaluation using a simple ranking and scoring technique. The procedure involves rating a system or a group of systems against a series of general evaluation criteria. This approach is quite similar to what Parker *et al.* (1989) refer to as 'information economics'. The evaluation criteria involve issues such as industry attractiveness, internal value chain, industry value chain, offensive or defensive thrusts, etc. Other issues not directly related to strategic concerns, but which affect equally important dimensions of a system may also be included.

10.2 Five steps to evaluation

There are five steps involved in an overview evaluation:

1 Select the criteria;

2 Associate weights to each criterion;

3 Score systems in terms of how they satisfy the criteria;

4 Calculate a system's rating by multiplying each score by the weight and then summing to a total.

5 Select the system with the greatest total score.

The key issues of ranking and scoring addressed here are:

♦ Strategic value

♦ Critical value

♦ Operational value

♦ Architectural value

♦ Investment value

♦ Risk assessment

Strategic value

The strategic value refers to the system's potential to create for the organisation a competitive advantage. This may be done in many ways, including effecting one or more of the five industry forces as described by Porter (1985). Competitive advantage may also be derived by improving the organisation's own value chain internally, or by changing the industry value chain. Strategic value may be derived from an offensive thrust or by a defensive reaction to other players in the market.

Critical value

The critical value of a system refers to its ability to improve the effectiveness with which the organisation competes. The attributes of the systems listed under this category will not *per se* deliver a new competitive advantage, but will generally improve the amount of basic advantage already available to the organisation.

Operational value

Operational value embraces both systems that relate to efficiency issues, as well as issues that are fundamental to the organisation's continued existence. These are not strictly strategic, although they are of vital importance to the organisation and are, therefore, considered at the same time as the strategic issues.

Architectural value

Architectural value considers major infrastructural systems without which the information systems department probably could not function at all.

Investment value

Investment value refers to a measure of the financial benefit that a system delivers to the organisation.

Risk assessment

Risk assessment represents both conceptual and practical problems. Although it is relatively easy to define risk it is difficult to actually assess its impact on a particular information system or project. The risk of a project is the potential for the actual values of the input and output variables to fluctuate from their original estimates. For example, although the list price of a new mainframe might be £250,000, by the time the organisation pays the invoice for it, the amount may be greater or less due to a price change or exchange rate fluctuation, or even a pre-installation upgrade. As original estimates may vary upward or downward, the measure of risk should reflect both the project's positive and negative potential. As most managers are averse to risk, risk is often only seen as a negative aspect of a system. The result of this is that risky investments tend to have their benefits understated and their costs overstated. Thus, risk is treated as a cost, resulting in a reduced estimated value of the system. In general, this is not a satisfactory way of handling risk as it does not reflect the up-side potential inherent in the risk, which is as intrinsic to the concept as the downside. Entrepreneurial managers may well wish to emphasise the up-side potential of the investment, making their judgement on that evaluation rather than on the negative downside evaluation.

10.3 A spreadsheet system for overview evaluation

A spreadsheet can be useful in assisting the evaluation of the strategic potential of IT investment using this ranking and scoring technique.

The primary function of the spreadsheet is to offer a checklist of issues that should be considered during an IT investment evaluation process. The secondary purpose of the spreadsheet is to calculate a total score, which represents the perceived value of the systems under review. The calculations involved are trivial, but the purpose of the spreadsheet is to offer a systematic approach to the ranking and scoring process.

The first task in using this system is to select the evaluation criteria that are most relevant in the organisation's particular circumstances. The criteria listed in Figure 10.1 are typical issues of concern, but of course they could change from organisation to organisation and with the type of information system being considered.

The second step is to allocate weights to each of these criteria or factors on a scale of 1 to 10. The objective of this is to effectively spell out the relative importance of the factors to the organisation. The final step is to score the system or systems under review on a scale of 1 to 5 for each of the criteria chosen.

Figure 10.1 shows the options from which the evaluation criteria are made and 10 evaluation criteria have been selected.

Each of the 10 criteria chosen from the list of 23 is then weighted on a scale of 1 to 10 and a weighted decision variable table is created that can be used as a checklist with which to compare competing information systems. Each competing system is then individually scored against the weighted decision variables using a scale of 1 to 5. For each competing system the weight of the decision variable is multiplied by the score, and these values are then summed.

IS selection system				
Indicate the **10** most relevant factors with an x.				
Strategic value		*Operational value*	*Risk assessment*	
Industry attractiveness		Administration improvement	New technology	x
Internal value chain	x	Legislative requirements	New application	x
Industry value chain	x		Application size	x
Offensive	x	*Architectural value*	Market damage	x
Defensive	x	Operating system		
		Comms. infrastructure		
Critical value		Languages		
Expense control				
Asset reduction		*Investment value*		
Equipment utilisation		Payback	x	
Sales increase		NPV/PI	x	
Production enhance-ment		IRR		
Waste minimisation				

Figure 10.1: Selecting the decision variables

Figure 10.2 shows the selected criteria, together with their weighted importance and the results of the evaluation for three different information systems.

		System 1		System 2		System 3	
Selected criteria	*Weighting*	*Score*	*Value*	*Score*	*Value*	*Score*	*Value*
Internal value chain	8	5	40	4	32	2	16
Industry value chain	9	4	36	4	36	5	45
Offensive	10	3	30	4	40	5	50
Defensive	7	2	14	4	28	2	14
Payback	9	5	45	4	36	5	45
NPV/PI	9	4	36	4	36	5	45
New technology	−8	3	−24	2	−16	1	-8
New application	−5	3	−15	2	−10	2	−10
Application size	−7	2	−14	5	−35	2	−14
Market damage	−6	5	−30	5	−30	0	0
			118		117		183

Figure 10.2: Weighted criteria with scores for three competing information systems

Figure 10.2 shows all the chosen decision variables as well as the weights, scores and results for each of the systems being analysed.

Note that the negative scores for the risk assessment criteria in Figure 10.2 reflect the risk aversion expressed by most managers. However, an entrepreneurial manager's view of the risk inherent in the investment opportunity could be expressed as a positive score.

Looking at the results in Figure 10.2, it would seem that System 3 best fits the requirements of the based on the selected criteria. However, a risk positive approach to the risk criteria could lead to quite a different system being indicated as the most appropriate selection.

The interpretation of results from a system such as the one illustrated here is not trivial, and neither is it necessarily obvious from these values which investment will be preferred.

10.4 Summary

In this chapter, one approach to using a ranking and scoring technique has been described. Such techniques are quite popular, and are therefore used extensively in business. However, the variables used and the weighting and scoring ranges employed may vary enormously. Readers are, therefore, invited to choose their own variables and use their preferred weighting and scoring measures.

11 | Value for money and health checks

If two people stand at the same place and gaze in the same direction, we must, under pain of solipsism, conclude that they receive closely similar stimuli. But people do not see stimuli; our knowledge of them is highly theoretical and abstract. Instead they have sensations, and we are under no compulsion to suppose that the sensations of our two viewers are the same. ...Among the few things that we know about it with assurance are: that very different stimuli can produce the same sensations; that the same stimulus can produce very different sensations; and, finally, that the route from stimuli to sensation is in part conditioned by education.

T. S. Kuhn, *The Structure of Scientific Revolutions* (1967)

11.1 Efficiency and effectiveness studies

A subject that is different, but relatively close to measuring IT benefits, is that of conducting value for money (VFM) and health check review (HCR) studies of the information systems department. These are very large subjects in their own right, and this chapter provides a brief overview of the area.

The aim of a value for money study is to establish whether the ISD is functioning efficiently, and whether the amount being spent on the department is proportionate to the service level being obtained. Questions such as 'Is the IS management making the most of the funds invested?', or 'Can the organisation obtain the same service cheaper?' are asked. A value for money study may also ask if different ways of managing the ISD could be applied, so that a better level of service will be obtained for the same expenditure. Thus value for money studies often attempt to identify opportunities for improvements and areas for general cost saving. Furthermore, pending resource requirements are often addressed in a value for money study to see if there is any way of minimising, or simply reducing, this expenditure. In fact, a value for money study can address any of the operative issues faced by the ISD.

Some value for money studies extend beyond considerations of the efficiency of the ISD to also look at the effectiveness of the information systems function. Such studies are usually much more extensive than the relatively straightforward efficiency reviews. Effectiveness studies are sometimes referred to as health check reviews and focus on strategic issues as well as operational issues. Therefore, a HCR requires a much broader view of the organisation and the role that the ISD plays.

11.2 A value for money study

It is important to establish that a value for money study is not simply an audit. The term audit has a very negative connotation and can produce very unusual behaviour in those members of staff who feel threatened by an external inspection. A value for money study is aimed as much at highlighting areas of excellence, as identifying those areas requiring remedial action. The study includes a discussion of the many different ways in which an ISD may be improved, and the selection of the most practical and cost-effective way of so doing with relation to the organisation in question.

The deliverables of a value for money study *inter alia* include:

1   A balanced report presented as objectively as possible highlighting the strengths and weaknesses of the ISD;

2   A better idea of how to use the resources available to the ISD;

3   A clearer idea of what the ISD budget can actually buy;

4 A more motivated ISD management team who, as a result of participating in the study, have been highly involved in assessing their own work and that of their colleagues;

5 A top management team who are likely to better understand the challenges faced by their ISD;

6 A list of action points.

VFM studies may be conducted either internally, i.e., by the organisation's own staff, or by external consultants.

There are a number of different approaches to value for money studies adopted by the large consultancies offering their own proprietary methodologies. Thus, Andersen Consultancy, Coopers & Lybrand Deloitte, Hoskins, Peat Marwick McLintock, to mention only a few of the larger organisations, have their own methodologies for value for money studies. Organisations who wish to conduct their own VFM studies should establish their own structured methodology before commencing.

If it is decided to use outside consultants to perform a VFM study, this must be approached in such a way that ISD personnel do not feel threatened. Failure to achieve this will lead to mis-information and inaccurate information being supplied. The most successful approach seems to be to use small teams involving both external consultants and selected internal personnel.

11.3 Setting up a value for money study

Once the study team has been selected, the first step is a meeting to agree the objectives and the scope of the study in direct relation to the organisation. Furthermore, the resources available for the study and the timescales must be clarified, and the deliverables defined. A team leader should also be appointed at this initial meeting. This should be someone from within the organisation who will be responsible for co-ordinating the work of the study with the other team members.

In defining the objectives, four main questions feature:

1 Is the ISD providing value for money?

2 Are pending resource requirements for the ISD reasonable?

3 What opportunities exist for cost savings, improved efficiency and effectiveness?

4 What is the ISD doing especially well and how can this excellence be extended?

The precise scope of the study categories will vary extensively depending on the organisation, but there are 12 identifiable areas that can be considered when setting up a study:

1 Hardware

2 Software

3 Staffing

4 Service levels

5 Security

6 Technical support

7 User support

8 Costs and charges

9 Application systems development

10 Networks

11 Integration with the rest of the organisation

12 The information systems plan.

The resources available for the study in terms of access to people, documentation, equipment, etc. must be clarified. In addition, the overall timescale for the study must be clearly identified. A traditional approach to performing value for money studies is for the study team to examine documentation, interview personnel and generally to observe the function of the ISD. Progress meetings will be necessary to review the on-going progress of the study and to discuss the results to date. A time limit should be set for completing personnel interviews, reviewing documentation and other procedures, and progress meetings should also be scheduled from the outset. This enables a date to be put on the submission of the final report.

In the setting up stage of the study, the required presentation approach for the deliverables should be agreed. This should include a succinct management report of the findings and recommendations of the study. The first part of the VFM report should provide an assessment of the current situation, whereas the second part of the report will focus on an action plan indicating how the performance of the IS function may be improved. Where necessary, appendices may be attached showing results of the analysis used to support findings and recommendations. In addition, an action plan should be provided with definitive practical suggestions for improved cost-effectiveness and department efficiency.

11.4 Detailed planning of the study

The operational issues listed in the scope of the study incorporated most of the areas that an ISD might be involved with. However, this list will vary to some extent from organisation to organisation, and the study must be structured to meet the specific needs of the organisation.

The following sub-sections indicate the type of information that the study team should aim to derive within each of the scope categories. In every case, having collected and analysed the information, an indication as to how well the ISD function is operating in that area should be reported, together with suggestions for improved costs-effectiveness and efficiency. By the end of the study a pattern should develop which will show the broad areas where most improvement can be gained.

11.4.1   Hardware and software

It is important to determine exactly what hardware and software exists in the organisation, and what is in use in the organisation. This will, in most cases, involve personal computers on the desks of end-users, as well as the equipment under the direct control of the data processing department. The range of hardware configurations and versions of software in use should be established. In many cases this is a non-trivial task and the establishment of a hardware and software asset register is a key component in any VFM study. Other aspects of the hardware and software inventory include what software is installed on machines, but not actually used by the user? What is the future plan for hardware and software growth? What is already on order, and what capacity planning techniques are employed? How effective is the data processing function?

If possible, existing statistics should be reviewed, and an indication as to the relevance and application of current configurations with relation to workload should be established. Performance monitoring tools may already be in use, and if so, data from these should be analysed to suggest the value for money currently being obtained. Other monitoring and modelling procedures might be suggested by the study, which could enhance cost-effectiveness.

The areas of hardware and software maintenance should be addressed. How much of this is outsourced and how much is performed internally? The study should examine the approach currently employed by the organisation and comment of the cost-effectiveness of this approach.

11.4.2   Staffing

A headcount of ISD staff should be taken, as well as an organisation chart for the department. ISD staff placed in user departments must also be counted. Manpower planning procedures should be examined in relation to the current workload.

It may also be useful to perform a study of the current working practices and conditions. This will involve reviewing rates of pay, leave entitlement, as well as training commitments. In so doing, 'good practice' may be identified and recommendations be provided as to how these may be implemented. The question of analyst, programmer and operator productivity must also be addressed, as well as the staff involved in data entry, data validation and information distribution. Key performance indicators should be identified for use in comparability studies in order that future objectives may be set and improvements be monitored.

11.4.3 Service levels

This involves looking at the current agreements and commitments that the ISD has to clients in terms of turnaround times, response times, availability, etc. If a service or help desk exists, its efficiency in terms of staffing and response time should be examined. What tools for recording problems and solutions are used? It may be appropriate to suggest the creation of such a service if it has not already been established. As even quite small organisations can benefit enormously from the introduction of sound service-level agreements, this area is frequently given considerable attention.

11.4.4 Security

The study should examine all levels of computer related security, including physical access as well as controls over input, processing, and output procedures. How computer security fits in with the general security of the organisation should be examined, and where the responsibility for security lies will be important. Physical access covers both controls over access to the premises, as well as to machines, software and data. Special attention to the control of operating software should be given. What, if any, written procedures are there, and what happens in actual practice? How does the organisation intend to minimise attacks from hackers and viruses? Potential problem areas should be highlighted. If the company has a disaster recovery plan, this should be reviewed and the methodology used compared to others. The cost-effectiveness of this and alternative approaches can then be assessed.

11.4.5 Technical support

The present practices and procedures should be reviewed. This will include looking at how hardware and software upgrades are handled, what standardisation is in place and how this can be improved. The commitment to training from the ISD should be examined as efficiency can be greatly enhanced if users are properly trained in the applications they should be using.

11.4.6 User support

How much support do users feel they get from ISD and how approachable do they feel ISD personnel are? Are requests dealt with promptly and sympathetically? Consider establishing departmental 'gurus' to filter trivial problems away from ISD.

11.4.7 Costs and charges

The costs incurred in the IT area by the organisation should be assessed and areas for potential savings highlighted. It is important that IT services are charged for. However, this implies that all IS users should have a budget and a certain degree of discretion as to how to spend it. Charging formulae should be evaluated together with algorithms for efficiency and fairness.

11.4.8 Application systems development

Examine the standards and methodologies currently in use for systems development and ongoing maintenance. Are CASE tools or other development aids being used? Evaluate the efficiency and effectiveness of these procedures. Compare the perceptions of the systems as seen by the users, user management and development staff. Derive a satisfaction quotient.

11.4.9 Networks

Examine the current design and configuration of online networks in terms of cost-effectiveness and efficiency. Determine whether alternative approaches such as PC networks could be applied, whether networks have enough capacity and are performing to an efficient level. What is the loading and the downtime of the network and can this be improved? How many users are currently connected and can this be increased? If the organisation has not established a policy to network PCs, this is a potential area for dramatic cost improvements as software, data and peripherals can be shared and accessed more readily.

11.4.10 Integration with the rest of the organisation

The study should clearly establish the relationship of the ISD to the rest of the organisation. A review of the history of the department, its workload growth, reorganisations, management changes, etc. is useful. Who is responsible for communicating with other departments within the organisation as well as with clients and suppliers? What is the reporting hierarchy within the ISD and to the rest of the organisation?

11.4.11 The information systems plan

If the organisation has undertaken the development of a strategic information systems plan (SISP), this will provide important information for the VFM study. The plan should be examined to see how many of the recommendations therein are in practice, and how successful they are. Has the information systems plan been linked to the overall corporate plan of the organisation? What monitoring of the plan has taken place and what results have been attained?

11.5 Analysing the results

The performance of the ISD in each of the categories may be assessed on a scale of perhaps four points. Such a scale would have the categories: excellent, good, poor and very poor, where 4 is excellent, 3 is good, 2 is poor and 1 is very poor. The scores could be derived by averaging views obtained at interviews, or by collecting data using a questionnaire. Figure 11.1 shows the results of a study showing a relatively high VFM, and Figure 11.2 represents the results of a study showing a low VFM.

Hardware	3.2	Costs	3.9
Software	3.4	Applications	2.9
Staff	3.6	Networks	3.5
Service	2.8	Security	2.1
Technical support	2.9	Integration	2.8
User support	1.9	IS planning	2.8

Figure 11.1: Results of a high VFM study

Hardware	2.4	Costs	0.9
Software	2.3	Applications	2.8
Staff	2.9	Networks	3.5
Service	0.9	Security	2.1
Technical support	2.2	Integration	2.2
User support	1.5	IS planning	1.8

Figure 11.2: Results of a low VFM study

The results of the scores may be presented in a number of different ways. One method of presentation, used by Coopers & Lybrand Deloitte, is that of a wheel diagram. In Figure 11.3 this concept has been adopted to accommodate the twelve scope categories using the ratings shown in Figure 11.1. Figure 11.4 uses the data from Figure 11.2. The area of the polygon produced by joining the scores is a reflection of the VFM the organisation receives. If the area is large, the VFM is considerable, whereas if the area is small the VFM is low.

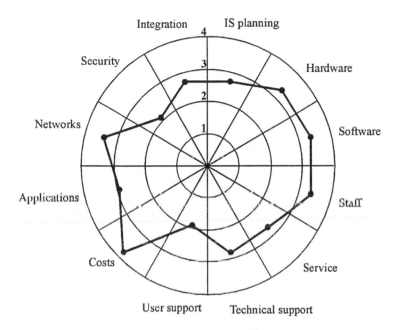

Figure 11.3: Wheel diagram showing high VFM

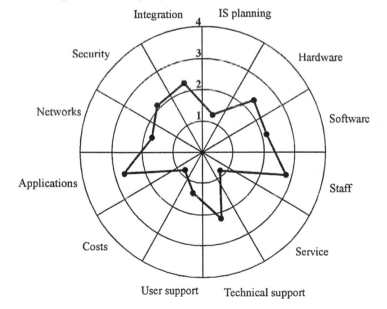

Figure 11.4: Wheel diagram showing low VFM

11.6   A list of action points

A VFM study must indicate how the performance of the ISD may be improved and this should be expressed through a list of action points. These may address such issues as:

♦ Increasing/decreasing the staff complement.

♦ Replacing hardware/software.

♦ Initiating training programmes.

♦ Implementing additional security procedures.

♦ Initiating strategic information systems planning.

♦ Controlling end-user computing.

The amount of detail that will be supplied with the action points will depend upon the terms of reference for the study. In some cases, the detail may be minimal, whereas in others the action points may be very specific

11.7   A health check review (HCR) study

Most of the topics discussed so far have been looked at from the point of view of assessing the level of efficiency in the ISD. Thus, the main focus has been on operational issues. In some cases, it can be useful to the organisation to measure the value for money they are getting from an effectiveness viewpoint. In this case, a more strategic view of the IS function is required.

Research has been conducted by The National Computing Centre (NCC) in a number of large UK establishments, with the aim of discovering how effective IT is in their organisations and how this can be improved. They defined effectiveness as the contribution made by the IS function to the organisation's objectives and the organisation's performance. Some aspects of the NCC study are described here to indicate how extensive a HCR study may be.

11.8 NCC HCR study

The main aim of the study was to define and measure what is meant by IT effectiveness. This was addressed by considering the following three key questions:

♦ What are the most important elements in effectiveness?

♦ How should each be defined?

♦ On what scale can each be measured?

The study was highly participative, comprising reviews, seminars, research projects, chief executives' conference, as well as regular reports of the findings. Participants in the study decided for themselves the subjects to be covered in seminars and briefings, arising from the findings of the reviews.

In order to approach these issues in some kind of structured way, the study prepared a pilot review of the IS function. Feedback from the pilot produced a second-generation set of questions, which formed the basis of a review procedure that could be applied and compared to each of the participating organisations.

The resulting review procedure was based around the following 12 elements of effectiveness, which were grouped under three headings of IT Policy, IT Contribution and IT Delivery. Each of the 12 elements had a definition and a list of issues to be discussed with each organisation during the review process.

IT Policy

♦ Corporate IT strategy

♦ IT planning and management

♦ IT investment

♦ IT budgeting

IT Contribution

♦ Customer relations

♦ Supply of IT services

♦ Evaluation of existing systems

IT Delivery

♦ Technology strategy

♦ Development planning

♦ Operations planning

♦ Human resources strategy

♦ Quality strategy.

From an independent assessment by a consultant, a qualitative scale of measurement was produced, consisting of five statements reflecting the level of sophistication, where A represented Advanced Practice and E represented Unsophisticated Practice. Ratings B to D represented points in between. The researchers emphasise that these results should not be taken purely at face value, seeing A as good and E as bad, but rather as a basis for discussion and refinement of the process.

An enhanced wheel or web diagram could then be produced giving a profile of each participant's response to the 12 elements. Figure 11.5 is an example of such a diagram, but does not reflect a particular participant in the study.

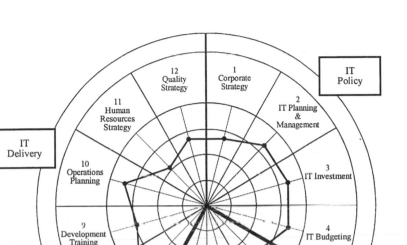

Figure 11.5: Wheel diagram showing 12 review elements

Although the individual results for each organisation were confidential, Figure 11.6 shows an example of the type of statements associated with the ratings.

Most advanced performance found:	IT and corporate strategies are closely integrated with effective feedback achievements.
Median performance:	Corporate and IT strategies are related but not integrated.
Least advanced performance:	Corporate and IT strategies are loosely linked.

Figure 11.6: Details of corporate IT strategy

The results of the reviews produced a number of significant points:

1 A set of definitions and measurements were produced which could be used to test effectiveness. Participants in the study

saw how they measured on a number of key issues alongside other partners. The following quotations are typical:

In our relationships with our customers, our practice is among the most advanced in the Joint Venture.

We thought we were doing a sound job on development planning, but most of the Partners are further advanced than us.

None of the Partners really has a handle on quality strategy; we are not alone.

The identification and presentation of best practice in information management has given us a standard to aim at.

2   A series of recommendations for each of the participants was produced. These provide an objective base for internal discussions on how the effectiveness of the IS function can be improved.

3   The reviews highlighted differences between participants' individual preoccupations and the current fashions. For example, fashionable IT issues included: using IT as a strategic weapon, user friendliness, and open systems. None of the participants considered these as a preoccupation.

4   Most organisations were still in the infrastructure phase, by which is meant automating clerical and routine operations, creating a communications network and establishing a base of routine transaction data. The IS department is forming a platform of understanding, confidence and comfort for users and, more importantly, for top management and line management. Superstructure refers to the adventurous, risk-taking, act-of-faith type of IS. Without substantial success on the infrastructure side, superstructure cannot be properly addressed.

5   The reviews showed that best practice is culture dependent. In a high-tech environment, where the top management are interested and involved in IS, performance expectations are

different to those organisations where top management are more involved in other issues.

The key issues for continued study as seen by the participants themselves were stated as:

- Effectiveness as top management see it
- Developing the definition and measurement of effectiveness
- Linking IS and corporate strategies
- Sharpening and promulgating IS policies
- Human resources
- Quality.

11.9 Summary

Value for money analysis is a key issue. Studies should be conducted on a regular basis, perhaps every two or three years. Using, at least partially, external consultants is recommended in order to retain a level of objectivity. The results of a VFM study should be presented to top management in order that findings can be incorporated into the on-going development of the ISD. However, VFM analyses are operational in nature and if strategic issues are to be included, then a HCR is required. These studies are much more comprehensive.

12 | Designing IT surveys for benefit measurement

All we can expect from one another is new and interesting information. We cannot expect answers. Solutions, as quantum reality teaches, are a temporary event, specific to a context, developed through the relationships of persons and circumstances.

Margaret Wheatley, *Leadership and the New Science* (1992)

12.1 Introduction

In order to measure IT effectiveness, most firms will need to administer a survey to staff, suppliers and customers/end-users. To do this, considerable knowledge and skill relating to survey design, sample choice and so on is required. If handled correctly, a survey can provide detailed information about systems effectiveness, but conducted poorly, the survey may be useless and a complete waste of time and money.

It is not possible to describe a single, concise way in which to conduct a survey using questionnaires. There are many different approaches to a survey, and the appropriateness of the approach is entirely dependent on the particular circumstances being addressed. Furthermore, survey design is still regarded as more of an art than a science. Unfortunately, much of what has been written about survey design has been in the form of admonishments. The focus has been predominantly on what not to do rather than on those things that will help.

It is generally agreed that each study using questionnaires is unique. Therefore, every study requires that a questionnaire be specifically designed to fit the study's peculiar needs.

In designing a survey there are three main issues to consider. These are:

1   The survey method

2   The sampling scheme

3   Questionnaire design.

Each of these components interacts with the others. In the following sections each will be discussed separately and the links that exist should become evident.

12.2   What is a survey?

A survey is a procedure for collecting information from individuals. The information sought can range from general background information such as age, income, size of the firm, the major areas of work of the firm, and the location of the firm, to that relating to beliefs, feelings, attitudes, life-styles and intentions, etc. Methods for obtaining such information usually fall into two categories, namely self-completion and interview administered. Self-completion methods include mail surveys, computerised surveys and so called on-board or in-company surveys. Interview administered surveys include personal interviews, telephone, and in-company/on-board surveys.

Each method possesses advantages and disadvantages. They do, however, all depend on the basic assumption that individuals subjected to questioning will be both willing and able to give truthful answers to the questions posed.

12.3   Approaches to data collection

12.3.1   Mail surveys

This method involves mailing the questionnaire to predetermined respondents with a covering letter. This form of survey is only necessary if there are many information system users and they are spread widely around the country or world.

Arguments for this method are that it allows a large sample, with wide locational coverage, to be easily obtained at a relatively low cost. Furthermore, it allows respondents to complete the form at their own pace and also ensures that they are free from being influenced by the interviewer. Generally speaking, these samples are easy to select.

Arguments against this method include the need for a very simple questionnaire, possible biased responses, and the low response rate. Many suggestions for improving the response rate have been put forward. A good covering letter, follow up questionnaire or reminder can boost response and so can the offering of incentives. Also, the problem of bias can be addressed through interviewing a small sample of non-respondents, or by comparing early returns with the returns from the follow-up questionnaire. The comparison is usually made on characteristics considered important to the study.

Typical response rates for this type of survey range from 1% to 60%.

12.3.2   In-company/on-board surveys

These surveys are carried out, for example, on board aircraft, in classrooms or in-company. In the information systems users' environment it may be possible to approach a group of IS users in the canteen, or perhaps a departmental head could be asked to bring his or her staff together for 25 minutes to fill out a questionnaire.

Arguments for this approach include that it provides a quick and cheap way of obtaining a large sample. This is because there is a captive audience. These surveys can be either interviewer or self-administered.

Arguments against this approach are that it invariably only includes users and that there may only be limited time available.

Typical response rates for this method range from 35% to 75%.

12.3.3 Telephone surveys

This method is a low-cost form of personal interviewing which can be used to obtain information quickly. With a small number of users this is a fairly practical way of being able to collect data. Of course, if the users are spread around the country, Europe, or the world, telephone costs can be very substantial and, therefore, a major consideration against this approach.

Arguments for this method are that it is a good compromise in that it combines personal contact with cheapness and wide coverage; it provides information quicker than face-to-face interviewing and mail questionnaires; and it is easy to supervise the interviewing process, thereby reducing interview error.

Arguments against this method are that the telephone interview must be short; that it could be biased since it is limited to listed telephone owners; and that it could be expensive. A way in which this bias is overcome is through digit dialling. One such scheme is the so called Plus-One sampling where a single, randomly selected number is added to each of a randomly selected sample of telephone numbers chosen from the telephone directory.

Typical response rates for this method range from 35% to 75%.

12.3.4 Personal interviews

This method requires a face-to-face conversation between the interviewer and the respondent. This approach is widely used in marketing research.

In the information systems users' environment, personal interviews are frequently used, especially to canvass the opinions of the decision-makers. It is an expensive means of collecting data in terms of time and money and therefore cannot be used with large groups where telephone or mail surveys are probably more appropriate.

The main argument for this approach is that in a long interview it is possible to probe complex issues that can be carried out in a relaxed atmosphere, developed by the interviewer. This should ensure a good quality response.

Arguments against this approach include the high amounts of time and cost involved. There is also the possibility of interviewer bias, and the difficulty in targeting users.

There are many factors that can influence the response rate but typical response rates for this method are between 50% and 80%.

12.3.5 Computer surveys

Where firms have electronic mail already established, a survey can be conducted across the network. This allows for instant data collection and summarisation. It is a relatively inexpensive method, easy to conduct and growing in popularity.

Arguments for this approach are that there is no need for printed questionnaires; interviewer bias is eliminated; checks can be built in so as to minimise response bias and optimise response consistency; and instantaneous analysis of the data is possible.

Arguments against this approach are that the design and programming of the questionnaire is likely to be a complex business involving considerable time and money up front; also respondents are restricted to e-mail users.

12.4 Sampling

All surveys require the selection of those individuals who are to provide the information. This set of individuals is called the sample. The sample comes from some much larger group of individuals or objects called the target population. The target population referred to as the *population* in the sequel, is that group about which it is intended to make generalised statements based on the sample findings. The sample is ideally chosen so that no significant differences exist between the sample and the population in any important characteristics. In other words, the sample serves as a model for the population, and thus, from a statistical analysis of the sample data, it is possible to generalise to the whole population with a specified degree of confidence.

Sampling might be carried out in order to save expense (it would be impossibly expensive, as well as unnecessary, to carry out an opinion poll among the whole electorate). Using a sample also enables results to be obtained more rapidly.

Sampling has problems, however. It must be ensured that the sample is representative of the whole population, or the results will be biased and therefore will not be applicable to the whole population. For example, an opinion poll carried out by knocking on doors in the afternoon is likely to result in a lot of people who work during the day being missed. If interviews are conducted in the canteen at lunchtime, staff who do not go to lunch will be missed. Similarly, the findings from interviewing accounting practices of 20 or fewer partners, with respect to software usage, cannot be extrapolated to larger accounting practices. Whether a sample is considered representative or not is a subjective assessment by those carrying out the survey or those using the results of the survey.

Sampling also has problems of variability. Even if great care is taken to avoid bias, the sample will never be exactly like the population. If another sample were chosen in exactly the same way, it would be different. This places a limit on how accurate the sample can be, and therefore how accurately statements can be made about the population.

12.4.1 Choice of sampling frame

The sampling frame is a comprehensive list of individuals or objects from which the sample is to be drawn. For example, the membership list of a major association of data processing professionals or, perhaps, the membership list of the Institute of Chartered Accountants in England and Wales (ICAEW) could form the sampling frame. Other examples of sampling frames are the postal address file, the electoral register, the telephone directory, and companies listed on the London Stock Exchange.

In practice, the findings of a simple up-to-date list are highly unlikely. Combining more than one list can possibly help improve matters.

12.4.2 Types of sample

Sampling techniques fall into two broad categories, namely non-probability samples and probability samples.

For a *non-probability sample* there is no way of estimating the probability of an individual having been included in the sample. Such a sample can occur when individuals are included in the sample on a ' first arrive first questioned basis' and as a consequence, it is not possible to ensure that the sample is representative. Examples of non-probability samples include *convenience samples, judgement samples,* and *quota samples.*

In *probability sampling* each individual has a known, not necessarily equal, probability of being selected. Examples of probability sampling include *simple random sampling, systematic sampling, stratified sampling, cluster sampling,* and *multi-stage sampling.* Probability samples can be rigorously analysed by means of statistical techniques, whereas for non-probability samples this is not possible.

12.4.3   Non-probability sampling

In non-probability sampling the subjective judgements of the researchers are used in selecting the sample. Clearly, this could result in the sample being biased. Non-probability samples are particularly useful in exploratory research. The more popular non-probability sampling methods are described below.

Convenience samples comprise those individuals that are most readily available to participate in the study. Such samples are extensively used in business school research, where the sample often comprises a group of MBA students or executives attending post experience courses at the time the research is being undertaken.

Judgement samples, also called purposive samples, are samples where individuals are selected with a specific purpose in mind. The composition of such a sample is not made with the aim of it being representative of the population. Such samples comprise individuals considered to have the knowledge and information to provide useful ideas and insights. This approach is extensively used in the exploratory research stage and is invaluable in ensuring a 'good' final questionnaire.

Quota samples are selected so that there is proportional representation of various sub-groups (or strata) of the target population. The selection of individuals to be included in the sample is done on a convenience basis. The interviewer is given information on the characteristics of those to be included in the sample, but the selection is left to the interviewer's judgement.

12.4.4   Probability samples

In obtaining a *probability sample*, use is made of some random procedure for the selection of the individuals or objects. This is done so as to remove the possibility of selection bias.

In *simple random sampling* each member of the population has an equal chance of being selected. Numbering individuals in the sampling frame and then selecting from these by some random procedure can achieve this. An example of such a sample is a questionnaire mailed to say 600 information systems executives chosen at random from a mailing list of 3000 executives.

A *systematic sample* is selected from the sampling frame of size N in the following manner. Having decided what size sample n is to be selected from the sampling frame, calculate:

$$\left[\frac{N}{n}\right] \text{ where } [\ ] \text{ denotes the largest integer } I \le \frac{N}{n}$$

Now select a random number i, say, in the interval $1 \le i \le I$. The sample size n then consists of the $i^{th}, (i+I)^{th}; (i+2I)^{th}$, and so on, up to the $(i+(n-1)I)^{th}$ item from the sampling frame.

Should there be some pattern present in the sampling frame, then such samples will be biased. For example, a systematic sample from the daily sales of a supermarket could result in picking out sales figures for Saturdays only.

In *stratified sampling* the population is subdivided into homogeneous groups, called strata, prior to sampling. Random samples are then drawn from each of the strata and the aggregate of these forms the stratified sample. This can be done in one of two ways:

♦ The overall sample size n can comprise items such that the number of items from each stratum will be in proportion to the size of the stratum.

♦ The overall sample size can comprise items from each stratum where the number of items from each of the strata are determined according to the relative variability of the items within each of the strata.

The first approach is the one invariably used in practice.

In *cluster sampling*, the population is made up of groups, called clusters, where the clusters are naturally formed groups such as companies, or locational units.

A cluster sample from a large organisation could be achieved by treating the various departments of a company as the clusters. A random sample of departments could then be chosen and all individuals in the departments sampled. In other words a census of the selected departments (clusters) is performed.

An extension of cluster sampling is *multi-stage sampling*. The simplest multi-stage sample involves random selection of the clusters in the first stage, followed by a random selection of items from each of the selected clusters. This is called two-staged sampling. More complex designs involve more than two stages. For example, in selecting a sample of accounting software users in accounting practices in England and Wales, a random sample of geographic areas may be made from the ICAEW membership list. Then, from within the areas, a number of accounting practices may be randomly selected, and finally, in the third stage, a random sample of software users is selected from each of the previously selected practices.

12.4.5 Size of sample

Determination of the sample size is a complex problem. Factors which need to be taken into consideration include: type of sample, variability in the population, time, costs, accuracy of estimates required, and confidence with which generalisations to the population are made.

There exist formulae for computing sample size, which are based on sound scientific principles. These were briefly considered in section 12.4.4.

In practice, the sample sizes resulting from the application of the formulae are not slavishly adhered to and are frequently ignored. In fact, the sample size chosen tends to be one that fits in with company policy or is are regarded as credible because it has been used by others conducting similar studies in the past. Such an approach is acceptable (Lehmann, 1989).

12.4.6   Statistical determination of sample size

This section describes two situations encountered in practice, namely, how to determine the sample size for estimating a population mean to a specified margin of error, or accuracy, with a specified level of confidence; and how to determine the sample size needed to estimate a population proportion (or percentage) to a specified margin of error, or accuracy, within a specified level of confidence.

These formulae only apply for probability samples taken from a very large population where the sample will be less than 10% of the population. Sample size calculations for more complex designs can be found in Lehmann (1989).

12.4.7   Sample size to estimate the mean

Suppose you wish to estimate the true average of a system's response time. In order to estimate this, a random sample of response times is taken and the average of these used to estimate the system's actual mean response time. The question now addressed is, what size of sample is needed to be 95% confident that the sample mean will be within E units of the true mean, where the unit of measurement of E can be in, say, seconds or minutes? E is therefore the accuracy required from the estimate. The sample size is given by:

$$n = \frac{3.84\sigma^2}{E^2}$$

where σ is the population standard deviation of response times and 3.84 is the constant derived from the normal distribution ensuring a 95% confidence level. In practice σ is inevitably unknown and will have to be estimated. This can be done by using response times for a pilot sample of size n_p, say, in the sample standard deviation formula:

$$S = \sqrt{\frac{1}{n_p - 1} \sum (x_i - \bar{x})^2}$$

where x_i is the n_p pilot response time, and x is the numerical average of the sample response times.

A simpler approach, often used, is to estimate σ from the range of the pilot sample values. This is done according to the following formula:

$$S = \frac{max(x_i) - min(x_i)}{4} = \frac{Range(x_i)}{4}$$

Some texts recommend dividing the range by 6. This is likely to result in an under-estimate of σ since pilots usually involve small samples. Of course a purely subjective estimate of σ is also possible.

Should it be required to estimate the mean to the same accuracy E as before, but now with a confidence level of 99% then the sample size is given by:

$$n = \frac{6.66\sigma^2}{E^2}$$

where 6.66 is the constant derived from the normal distribution ensuring a 99% confidence level and σ can be estimated as described above.

12.4.8 Sample size to estimate a percentage

Suppose you wish to estimate the actual percentage, p, say, of your customers who purchase software from a competing company. Suppose further that you require to know what sample size is needed to be 95% confident that the estimate of p resulting from the sample will be within E% of the actual percentage, p:

$$n = \frac{3.84p(100 - p)}{E^2}$$

The caveat in this case is that p is not known, as it is the parameter being estimated. In practice the value of p used in the above formula can be estimated in a number of ways. It can be estimated subjectively, or from a pilot sample or taken to be 50%. The latter results in the most conservative sample size estimate.

For a 99% confidence level:

$$n = \frac{6.66p(100 - p)}{E^2}$$

where p can be estimated as described above.

12.4.9   Sample size correction factor

As previously stated the above formulae hold strictly only should the target population be infinite, and will provide good approximations should the calculated sample size n be small relative to the target population size N. By small we understand the sample size to be 10% or less of the population size. That is,

$$\frac{n}{N} \times 100 < 10\%$$

In situations where the sample size (n), as determined by the formulae above, exceeds 10% of the population size (N), n has to be adjusted downwards by applying a sample size correction factor (see Lehmann, 1989: 301). In this case the required sample size n is given by

$$n' = n \times \frac{N}{N + n - 1}$$

where ($N/(N+n-1)$) is the sample size correction factor. Thus use of the sample size n will provide the desired accuracy E.

The need for correction often arises in practice. For example, it is likely to occur should a firm decide to conduct an internal survey among staff using the computer network. In practice, all that needs to be done is to apply the sample size calculation under the infinite population size assumption and then should $((n/N) \times 100)$ be greater than 10% the calculated sample size n has to be multiplied by the sample size correction factor.

Another situation that arises is the need to calculate the accuracy E, say, associated with a specific confidence level given a sample size n.

For estimating the percentage accuracy associated with 95% confidence and sample size n´:

$$E' = \sqrt{\frac{3.84P(100 - P)}{n'} \times \frac{N - n'}{N - 1}}$$

and for estimating the accuracy of the mean associated with 95% confidence and sample size n:

$$E' = \sqrt{\frac{3.84\sigma^2}{n'} \times \frac{N - n'}{N - 1}}$$

Examples of the application of these formulae can be found in Appendix E.

Sample size calculations for more complicated sampling schemes (e.g. stratified sampling) can be found in Lehmann (1989) and Churchill (1994).

12.5 Questionnaire design

A questionnaire is not just a list of questions to be answered. It has to be designed with specific objectives in mind and is essentially a scientific instrument for measurement of the population characteristics of interest.

In designing the questionnaire consideration must be given to such issues as (Churchill, 1987):

♦ What does the firm want to achieve with the results of the questionnaire?

♦ What information is sought?

♦ What type of questionnaire will be used?

♦ How will the questionnaire be administered?

♦ The content of individual questions;

♦ The type of response required to each question;

♦ The number of questions to be used;

♦ The manner in which the questions are to be sequenced;

♦ After testing, by means of a pilot study, what revisions are needed?

Some of the above issues were dealt with in previous sections.

12.5.1   Prior to the main survey

The main survey makes use of a questionnaire comprising mainly structured pre-coded questions. The construction of the main questionnaire is generally preceded by some qualitative or exploratory research involving the use of such informal techniques as unstructured interviews, brainstorming and focus groups. These activities include group discussions addressing many open-ended questions. These activities combine not only to 'firm up' the study objectives, the method of data collection, and the definition of the target population, but also help identify appropriate questions to include in the survey and help ensure that the various concepts used in the survey are properly defined. A first draft of a questionnaire should then be tested by means of a pilot survey. Pilot surveys are used to test the structured pre-coded questions. It may include some open-ended questions.

12.5.2 Things which help

A good starting point is to have clear terms of reference and objectives for the study, and to have made a thorough study of past surveys similar to the one being undertaken. In designing the questionnaire, consideration should be given to composing a good letter of introduction, the offering of incentives such as a draw for a magnum of champagne, an attractive design, using no jargon, together with an easy to understand and relevant wording of the questions.

Also important is the sequencing of questions. This should be done so that the demographic and other potentially embarrassing questions are placed at the end of the questionnaire. Also, questions on the same topic should be kept together. The opening questions should be carefully designed so as to ensure the respondent's early co-operation, thereby increasing the chances of obtaining truthful and quality responses to all questions.

Pilot surveys are essential. Authors of questionnaires can never rely on knowing how clear a question is. This can only be established through pilot studies, which should be completed by a range of possible respondents, including those least familiar with completing questionnaires. Every single question should be examined on the basis of how the answer will lead to a better understanding of what is being studied.

Questions that do not contribute to the specific objectives of the study should be removed. Furthermore, more sophisticated surveys may involve complicated terminology and concepts that could mean different things to different people. In such cases precise definitions of these concepts must be provided.

Special attention should be given to the inclusion of demographic and usage questions so that adequate segmentation and cross tabulation can be performed. For example, of especial importance in IS studies is knowledge of who are the extensive users, minimal users and clerical users.

12.5.3   Things to avoid

The design should ensure that the questionnaire is not unduly long. Mail questionnaires requiring more than 15 to 20 minutes to complete are likely to have a dramatic impact on the response rate. Further, the design should ensure that there is no vagueness in the questions posed, that there are no loaded or leading questions, no double-barrelled or double negative questions, no one-sided and not too many open-ended questions. Good quality responses to open-ended questions require the respondent to be articulate. Also, such questions are difficult to code for computer analysis. These two factors combine to produce problems in analysis and summarisation. The questions should not be too complex or involve concepts that are likely not to be clearly understood. Where jargon has to be used it is essential to supply a detailed glossary. Should the questionnaire involve branching type questions, then the branching instructions must be clear so as to ensure that the respondent does not become confused.

12.5.4   Techniques for questioning

The manner in which questions are structured, ordered, presented and coded can affect the response rate and the quality of response, make accurate data capture easy, and facilitate statistical analysis. Some of ways in which this is done are set out below.

For more detailed discussions on this topic, the reader is referred to Churchill (1994), Dillon, Madden and Firtle (1987), Lehmann (1989) and Parasuraman (1991).

12.5.5   Sequencing of questions

It is generally agreed that the best way in which to order the questions is to place general questions first, specific questions next and attitudinal questions later. Hard questions should be placed fairly early interspersed with easy questions. Further, there is a need to ensure that the questions are structured in such a way that the respondent will find it easy to answer questions within a topic, and also not be burdened with questions that are irrelevant to him or her.

Funnel Questions are used to sequence within a particular topic. For example, consider the sequence of questions:

Which of the following high-level languages do you use?
(Please tick appropriate box)

Cobol ☐   Fortran ☐   APL ☐   C ☐   BASIC ☐

Which of the following high-level languages do you like most? (Please tick appropriate box)

Cobol ☐   Fortran ☐   APL ☐   C ☐   BASIC ☐

Which of the following high-level languages did you not use in the past seven days?
(Please tick appropriate box)

Cobol ☐   Fortran ☐   APL ☐   C ☐   BASIC ☐

In this type of question the respondent is guided from a general question to a specific question.

Filter Questions are used to exclude the respondent from being asked questions that are irrelevant to him or her. For example, consider the question:

Do you ever use Cobol?

If YES: When did you last use Cobol?

Within last 10 days ☐ 8-14 days ☐ More than 14 days ago ☐

If NO: Why is that?

The above filter question also illustrates the use of what can be referred to as a specific time period question.

Specific Time Period questions are used to avoid memory problems with respondents. Consider the question:

How often do you use high level programming languages? ☐

which is open-ended and has no prompt, against:

When did you last use a high level programming language? (Please tick appropriate category)

Within last 10 days ☐ 8-14 days ☐ More than 14 days ☐ Never ☐

12.5.6 Examples of pre-coded questions

Coding is the procedure for assigning numerical symbols to the categories or classes into which the responses are to be placed. This is usually decided when designing the questionnaire. For example:

Which of the following best describes your position in the management structure? (Please circle the appropriate number)

1	Upper	4	Lower middle
2	Upper middle	5	Lower
3	Middle		

It is recommended that not more than six or seven categories be used. Also one must make sure that the categories fit, otherwise the respondent can become irritated.

12.5.7 Particular questions

The typology of data used in IS studies includes demographics, attitudes, beliefs, interests, preferences, product, software and systems usage, determinants of usage, perceived benefits and desired benefits. Below are examples of questions for some of these categories (see also Appendix F):

Demographic variables provide factual information about the individual or company and include information on:

♦ Industry in which the firm operates

♦ Number of IT staff employed in your firm

♦ Total investment in IT in the firm

♦ Degree of specialism of respondent
  (e.g. whether IS specialist or managerial user)

Socio-economic variables relate to the economic status of the individual or company. Examples of variables that reflect this include:

♦ Income

♦ Turnover

♦ Market share

♦ Profits

♦ Education

♦ Spend on IT training as percentage of annual income

♦ Position in the company

♦ Function within the firm

Attitudes relate to a latent state of mind, which in turn relates to feelings, which can subsequently influence behaviour. Attitude measurement is usually achieved by use of a five-point or seven-point scale. For example:

(7) Strongly agree
(6) Agree
(5) Slightly agree
(4) Neither agree or disagree
(3) Slightly disagree
(2) Disagree
(1) Strongly disagree

Use of a scale with an odd number of points allows a neutral response. When using a five-point scale leave out 'slightly'. Should it be desired to force the respondent to reveal his or her inclination, an even number of points is used. In the case of a five-point scale leave out the 'neutral' category. Sometimes a four-point scale is used. This can be achieved by leaving out the three central categories.

Example: *Attitudes*

To what extent do you agree that the following should be used by/introduced into your organisation?

Use the scale:

(5)   Strongly agree
(4)   Agree
(3)   Uncertain
(2)   Disagree
(1)   Strongly disagree

Q1 ☐ Computer assisted learning techniques

Q2 ☐ Public availability of financial information on public companies

Beliefs relate to an individual's subjective assessment, or opinion, of the likelihood of a statement holding.

Example: *Beliefs*

Indicate the strength of your opinion in terms of the use of your computer network if the following were available to you:

Use the scale:

(1)   Very likely to use it
(2)   Somewhat likely to use it
(3)   Neither likely or unlikely to use it
(4)   Somewhat unlikely to use it
(5)   Very unlikely to use it

Q1 ☐ Access to the Internet through the system

Q2 ☐ Close collaboration with colleagues

What do you see as the main benefits of IT for your firm?

Use the scale:

(5)   Very great benefit
(4)   Great benefit
(3)   Some benefit
(2)   Little benefit
(1)   No obvious benefit

Q1 ☐ Providing better management information

Q2 ☐ Improving access to external sources of information.

Incidentally, the above scale can be regarded as unbalanced in that the emphasis is placed on the extent of belief and is loaded towards the respondent indicating a degree of benefit. In the previous example the scale is regarded as balanced in that there are an equal number of negative and positive categories.

Usage of Product/Software/Systems questions describe what is used, how it is used, the purpose of use, the benefit from use, the frequency of use and so on. Common variables include:

System used/planned to use
Usage rate of reports
Time between use
Satisfaction

Example: *Areas of use and amount of use*

Q1 In which areas do you use SIS (Strategic Information Systems)? (Please tick appropriate box)

☐ Sales and Marketing Systems

☐ Financial Planning and Mgmt Systems

☐ Inter-organisational systems

☐ Office automation

☐ Artificial intelligence based systems

☐ Other (Please specify)

Q2 How many hours per week do you use a workstation?

_____   Hours

Q3 Of these hours what percentage (whole numbers) do you use the following?

_____   % Word processing

_____   % Spreadsheet

_____   % Database

_____   % E-mail

_____   % Time management

_____   % Other (Please specify)

Example: *Benefit Identification*

Q1 Can you cite an instance in which ICON can be directly credited with giving the firm a competitive advantage? (Please tick appropriate box)

☐ Yes

☐ No

If yes please give a brief description _____

Example: *Satisfaction with software*

Q1 Look through the following list and state how satisfied you are with your firm's applications software in the following areas. Use the scale:

(1) Very dissatisfied
(2) Dissatisfied
(3) Not sure
(4) Satisfied
(5) Very satisfied

☐ Preparation of Accounts

☐ Tax Planning

☐ Stock Control

☐ Payroll

☐ Novell Network

☐ Other (Please specify):

Determinants of use questions are included with the view to explaining behaviour relating to the use of products, software or information systems. Variables used include:

Knowledge and understanding of the system
Ease of use
Influence of others
Relevance of report contents
Information systems needs
Information systems capabilities

Example: *IS needs*

Evaluate how *important* you feel that each attribute is in ensuring that the overall computer based system will be effective? Use the scale:

    (1)   Irrelevant
    (2)   Possibly useful
    (3)   Of some use
    (4)   Important
    (5)   Very critical

Q1 ☐ Availability and timeliness of report delivery

Q2 ☐ Communications between IS staff and managerial users.

Example: *IS capability*

Evaluate the degree of IS *performance* attained within your organisation on the following scale:

    (1) Very poor
    (2) Poor
    (3) Adequate
    (4) Good
    (5) Excellent

Q1 ☐ Availability and timeliness of report delivery

Q2 ☐ Communications between IS staff and managerial users.

12.6 Measurement scales

Section 12.5 reveals that the nature of data obtained from respondents is both qualitative and quantitative. Meaningful analysis requires that the responses be quantified.

There are four scales (or levels) of measurement that can be used. These are the nominal (or categorical), ordinal, interval and ratio measurement scales.

Nominal scales are used to identify the categories to which a respondent belongs. An example of such a scale can be found in Appendix G, question 1 where the response can be either yes or no. A nominal rating of '1' is assigned to a yes answer and a '0' to a no answer. A '1' therefore categorises the respondent as *'having a formal procedure for identifying business opportunities or problems'.*

In this case the numbers assigned are arbitrary and are no more than labels for the categories. Counting is the only analysis possible on such data.

Ordinal scales are used when the respondent is asked for responses in the form of a rank ordering. An example of the use of such a scale is:

Q1   Rank the following areas of benefit in the order you think that the proposed system will have the most impact on our organisation.

(1) Efficiency (doing more things, doing things faster) ☐

(2) Effectiveness (doing the right thing) ☐

(3) Innovation (new ways of work ☐

(4) Utilisation (hours billed to client) ☐

(5) Job satisfaction (work environment) ☐

The ranks in this case provide information on the relative standing of the benefits when compared with the impact of the proposed system on the organisation. For example, should efficiency be ranked '1', and effectiveness '2', then the system is considered to have a greater impact on efficiency than on effectiveness. However, how much more impact it will have cannot be inferred from such numbers. Therefore the difference in the ranks does not provide information on the actual extent of the impact. Such scales do allow for more sophisticated analysis than was possible for the nominal scale. For this data it is meaningful to compute such non-parametric statistics as the median, quartiles and rank correlations.

Interval scales possess the property that the difference between the numbers on the scale can be interpreted meaningfully. Examples of a scale that can be treated as an interval scale (Parasuraman, 1991: 410) are to be found in Appendix F, parts B and C. For these questions the rating system is such that a score of 1 denotes strongly disagree and a score of 9 denotes strongly agree.

In this case, the difference between the ratings of two individuals on the same item gives an indication of the extent to which the two individuals agree or disagree on the item. In other words, the difference between the numbers of such a scale can be interpreted as an absolute measure of how far apart individuals are with respect to the item. For example, in this case the difference between a rating of '1' and a rating of '2' is equal to the difference between ratings of '3' and '4'. Also the difference, say, between '1' and '2' is half the difference between '1' and '3'. This thinking also applies between '4' and '5', '6' and '7', etc.

Interval scale data can be analysed by virtually the full range of statistical procedures. For this scale the calculation of means, standard deviations and Pearson correlation coefficients provides meaningful statistics.

Ratio scales are scales such that the numbers on the scale possess not only the properties of the nominal, ordinal and interval scales, but in addition, ratios of numbers on this scale have meaning.

This scale possesses the property that intervals between points on the scale are comparable. For example, the difference between an average workstation usage of 10 hours per week and 12 hours per week is the same as the difference between say 15 hours per week and 17 hours per week.

In addition, it is meaningful, for example, to compare an average usage of 15 hours per week with an average usage of 10 hours per week, by stating that the former usage of the workstation is 1.5 times that of the latter. For a ratio scale 'zero' has a physical meaning. In this case a response of zero is taken to mean that the individual does not use the workstation. Ratio data is the highest level of data and can be analysed by the full range of statistical techniques.

In practice, surveys generally make most use of data at the nominal, ordinal and interval level.

12.7 A guide to conducting a survey

The following is a step-by-step guide to conducting a survey of the use of IT in the firm.

Terms of reference

Accurately define the purposes of the survey. These should be stated as the survey's terms of reference.

Data collection

Establish how the data will be collected, i.e. personal interview, mail, telephone, etc.

Determine the sample size and the sample frame

Estimate the response rate that will produce the appropriate sample size.

Focus groups

Form a focus group in order to identify the key issues to be addressed by the survey. Focus groups may be from six to ten informants.

Produce questions

From the key issues develop a list of appropriate questions.

Questionnaire design

From the questions draft a questionnaire. This task includes the selection of an appropriate scale.

Conduct a pilot study

Perform a pilot study using the questionnaire to determine initial responses. The pilot study may encompass between six and 10 individuals.

Revise the questionnaire

Using the results of the pilot study, revise the questionnaire so that it focuses more closely on the key issues.

Distribute questionnaire

Distribute the finalised questionnaire to the chosen sample. Each respondent should be notified of the date by which return of the completed questionnaire is required.

Collect results

The completed questionnaires should be collected. It may be possible to discard partially complete questionnaires in favour of complete ones, depending on the response rate achieved.

Code results

The results of the questionnaires should be coded appropriately, in order to make analysis and interpretation easier.

Analyse and interpret

The coded results should be analysed to determine the overall results of the survey. Careful analysis will reveal both whether the survey was successful as well as whether the IT systems are meeting the requirements of the respondents.

Two sample questionnaires are provided in Appendices F and G.

12.8 Summary

Survey design is very much an art and invariably results in economic considerations forcing the researchers to sacrifice what they ideally would require for what is practical in terms of the time and money available. It must be accepted that no survey will be found to be perfect. The key to a successful survey is the care taken in carrying out the time-consuming and costly up-front work. This includes tasks such as clearly defining the purpose and objectives of the study, the running of focus groups, analysing transcripts of the focus group meetings, conducting fairly open-ended interviews with appropriate persons, and the development and thorough pilot testing of the questionnaire. Also there is the need to ensure that the sample is representative and of credible size.

13 Evaluation and project management

You can manage an IS project just as well as you can manage a capital building project. Even if you're using the bleeding edge of technology, you can still succeed through careful planning, scheduling and monitoring.

T. Winter, cited in Scheier R, *From Hard Hat to Hard Drive* (1995)

13.1 Introduction

IT projects can be successfully managed in much the same way as any other project. However to do this the project management needs to carefully focus on the continuous evaluation of the project. In fact the measuring and management of IT costs and benefits needs to be an integral part of IT project management as well as the day-to-day management of an organisation's computer-based systems. The purpose of this chapter is to explain how to set up evaluation as part of project management.

The process of management, and especially project management is a repeated cycle of planning, resourcing, execution and control activities, which can be seen in Figure 13.1.

The control phase involves the evaluation of what has gone before and decision making to support the renewal of the planning and management exercise. The cycle of resourcing and execution is then repeated.

Central to evaluation is the process of measuring or assessing the merit or deficiencies of past performance.

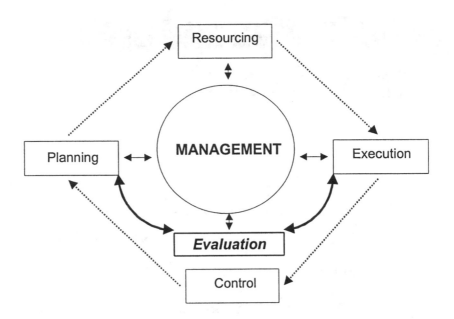

Figure 13.1: Evaluation as a central issue in the management process cycle

The key practical issues of an evaluation process, especially from a project management point of view are *when* the evaluation is done, *who* does the evaluation, and *how* is the evaluation done. This last issue involves deciding *what* characteristics of the information system are to be evaluated and which techniques are appropriate for the evaluation process.

13.2 The traditional approach

This section presents the traditional IT project management approach and underpins the fact that there have been developments as to how the IT evaluation process needs to be incorporated in IT project management.

The traditional IT project management approach was based on the concept that an IT project was purely a technical engineering type activity.[1] The following diagram, Figure 13.2, adapted from Zehnder (1990) illustrates the traditional project approach, which is sometimes referred to as the 'waterfall' approach.[2]

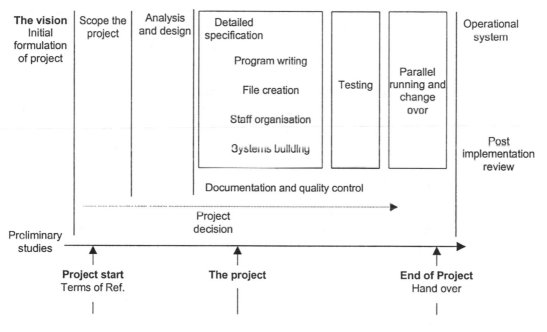

Figure 13.2: The stages of IT project development

---

[1] A participant attending an executive programme on IT management pointed out recently that IT was originally seen as much the same thing as civil engineering and that programmers were regarded by management much like bricklayers. Although this is perhaps a little exaggerated it certainly does capture the spirit of the traditional attitudes towards information systems development. With such an approach to programmers and programming it is hardly surprising that there have been so many failures.

[2] It has been well known for some considerable time that projects seldom operate in as linear a fashion as the 'waterfall' approach or model suggests. Nonetheless it has been regarded as a useful description on the components of an IT project.

The issues of project management have been, and are still sometimes associated with delivering a number of completed and possibly integrated work packages (building blocks of the information system) on schedule. This involves managing the cost of delivering the information system within a budget and ensuring the quality of the build of the system components. The issues of evaluation for a project with this profile were the following:

◆ *When:* An initial evaluation was carried out at the feasibility stage when the project was scoped and the terms of reference for the project prepared. A second evaluation was carried out at the end of the design stage and a review was carried out after implementation. Then sometimes a post-implementation audit was conducted.[3]

◆ *Who:* At the feasibility stage, user management[4] was usually involved to support[5] the project leader in decision-making.[6] The second evaluation involved the technical project team and sometimes the eventual users of the information system. The post-implementation review (if carried out at all) was an accounting type evaluation involving management and their accountants. Sometimes a user survey, evaluating of their satisfaction with the system was carried out (see user surveys: Chapters 9 and 12).

---

[3] Research on the issue of post-implementation audits suggests that perhaps as few as one third of projects are ever subjected to such a review.

[4] User management may sometimes have been just about the only other primary stakeholder represented here.

[5] The notion that the user manager would support the project leader actually put the emphasis of the activities of these two stakeholders the wrong way around.

[6] Sound project management dictates that the feasibility study should be compiled with the direct support of a senior sponsor who should ensure that the process change underlying the information system clearly is beneficial to the organisation.

♦ *How and What:* The measurable characteristics for evaluation were the following:

Time: A schedule of activities was proposed and controlled. There are well-established and sophisticated techniques available for managing time in the context of project management.

Cost: A budget was proposed and standard budgetary control techniques were used to evaluate and control tangible costs.

Quality: Building quality software is sometimes still a problem even today, but there are techniques available used by software engineers to support quality assurance and control.[7]

The basic issues of evaluation outlined above are still an integral part of setting up and managing a project and should never be ignored as part of any IT project management programme.

13.3 Moving away from the traditional approach

In current business practice IT is now inextricably integrated into the fibre of an organisation's functions. The effective use of IT underpins the business and the organisation's ability to be successful in its operation. Over and above this, the environment in which an organisation is operating is continually changing and so the organisation needs be much more adaptable. This integration of IT and the climate of continual change have had a major impact on management thinking for IT projects.

---

[7] The issue of quality today is more to do with whether the information system is fit for its purpose as opposed to the traditional view of quality being to do with minimising the number of bugs that are present when the system is commissioned.

Furthermore, there have been two key changes in the way IT projects and their management are perceived. First, by and large computer-based systems are not measured in terms of just the old ideas of quality of build, but in terms of the value of the system to realise business benefits for the organisation.

Second, the development of computer-based systems is no longer viewed as an engineering project with development and build phases, a delivery point, and then an extended period of use for the delivered application. The development of a computer-based system is viewed more in terms of the introduction and evolution of organisational processes. The systems development may be characterised as having a set-up phase and then the system evolves to meet the changing needs of the organisation to deliver enhanced processes, which lead to improved efficiency and effectiveness, and thus produce business benefits for that organisation. The setting up of an evaluation process as part of project management needs to focus on the participation of the business people involved, on identifying the improved processes and on the continuous evaluation of the evolving system and its use. The evaluation activity of the management process involves setting up a group consisting of owners and managers and technical people who have a genuine stake in the future of the computer-based system and a concern for its success, to participate in the management process. The evaluation activity should be supported by information that evidences the performance of the system in terms of it supports process changes, which make an improved contribution to the business's goals. The evaluation activity should be part of a continuing management activity over the useful life of the system and not just the project itself.

13.4 Active benefit realisation

The process described in this chapter for setting up evaluation as part of IT management, has been called Active Benefit Realisation (ABR) it is based on the approach proposed by Remenyi, *et al.* (1997).[8] This involves the integrating of a continuous participative evaluation activity into the project management process.

The participation and delegation of some aspects the project control activity to the stakeholders, rather than focusing on technical issues, suggests a mind-set shift. It requires more of a partnership and a co-evolution in systems building and a much broader focus on business processes rather than just technical project management issues. As the development and use of the systems progress, all the principal stakeholders appreciate the business problem more fully and understand the opportunities of the information system better. They will then guide the IS development towards a system that delivers real improvements. The ABR process complements the recognised and well understood project management and financial management techniques that are necessary to satisfy top management sponsorship of an information system and are increasingly accepted as sound management practice for successfully delivering an information system.

13.5 The evaluation process

The ABR evaluation process for information systems development is illustrated in Figure 13.3. This figure shows that the evaluation needs to accommodate the evolving nature of the information systems investment and that a participative[9] approach is required.

---

[8] ABR is the main theme of another book referred to above by two of the authors of this book and thus is not discussed in any real depth here.

[9] According to Brunner and Guzman (1989), 'Participatory evaluation is an educational process through which the social groups produce action-oriented knowledge about their reality, clarify and articulate their norms and values, and reach a consensus about future action.' A participative approach is not at all easy. Participative evaluation implies that a group of stakeholders is involved. The fundamentals of evaluation and all the complexities of individual

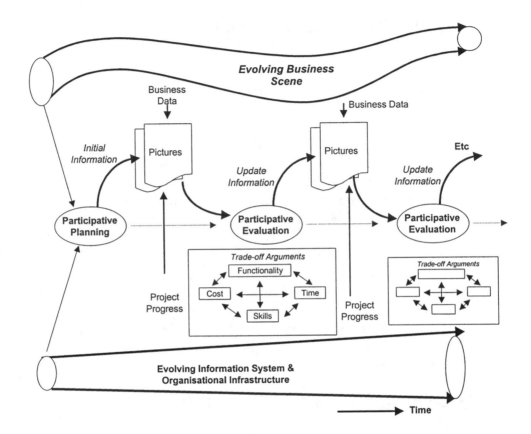

Figure 13.3: A continuous and evolving participative evaluation process

At the start of the project there is an initial peak of activity when stakeholders together set up the plans for the project and the framework for evaluation.

interpretation of value persists for a group situation and often further complexity is added. Each individual group member's understanding of the information system will be different, the desirability of the system will be different and in a group situation the personal behaviour and stance of each individual member may influence the evaluation. A common understanding should be arrived at and then an agreed course of action negotiated.

The documents that are used for summarising the evaluation information are called 'pictures'. These documents are discussed in more detail in the next section.

The frequency of the participative evaluation reviews is decided when setting up evaluation in project management. During the most active phases of systems development and implementation these could be fortnightly or monthly. The evaluation process continues during the whole life of the project, and even continues beyond the project as part of operational management for the information system.

Broken down into separate activities, this evaluation process consists of the following seven major activities which are illustrated in Figure 13.4:

1   Initialisation, i.e. validation of the project

2   Production of pictures

3   An agreement to proceed

4   System development

5   Evidence collection

6   Review: participative evaluation

7   Development of updated pictures.

Repeat cycle from step 3.

The ABR process usually begins with the vision by an executive that IT can transform one or several of their business processes. The use of IT to support a business activity and the launch of the development of a computer-based system is the appreciation by the organisation of a primary business problem that can be resolved or an opportunity which can be grasped by using information technology. The evaluation cycle starts from the point when the problem is first defined or the vision of the opportunity described.[10] This is the entry point into Activity 1.

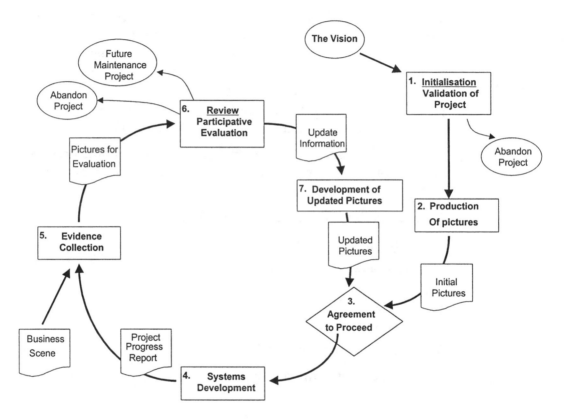

Figure 13.4: The ABR evaluation process

Activity 1. *Initialisation of project*: The first task is to make a clear statement of the problem that the envisaged information system is planned to overcome or of the opportunity to be grasped. One of the primary objectives of the initialisation activity is to

---

[10] Research suggests that about one half of information technology investments are initiated through the process of formal strategy planning. The other half occur as the result of impromptu commercial insights and are totally opportunistic in nature.

validate that an IT investment is worthwhile and that the project is worth tackling. The validation depends on a clear statement of the business objectives of the investment.

Some initial analysis is necessary during this first activity. The analysis involves gaining a clear understanding of the organisational objectives that are to be realised as a result of the proposed process change and the information system development. From this analysis, the context for the information system development, as well as the goals and expected benefits of the proposed system, will become clear. The business opportunity is validated by ensuring that it is aligned to the strategy of the organisation as expressed by its critical success factors. The deliverable at the end of step 1 will be a document that will contain the terms of reference and an authorisation to proceed with the detailed exploration of the proposed project.

Activity 2. *Production of pictures*: This activity requires the preparation of what is termed the initial business picture (IBP) and two supporting pictures the initial financial picture (IFP) and the initial project picture (IPP). For the purposes of describing this process, these pictures can be viewed as a formalised expression of the process or practice changes and the information systems development project targets in business benefits terms, with the supporting financial budget and the supporting development project plans. Once the pictures have been prepared a key decision making point is reached. The pictures are a model of the business opportunity, the context, the financial impact of an information system and a project plan. The deliverable at the end of step 2 will the three pictures required for the management of the project. These documents are prepared, discussed and agreed in a participative forum.

Activity 3. *An agreement to proceed*: Based on the information provided by the pictures, a decision can be made and an agreement to proceed may be reached.

Activity 4. *System development*: The actual building and setting up of the organisational infrastructure for the information system is now started. Once a part of the information system has been developed some deliverables exist. At first this may simply be a paper based report, an analysis report or a systems design specification, but as systems development advances this may be a prototype and eventually will be the results of live testing of the system. The project management will deliver progress reports from this systems development activity.

Activity 5. *Evidence collection*: The stakeholders familiarise themselves with the evidence of progress in the project and bring their expertise of the evolving business scene together. If the stakeholders have genuinely exercised active participation they will be familiar with project progress, they will have looked at prototypes and they will be aware of organisational issues. Evidence collection for senior management may take the form of reading a clearly expressed management summary or the oral presentation of project progress by the project team.

Activity 6. *Review – Participative Evaluation*: The stakeholders review and evaluate progress. Progress is evaluated against the business, financial and project targets, with specific emphasis on the process change and the resulting business benefits. Regulatory action, to ensure information systems development stays on course to deliver business benefits is at the heart of the evaluation process. Evaluation for specific aspects of the information system will be supported by techniques that will evidence the evaluation information in an easy-to-understand way. The business stakeholders participate in the process, to ensure that business and not technological issues come to the fore.

Activity 7. *Development of updated pictures:* Making decisions and formulating new agreed plans for continuing the project to its next phase completes the participative and formative evaluation cycle. This activity involves updating the pictures to reflect the new targets and plans for systems development and updating the budget in accounting terms. In this process targets are updated, but another key aspect of this process is that the stakeholders learn to understand better each other's requirements and what is possible. The development process continues by returning to Activity 3 with an agreement to proceed.

13.6 The ABR pictures

ABR requires the production of three pictures. These pictures have a hierarchical nature. Some items on the pictures are simply a statement of a contextual situation or a target that the system development is expected to achieve. Other items are numbers and some may be graphical representations. They are expressed in these pictures in a summary form. Where necessary for the project the higher-level figures or statements are underpinned by more detailed information. This is shown in Figure 13.5.

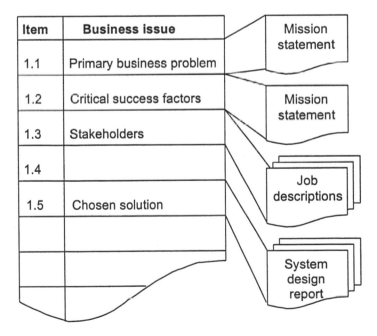

Figure 13.5: The hierarchical nature of the business picture (BP)

The three pictures are produced initially as part of the development of the business case for the investment in a process change and the accompanying information system and are used to support the decision to launch the project.

13.6.1 The business picture (BP)

Figure 13.6 lists the issues that need to be addressed in the BP and together these items may be regarded as a business case for the project.

Item	Business issues
1.1	Primary business problem or opportunity
1.2	Critical success factors
1.3	Stakeholders
1.4	Outcome definition
1.5	Chosen solution
1.6	Rationale
1.7	Solution champion
1.8	Ideal term report
1.9	Specific benefits and metrics
1.10	Stakeholder–benefits matrix
1.11	Critical success factor–benefits matrix
1.12	Major risks
1.13	Major risks–benefits matrix

Figure 13.6: Business picture

1.1 Primary business problem or opportunity: Item 1.1 expresses the opportunity or the problem that the organisation faces. It is a succinct statement and/or list of problems being addressed by the proposed process change and information systems initiative. An example of a problem stated clearly and simply might be 'Gross sales invoice value too small and as a result administrative overheads are too high to provide the required return on investment'.

The statement of the primary business problem or opportunity is an important issue for any project. If the primary business problem or opportunity is not correctly understood the resulting information system will probably be of little value.

1.2 Critical Success Factors (CSF): Item 1.2, which is entered at the initialisation stage of the project, lists the key CSFs for the business or organisational units that are being addressed by the process change. In the context of the BP, CSFs are used to check the relevance of the proposed business opportunity to the stated organisational mission. They help to identify the significance of the possible associated benefits.

CSFs are derived from the organisation's objectives, goals and corporate strategy. To deliver real benefits for the organisation, the information system needs to be aligned to one or more CSF.

CSFs may have been prepared for the organisation during its planning procedures, but if this has not been the case, time needs to be spent on this issue, as it is a key technique for assisting in the validation of information systems opportunities.

1.3 Stakeholders: Item 1.3 lists the primary stakeholders in the project. This item supports one of the key principles of ABR for setting up evaluation successfully in IT project management. This item records the agreed result of the management discussion and decisions as to who will be ultimately responsible for IT investment and who will participate in the evaluation (and consequently the control) process for the systems development.

Agreeing participation in an IT systems development project is a difficult and sometimes controversial task.

1.4 Outcome definition: Item 1.4 is a statement or a list of the expected results of the process change or information systems initiative expressed in business terms. It relates to the primary business problem or opportunity and represents in concrete terms the vision of how the opportunity will be realised. It is derived directly from the primary business problem or opportunity statement given in Item 1.1 of the picture.

The outcome statement should be comprehensive and thus carefully thought through. A brainstorming session involving the principal stakeholders is a useful way of tackling this issue.

1.5 Chosen solution: Item 1.5 is a summary description of the chosen solution. The task of selecting the solution will involve some systems analysis and design work by information systems or business analysis professionals. This work is complementary to the work of reviewing solution alternatives.

1.6 Rationale: Item 1.6 provides a brief statement as to why the particular solution was chosen in item 1.5.

1.7 Solution champion: Item 1.7 records the name of the champion of the chosen solution. If there is no champion for the chosen solution then the business process change and accompanying information systems development is unlikely to realise business benefits.

1.8 Ideal term report: Item 1.8 in the BP is a series of statements expressing the ideal situation the organisation hopes to realise in terms of the information systems development project. This is to be expressed in business and organisational terms and an example of such a report is shown in Figure 13.7.

1	Within one year of the commissioning of the systems the sales revenues have increased by 20%, while.
2	The number of clients has been reduced from 10,000 to 8,000.
3	The average value per invoice has increased by at least 20%.
4	There are fewer bad debts both in absolute terms and as a percentage of sales.
5	Sales managers and representatives claim that the system has played a major role in achieving the above.
6	Sales managers and representatives claim that they find the systems easy to use.
7	There is a growing feeling among the sales staff at all levels that information systems can play a major role in helping them do a more efficient and more effective job.

Figure 13.7: An example of an ideal term report

1.9 Specific benefits and metrics: Item 1.9 is derived from the outcome definitions specified in Item 1.4 of the business picture, and the chosen solution. It identifies the specific benefits that the chosen solution will deliver in business terms. These benefits will not be stated here in financial terms, as financial estimates will be produced for the financial picture (FP).

Business benefits will be stated in terms of the effect of the organisation's processes. Thus a sales order process system could have business benefits attributed to it.

For benefits to be achieved they need to be measurable, i.e. a stakeholder should be able to assess whether the planned benefits have been delivered. Virtually all process change benefits are measurable, even intangible ones.

The completion of this item of the business picture is at the heart of setting up an evaluation of an IT project. It is by participatively looking at, and planning for, the achievement of the stated benefits, using the prescribed metrics, that business benefits will be realised.

1.10 Stakeholder-benefits matrix: The stakeholder–benefits matrix, item 1.10, lists all the benefits identified in item 1.9 (above). The stakeholder–benefits matrix cross-references each benefit to one or more stakeholders. It is a control item in the BP. It identifies, with an explicit model, the individual stakeholders who will be affected by the realisation of that particular benefit during the implementation and from the realisation of each different aspect of the proposed process change and information system.

This process allows stakeholders to identify with the targeted benefits of the information system development. Furthermore, it helps draw the stakeholders' attention to the issues and focuses their attention on a more comprehensive statement of possible benefits. It also identifies stakeholders with no benefits accruing from the information system development, which may mean that they have been mistakenly included as primary stakeholders. An example of a stakeholder–benefit matrix is shown in Figure 13.8.

From the matrix it is clear as to who is associated with what benefit and vice versa. Instead of simply putting an asterisk in the matrix, it is possible to weight and/or score the relative importance of the benefits.

Stakeholder	Increase in sales	No. of clients reduced	Fewer bad debts	Increase in staff satisfaction
Sales manager	*	*	*	
Marketing manager	*			
Credit manager			*	
Sales staff	*	*	*	
Office manager				*

Figure 13.8: Stakeholder – benefit matrix

1.11 Critical success factors-benefits matrix: The CSF–benefits matrix, item 1.11, lists the benefits identified in item 1.9 (above). The matrix cross-references each benefit to one or more CSFs and identifies which corporate CSFs are supported by that benefit. This is another control item in the BP.

Process change and the accompanying benefits accruing from the information systems' development should be aligned to corporate strategy. If an anticipated business benefit does not support a corporate CSF[11] then it may not be a benefit at all or at least one of low priority. On the other hand if some relevant identified CSFs are not supported by any business benefits of the information system, then it is possible that the information system development is not adequately targeted. The CSF–

---

[11] CSFs are viewed here as the detail supporting the organisation's corporate strategy and as such CSFs are much easier to work with when discussing process changes or information technology investments than the overarching corporate strategy.

benefit matrix can be presented in a similar way to the stake-holder–benefit matrix, as shown in Figure 13.8.

1.12 Major risks: Item 1.12 lists the major risks involved with the process change. Risk should be identified in the BP when setting up an evaluation. Its importance as an item on the BP for systems development is that process change involves new activity and new activities are always risky. The major risks to the non-realisation of business benefits and to the negative impacts of the information system development are listed so that the stakeholders can evaluate them as acceptable or not. They can also be monitored during the development of the information system and re-evaluated.

1.13 Major risks–benefit matrix: The major risks–benefits matrix, item 1.13, lists the benefits identified in Item 1.9 (above). The matrix cross-references each benefit to one or more of the major risks and identifies to what risks benefit realisation is exposed. It also indicates whether systems development is exposed to risk where there is no obvious benefit indicated.

Figure 13.9 illustrates some of the detail of the development process and sequence for the business picture.

13.6.2 The financial picture

The financial picture (FP) summarises the costs and benefits figures discussed in previous chapters of this book.

This statement shows in money terms the benefits and costs of the project and includes some financial ratios that need to be evaluated and monitored to help manage the financial health of the project.

The FP includes the recognised cost categories for financial planning in information systems development. It also contains a comprehensive list of benefits.

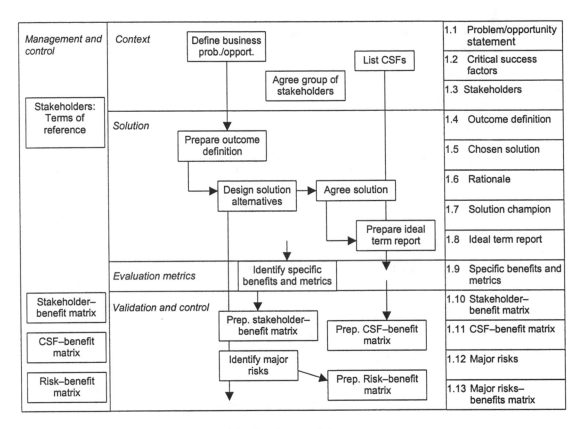

Figure 13.9: Development of the business picture

Only the summary of these calculations is included in the FP. The detailed financial information will be available in the form of budgets and costings within the organisation's accounting system. Of course the ABR process proposed here does not prescribe the accounting conventions to be used. The FP complements the current financial controls of the organisation.

Figure 13.10 lists the issues that need to be addressed in the FP.

Item	Financial issues
2.1	Project duration
2.2	Hardware costs
2.3	Software costs
2.4	Data communications costs
2.5	People costs
2.6	Commissioning costs
2.7	Group productivity tools
2.8	Individual or personal productivity tools
2.9	Informate the organisation
2.10	Reduce time and space in business processes
2.11	Create a corporate memory
2.12	Bind the organisation closely with clients and suppliers
2.13	Induce discontinuities by BPR
2.14	Required payback
2.15	Required return on investment
2.16	Required net present value
2.17	Major financial risks

Figure 13.10: The financial picture

2.1 Duration: Item 2.1 of the initial FP is a statement of the anticipated duration of the project.

2.2–2.6 Systems cost: The next five items from 2.2 to 2.6 are the estimated cost of the hardware, software, data, communications, people costs and commissioning costs. It is common practice to supply these forecast costs as a series of single budget, or estimate items. It is expected that these costs will be reasonably accurate, i.e. within about 10% of the final costs. If there is a high degree of uncertainty about these cost estimate numbers then, instead of supplying single point estimates, range values may be used and a process of financial risk analysis may be employed to perform the subsequent calculations.

2.7–2.13 Systems benefits: The initial FP provides a list of the major tangible benefits that can be derived from an information system. These are listed from points 2.7 to 2.13 and need to be addressed individually.

2.14–2.16 Required payback, return on investment and net present value: Items 2.14, 2.15 and 2.16 of the FP refer to three classical measures of investment performance. These three statistics payback, return on investment and net present value are only examples of a much wider range of financial measures which may be used by accountants to assess the viability of an investment.

2.17 Major financial risks: Item 2.17 lists the major financial risks that an information system development project could face. These are primarily related to escalation in the prices of the various inputs to the project. Thus the cost estimates for the hardware costs, the software costs, the data communications costs, the people costs and the commissioning costs are all potential financial risks. If elements of the system are being imported from a different currency area then the foreign exchange rate constitutes a potential risk area, as does the interest rate if the project is being financed out of borrowed funds. There are of course other possible financial risks that are beyond the scope of this section.

13.6.3 The project picture

Different project management approaches or methodologies will emphasise different instruments for planning and control of a process change. ABR does not prescribe a definite instrument for project management at this level. ABR suggests an outline of what should be included in a project management summary. The items touched on are: the work packages, resource management to deliver the packages, time scheduling and management, and the identification of problems and risks. These facts should be characterised and evidenced in a way the non-technical management can understand and appreciate. They should be presented to give the evaluator the holistic view required by continuous participative evaluation. They should be presented for frequent review and evaluation synchronised with the cycle of the project evaluation process. In order to satisfactorily complete the project picture (PP) it is necessary to apply the skills and techniques of project management.

Figure 13.11 lists the issues that need to be addressed in the PP. The PP highlights for the primary stakeholders and project management the key project planning issues for an information systems development project. The PP by itself is not a substitute for a comprehensive project plan, which is, of course the responsibility of the project manager. Effective and efficient project management is a critical success factor for any project and it is assumed that the necessary skills for this are in place.

Item	Project issues
3.1	Project manager
3.2	Project deliverables – major products
3.3	Project activities – detailed tasks
3.4	Resources available
3.5	Project duration, time consumed and target completion date
3.6	Current best estimate of completion date, with rationale
3.7	Budget, actuals and cost variances-to-date
3.8	Percentage of job finished by time, cost and by specification
3.9	Forthcoming bottle necks identified
3.10	Changes identified by formative processes
3.11	Additional funds and time available
3.12	Major risks

Figure 13.11: Project picture

13.7 Using the pictures

The presentation of information in an easy to understand and yet rigorous format is essential to setting up the participative evaluation activity in process change or IT project management. The three pictures are offered as a comprehensive framework for this.

13.7.1 Continuous participative evaluation

When setting up an evaluation process for IT project management it is necessary to organise the review and participative evaluation activity. To monitor an activity at weekly intervals, weekly data collection is necessary and to monitor the activity on a monthly basis involves monthly data collection on progress. Consequently when setting up evaluation the frequency of the review is significant and the volatility of the data is also significant. As has been highlighted in Section 13.6, the most volatile data for monitoring progress stems from the project picture (work package progress, performance measures, time management and cost management) and from the cost management heads of the financial picture. Collecting this data is onerous but is a recognised activity of project management. The evaluation activity piggybacks the regular project management activity. The benefits calculations of the FP (i.e. benefits from increased in-group productivity) are to a certain extent persistent and would only be reviewed as part of continuous evaluation if one of the significant parameters of the calculation changes. So, for example, if one of the identified risks was that the 'sales function' might be outsourced, thus invalidating the projected benefits on calculations sales costs, then new benefits calculations might have to be undertaken.

The data of the business picture is essentially not volatile. Item 1.9 (specific benefits and metrics), depending on what is being measured, may require some more frequent data collection. So when setting up evaluation and developing the BP a realistic view should be taken of the specific benefits to be measured and the metrics to be used. The setting up of the BP and the continuous evaluation activity go hand in hand. The purpose of frequent, say monthly, formative evaluation is to keep the stakeholders informed, identified with and committed so that if one of the items of the BP does change fundamentally or can be seen to be drifting then this can be discussed and formally re-evaluated. It is the stakeholders, through participation, who will bring evidence to the evaluation process, either from their own areas of responsibility if business conditions are changing or from observation and discussion when progress on the project development or day-to-day running is reported on during monitoring sessions.

In the end the challenge for continuous participative evaluation is that the information should be presented for frequent review and re-evaluation.[12] The length of time between review will obviously always vary from project to project but they should not be allowed to extend beyond a few months. According to Wick and León:

We found that goals that take 4 months to accomplish work best. If the time required is shorter, that's fine. If your goal will take longer, then break it into smaller pieces and select a milestone along the way that you can attain in 4 months. (Wick and León, 1993)

Once properly set on course through the preparation and discussion of the initial pictures, the cost and management effort of continuous participative evaluation is limited. The advantage of the effort put in initially into preparing a business case through pictures is that the monitoring is continually focussed on the business case for little effort. The continuous participative monitoring effort is not costly.[13] If the organisation is operating in a volatile environment then the use of continuous participative evaluation is even more essential. It is clear in these circumstances that collecting data and reworking the business case will involve costs, which should be budgeted for as part of setting up project management for the volatile environment. Without frequent evaluation sessions it is nearly certain that the computer-based system will not meet the changing needs of the organisation.

---

[12] It is never an easy task to bring the principal stakeholders together for review sessions and thus the politics of the process change may actually dictate how often this actually happens.

[13] Of course management time is a hidden cost but it may be argued that if management does not put the time into seeing that the IT projects is run competently then it will have to put the time into deciding if the project should be repeated or just simply abandoned.

13.8 Summary

Setting up evaluation as part of a business process change or IT investment project is a key part of establishing a sound approach to project management. The focus of this evaluation is the realisation that business process change and the accompanying IT investment result in improvements to business efficiency and effectiveness, which in turn lead to benefit streams.

The ingredients of success in this endeavour are participation in the production of the business case using the three pictures described here and the focus on business process changes and improvements through continuous participative evaluation. Participation, by senior management and by business user-owners at whatever level is necessary for the project, and is one of the keys to motivating benefits realisation. Keeping a focus on the efficiency and effectiveness improvements stemming from the investment and not on the technological hype and niceties directly supports the delivery of improved business results and thus benefits.

This chapter has presented the process and the instruments of ABR for initiating a continuous evaluation approach. This evaluation is set up in a way to complement the necessary project management and financial management activities. The cost in management time and in data collection is limited and the pay off in terms of realising business benefits is often very substantial indeed.

14 | Final thoughts

The computer press is littered with examples of information technology fiascos or near disasters. An example is the computer aided dispatch system introduced into the London Ambulance Service in 1992. The £1.5 million system was bought into full use at 07:00 hours on 26 October and almost immediately began to 'lose' ambulances. During that and the next day less than 20% of ambulances reached their destinations within 15 minutes of being summoned, a very poor performance when compared with the 65% arriving within 15 minutes the previous May and the target set by the Government of 95%. The service reverted to semi-computerized methods during the afternoon of 27 October and then right back to manual methods on 4 November when the system locked up altogether and could not be re-booted successfully (South West Thames Regional Health Authority, 1993)

Joyce Fortune and Geoff Peters, *Learning from Failure: The Systems Approach* (1995)

14.1 Introduction

It is not an easy task to measure or manage IT costs and benefits. Many of the problems or challenges associated with this task have been spelt out in some detail in earlier chapters in this book. In general it may be said that some of the challenges are philosophical, such as those that relate to operationalising the meaning of value,[1] and some of them are practical, such as those involving the quantification of certain types of benefits. It

---

[1] With regards this issue the comment, which has been attributed to the Nobel laureate George Bernard Shaw 'If all economists were laid end to end, they would not reach a conclusion' immediately comes to mind.

is interesting how the question of the struggle for the meaning of value reoccurs so frequently in the IT evaluation literature. Bannister and Remenyi point out:

It is argued that a weakness in much of the current research is the fact that the definition of value is usually unclear, frequently inadequate, often partisan and sometimes completely absent from the discussion. Until there is a better understanding in the IT community of what value is and how managers attempt to optimise it, current IT evaluation methods for complex decision making purposes will often be neither credible nor effective. (Bannister and Remenyi, 2000)

It does appear that few IT professionals, be they practitioners, academics or consultants have explored and understood the concepts in this interesting field.

14.2 No obvious methodology

One of the conclusions that it is hoped will be drawn from a close examination of this subject area is that there is no obvious methodology for the measurement or management of IT costs and benefits. There are, of course, a number of different approaches to the problem, but there is not much agreement between academics, consultants and practitioners. However it is hoped that this does not necessarily lead to inaction in this endeavour, as organisations do really need to be able to evaluate their business process change and the accompanying IT investment. Thus the spirit of Edison' s words is relevant:

There aren't any rules here, we are trying to get something done. (Edison 1995)

And there are, as described in this book quite a lot of tools with which something can be done.

However it needs to be borne in mind that some organisations do not have a measurement culture. These organisations do not see much need to spend time and resources on attempting to calculate numbers that reflect their activities. They believe that it is the action that counts and not the estimates made in advance. This type of organisation also tends to say that poring over reports of past performance is also a distraction from effective management. It is perhaps fortunate that there are not many organisations that fall into this category.

14.3 Start with the high level view

One of the features of the work previously undertaken to measure and manage IT cost and benefits was a considerable focus on detail. IT investment were costed[2] at the feasibility stage and estimates of some of the possible benefits were made without necessarily really understanding the full set of implications of the system and its role in supporting the process changes that would lead to business benefits. In dealing with this type of situation or problem the advice of Wittgenstein seems most appropriate:

Don't get involved in partial problems, but always take flight to where there is a free view over the whole single *great problem, even if this view is still not a clear one.* (Wittgenstein 1914)

The suggestion of focusing on the business process change, which when supported by appropriate IT investment leads to improvements in efficiency and effectiveness, and thus business benefits is essentially the same as obtaining ' *a free view over the whole* single *great problem*'. This approach places the costs and benefits analysis above the clutter of the detail and allows the big picture to be revealed.

It is only in the bigger picture that the real benefits of process change and IT investment can be seen.

---

[2] The emphasis here was on low level detail that did not address the important issues as discussed in Chapter 1.

14.4 Know the purpose of the evaluation

The first question that needs to be addressed in developing any programme to measure or manage IT costs and benefits is what is the corporate objective in doing this. Without a specific objective the energy and the cost of the evaluation is likely to be dissipated, if not entirely wasted. Establishing the objectives of the evaluation exercise may not be a simple matter as Walsham pointed out:

A key element of the evaluation ..is the purpose for which the evaluation is being carried out; this purpose may be explicitly stated or may be implicit..(Walsham 1993)

And this view was supported by Farbey *et al.* who said:

The process of appraising new investment is always a political process in so far as it touches on the diverse interests of many people and groups. (Farbey *et al.* 1993)

Having a clear set of operationally-based objectives generally makes the evaluation process more straightforward. Also, if there are any hidden agendas in the evaluation, these will lead to questionable results, both from a practical point of view as well as from an ethical viewpoint.

Thus there is always the question of how objective an evaluation is. Even when working consciously to be as non-partisan as possible it is sometimes difficult to produce a fully objective view of the process change and the accompanying information systems investment. It is well to remember the words of Gould who points out:

Facts are not pure and unsullied bits of information; culture also influences what we see and how we see it. (Gould 1992)

And corporate culture is every bit as strong as any national culture.

Of course it is not difficult to perform an evaluation to ensure that a proposed system is rejected or that the information systems department appears in a poor light.

14.5 Evaluation is never trivial nor inexpensive

At the centre of the evaluation process is a management information system. Hopwood, in his discussion on 'Evaluating the Real Benefits' of information technology, points out that an evaluation is a complex information processing exercise:

Be aware that the evaluation exercise is itself a complex information processing activity, subject to all the problems and opportunities which characterise this area. (Hopwood 1983)

Thus it is important to always bear in mind that an evaluation exercise requires the establishment of an inquiring system,[3] the purpose of which is to produce knowledge to support the assessment of the business process or IT investment. This is never a trivial task and therefore should not be undertaken without due care to the resources required to do it properly.

There is no obvious research related to neither how much the evaluation process should cost nor how long it should take. However, it is generally agreed that the evaluation process should be easy to use and the evaluation activity relatively economical in terms of management time and evidence collection effort.[4] When setting up an evaluation process, the importance of the evaluation effort should reflect the importance and be in

---

[3] An inquiring system is 'A system which produces knowledge'. A complete discussion can be read in Churchman's book (1971). The term is used here in the sense that to support the final act of evaluation it is necessary to produce knowledge about the substance and the qualities of the system to be evaluated and to produce knowledge about the measurement norms.

[4] It is worth noting that it is quite possible to evaluate the costs and benefits of the evaluation process itself. As Shadish *et al.* (1991) point out: 'We can evaluate anything including evaluation itself.'

proportion to the size of the project itself. The evaluation effort should only be a small part of the project management effort.

14.6 A tool kit

This book offers a wide range of tools and supporting techniques with which IT costs and benefits can be measured and thus managed. These range from business case accounting approaches, to value for money studies to user information satisfaction surveys. Some of these tools are designed to be used before the IT investment are made in the so-called ex-ante mode, while others are only appropriate to be used once the information system has been in place some time and an ex-post evaluation is required. Furthermore, some of the tools are used to evaluate a process change or a single system while other are intended to help in the overall assessment of an information systems' function or department or a section thereof. The book leaves it up to the reader to choose which tools are the more appropriate to his/her own circumstances.

14.7 A change in culture

However the section on ABR described in Chapter 13 is not a tool *per se*, but rather a framework for improving the rate of success with the implementation of process change-based IT projects. Although the tools (or perhaps pictures) described in this chapter are important, the approach of employing continuous participative evaluation is perhaps much more important. But this is sometimes more difficult than it first appears and may well require a distinct change in corporate culture, which embraces a higher degree of glasnost or openness than the organisation has been accustomed to.

14.8 Summary

Of course, the work involved in developing a comprehensive understanding and approach to the identification and the management of IT costs and benefits is not complete and is unlikely ever to be so. There are too many issues and concepts and there are too many different ways of thinking about these issues and concepts. Nevertheless, this should not discourage those who are interested in improving our understanding of this challenging, and at times exasperating, subject. In the words of Checkland when writing about systems thinking:

Obviously the work is not finished, and can never be finished. There are no absolute positions to be reached in the attempt by men to understand the world in which they find themselves: new experience may in the future refute present conjectures. So the work itself must be regarded as an on-going system of a particular kind: A learning system which will continue to develop ideas, to test them out in practice, and to learn from the experience gained.' (Checkland 1986)

But the secret is to do something and to learn as one goes.

Appendix A

Glossary of terms

Artificial intelligence (AI)

An approach to developing systems so that they will function in a way not dissimilar to the human brain. The most frequently encountered application for artificial intelligence is expert systems, which allow very efficient rule processing to be performed.

Benefit

A term used to indicate an advantage, profit or gain attained by an individual or organisation.

Bottom-up planning

Bottom-up IS planning is an approach which addresses the current IS requirements and focuses on priority settings and resource allocation to achieve these requirements.

Business vision

The business vision is what the management wants to achieve with the enterprise in the future. A business vision usually refers to the medium to long term. It is often expressed in terms of a series of objectives.

CAD (computer aided design)

A computer system or software package providing facilities for simplifying the design of items. Systems may be specialised towards engineering, architectural or electronic applications.

CAM (computer aided manufacture)

Wide ranging term to describe computer systems that improve the firm' s ability to improve it' s manufacturing efficiency.

CASE (computer aided systems engineering)

Term used to refer to software products that improve the efficiency of systems planners, systems analysts and systems designers. Some CASE tools will also include code generators that can produce final programs in Cobol.

Corporate strategy

The method through which the firm finds, gets and keeps its clients. In a broad sense it refers to how the firm relates to and interacts with its environment, including its stakeholders.

Cost benefit analysis

The process of comparing the various costs associated with an investment with the benefits and profits that it returns.

Cost leadership

A generic strategy by which the firm presents itself to the marketplace as a low-priced, no-frills supplier.

Critical success factors (CSF)

Those aspects of the business that must be right for the enterprise to succeed in achieving its objectives. It is also sometimes said that even though all other aspects of the business are going well, if the critical success factors are not, then the business will not succeed.

Data processing (DP)

Early term given to the use of computers in business for the purposes of record keeping and providing regular reports to assist in the functioning of the firm. The term was originally referred to as Electronic Data Processing (EDP), but the E was dropped by most members of the industry.

Decision support systems (DSS)

Information systems that support semi or unstructured decisions in the area of strategic planning, management control or operations control.

Differentiation

A generic strategy by which the firm presents itself to the market as a high quality supplier, and therefore asks for a premium price for its goods or services.

Electronic data interchange (EDI)

Technology that facilitates computer application to computer application communications. EDI is designed to allow structured messages to be transmitted across a network. It relies on adherence to data communications standards. These standards have to include details of how EDI partners are prepared to receive standard business documents such as purchase orders, sales invoices, etc. This means that careful attention must be given to the definition of such documents.

Electronic point of sale (EPOS)

Technology for recording retail sales directly onto a computer. This can be achieved through a variety of devices ranging from computerised tills where operators enter the data, to various forms of scanning machines. EPOS produces instant updates to inventory records as well as valuable sales information. It can also have a very much lower error rate than traditional systems.

Electronic trading opportunity (ETO)

Use of computers to buy or sell in the marketplace. This is a wide-ranging term and includes systems such as airline reservations through which organisations can sell their services, as well as applications used for purchasing from a vendor or vendors.

End user computing (EUC)

Term referring to the supply of computer power to management in order to increase its efficiency and effectiveness.

Enterprise Resource Planning (ERP)

An information system whose scope can potentially embrace all aspects of an organisation in a highly integrated manner.

Executive information systems (EIS)

Systems used by top executives to assist in the planning and control process of the firm. It involves the use of an information warehouse or repository, which is accessed through a series of easy-to-use tools. EIS also normally implies the use of communications to address external databases.

Factory system

A computer system that assists the firm in achieving its required level of efficiency and effectiveness. These systems are also sometimes referred to as critical information systems (CIS).

Gantt chart

A chart on which activities and their durations are represented by lines drawn to a time scale.

Generic strategy

One of the basic ways in which a firm can find, get and keep its clients. There are two generic strategies, which are *cost leadership* and *differentiation*. A generic strategy may be broad-based or focus on a niche in the market.

Hard cost

Costs associated with an investment that are agreed by everyone to be directly attributable to the investment, and which can be easily captured by accounting procedures.

Hidden cost

A non-obvious cost associated with an investment that may in fact appear to be due to another source.

Industry driver

Condition which directly influences or affects the performance of all the firms in the industry. Examples include major changes in competition, deregulation and new technology developments.

Industry value chain

A concept developed by Michael Porter (1985), which shows how the value chains of individual firms within an industry are related. It is an excellent basis from which to find SIS opportunities.

Information System (IS)

General term to describe the use of hardware and software to deliver information to businesses.

Information Systems Department (ISD)

Department in the firm responsible for managing the information systems function. Sometimes also referred to as the information technology department (ITD).

Information Technology (IT)

Wide-ranging term to describe the use of computers and telecommunications.

Information weapon

A term used by a number of authors to describe the firm's efforts to gain a competitive advantage through the use of IT.

Intangible benefit

Benefits produced by an investment which are not immediately obvious and/or measurable.

Internal Rate of Return (IRR)

The return generated internally by an investment throughout its life, also referred to as the Yield of the Investment.

IT benefit

The benefit produced by an investment in information technology. It is likely that such an investment will produce both tangible and intangible IT benefits.

Just In Time (JIT)

Approach to manufacturing which requires raw material to be delivered to a firm exactly when required. The objective of a Just In Time system is to minimise raw material inventory and work in progress.

Local Area Network (LAN)

The joining together of a number of personal computers or other devices in a network that operates within a limited geographical area.

Management Information System (MIS)

There is no general agreement in the industry as to a precise meaning of the term MIS. Initially, it was used to describe systems that would play an active role in assisting managers make decisions. However, with the arrival of Decision Support Systems and Executive Information Systems, the term MIS has been used to describe information systems that perform routine data processing and supply regular reports.

Management Support System (MSS)

Information system which provides reports which assist management in its decision making function.

Network

A series of important points connected together. In IT terms a network may be defined as a number of computing devices connected together electronically.

Niche

A clearly defined market segment at which the firm aims its corporate strategy.

Office automation (OA)

Provision of computer power to white-collar workers in order to improve their efficiency and effectiveness. The key to an office automation system is its connectivity whereby data is shared between a group of people working in the same office or the same firm.

Opportunity cost

The opportunity cost of an investment is the amount the organisation could have earned if the sum invested in IT was used in another way.

Payback

The amount of time, usually expressed in years and months, required for an original investment to be repaid by the cash-in flows.

Project management workbench (PMW)

Software product used to plan and control projects. It produces various forms of Gantt chart etc.

Return on investment (ROI)

Accounting or financial management term to describe how well the firm has used its resources. It is usually calculated by dividing net profit after tax by total net assets.

Soft cost

Costs associated with an investment that are not readily agreed by everyone to be directly attributable to the investment, and which are not easily captured by accounting procedures.

Software platform

An already existing IS which may be extended so that it acquires a strategic dimension. An example would be a sales order entry system to which clients are given access through an external network so they can monitor the progress of their orders.

Strategic information system (SIS)

An information system that directly assists the organisation in achieving its corporate strategy. These applications are sometimes referred to as competitive edge systems.

Strategic option generator (SOG)

A system application developed by Charles Wiseman (1985), which may be used to identify SIS.

Strategic vision

How the top management of an enterprise believes it can achieve its objectives in the medium- to long-term.

Strategy

The formal use of this word refers to the way a firm finds, gets and keeps its clients. Common usage has reduced the meaning of strategy to be synonymous with plan. See also 'corporate strategy' and 'generic strategy'.

Support systems

Basic record keeping systems that the firm requires to function. These systems are also sometimes referred to as vital information systems (VIS).

Tangible benefit

Benefits produced by an investment which are immediately obvious and measurable.

Technology vision

How the organisation considers the application of technology within the business. This term is usually used to refer to a relatively mechanistic application of technology within the firm.

Top-down planning

Top-down IS planning attempts to develop IS which support business objectives and strategies.

Top management

A term used to refer to the chief executive and other senior members of the board of directors.

Transaction processing system (TPS)

Computer system that processes large volumes of data. These systems are normally online or real time.

Turnaround system

Experimental information systems developed by the organisation. This is the research and development aspect of the information systems department. It is hoped that turnaround systems will eventually become SISs.

Value activities

The term used by Michael Porter (1985) to describe the individual aspects or functions of an enterprise.

Value chain

A value chain is a method described by Michael Porter (1985) for the detailed analysis of an enterprise.

Value added network (VAN)

A facility whereby an organisation can sell its network to third parties, thus allowing them the facility of large-scale data communications without its initial set-up costs.

Vision

Sometimes referred to as strategic vision or business vision, this term refers to how the firm can successfully function in the marketplace in the medium to long-term. It usually encompasses how the firm will find, get and keep its clients.

Appendix B

Acronyms

ABR	Active benefit realisation
BP	Business picture
CAD	Computer aided design
CAM	Computer aided manufacturing
CASE	Computer aided systems engineering
CBA	Cost benefit analysis
CEO	Chief executive officer
CIS	Critical information system
CSF	Critical success factor
CUI	Character user interface
DCF	Discounted cash flow
DP	Data processing
DSS	Decision support system
EDI	Electronic data interchange
EIS	Executive information system
EPOS	Electronic point of sale
ERP	Enterprise resource planning
ETO	Electronic trading opportunity
EUC	End user computing
FP	Financial picture
GP	Gross profit
GUI	Graphical user interface
HCR	Health check review

IBP	Initial business picture
ICAEW	Institute of Chartered Accountants of England and Wales
IFP	Initial financial picture
I/O	Input/output
IPP	Initial project picture
IRR	Internal rate of return
IS	Information system
ISD	Information systems department
IT	Information technology
ITAM	Information technology assessment metric
ITB	Information technology budget

JIT	Just in time

KMO	Kaiser-Meyer-Olkin
KPI	Key performance indicators

MBA	Master of business administration
MD	Managing director
MIS	Management information system
MIT	Massachusetts Institute of Technology
MSS	Management support system

NP	Net profit
NPV	Net present value

OA	Office automation
OECD	Organization for Economic Co-operation and Development

PC	Personal computer
PI	Profitability index
PIA	Post implementation audit
PIN	Personal identification number
P&L	Profit and loss
PLC	Public listed company
PMW	Project Manager Workbench
PP	Project picture
PSIS	Potential strategic information system

R&D	Research and development
ROE	Return on equity
ROI	Return on investment
ROM	Return on management

SD	Standard deviation
SIS	Strategic information system
SISP	Strategic information systems plan
SOG	Strategic options generator
SPSS/PC	Statistical Package for the Social Sciences/PC-Based
TIMIS	Totally integrated management information system
TPS	Transaction processing system
TQM	Total quality management
UIS	User information satisfaction
US	User satisfaction
VAN	Value added network
VDU	Visual display unit
VFM	Value for money
VIS	Vital information system
WAN	Wide area network

Appendix C

Financial measures used in cost benefit analysis

Payback

The payback may be defined as the amount of time, usually expressed in years and months, required for the original investment amount to be repaid by the cash-in flows. This measure is sometimes used with nominal cash-in flows and sometimes used with discounted cash-in flows. Nominal cash flows are the amounts unadjusted for the time value of money. The most popular form of payback used today is referred to as the exhaust method. The exhaust method of payback calculation involves the deduction of each year's cash-in flow from the original investment until the original amount is reduced to zero. This method should be contrasted with the average payback method which only gives a rough approximation of the period of time required to recover the investment amount when the cash-in flows are relatively constant.

Exhaust method

Payback in time (years, months, etc) = Investment – Cumulative benefit

The calculation of the payback by the exhaust method is a reiterative process which requires the cumulative benefit to be subtracted from the investment until the result is zero. The time at which the result is zero represents the period that is required for the investment amount to be returned.

Average method

$$\frac{\text{Payback in time}}{\text{Average annual benefit}} = \text{Investment}$$

If there is any substantial variability in the annual benefits this method will produce meaningless results. Many organisations use the payback as the primary criterion for deciding whether an investment is suitable or not.

It is generally considered that the cash flows used to calculate the payback should have first been discounted. This is referred to as a discounted payback. If this is done it will produce a time value based payback measure that will reflect the cost of capital. A discounted payback will always show a longer period than those based on nominal values.

Net present value (NPV)

The net present value may be defined as the difference between the sum of the values of the cash-in flows, discounted at an appropriate cost of capital, and the present value of the original investment. Provided the NPV is greater than or equal to zero the investment will earn the firm's required rate of return. The size of the NPV may be considered as either a measure of the surplus that the investment makes over its required return, or as a margin of error in the size of the investment amount.

$$\text{Present value of benefit} = \frac{\text{Benefit}}{(1+i)^n}$$

Where i = rate of interest

n = number of years

NPV = $\sum$ Present value of benefit − Present value of investment

The interpretation of the NPV should be based on the following rules:

If NPV >=0 then invest

If NPV < 0 then do not invest

The size of the NPV represents the margin of error which may be made in the estimate of the investment amount before the investment will be rejected.

Profitability index (PI)

The profitability index is defined as the sum of the present values of the cash-in flows divided by the present value of the investment. This shows a rate of return expressed as the number of discounted pounds and pence that the investment will earn for every pound originally invested.

$$PI = \frac{\sum \text{Present value of benefits}}{\text{Present value of investment}}$$

Internal rate of return (IRR)

The internal rate of return is the rate of interest that will cause the NPV to be zero. It is the internally generated return that the investment will earn throughout its life. It is also frequently referred to as the yield of the investment.

IRR = i such that NPV = 0

Rate of return or return on investment (ROI)

The rate of return or return on investment, which is sometimes referred to as the simple return on investment, is calculated by considering the annual benefit divided by the investment amount. Sometimes an average rate of return for the whole period of investment is calculated by averaging the annual benefits while on other occasions the rate of return is calculated on a year-by-year basis using individual benefit amounts.

$$ROI = \frac{\text{Annual benefit}}{\text{Investment amount}}$$

Appendix D

Factor analysis

Factor analysis is the generic term given to a group of multivariate statistical techniques that can be used to identify, from a large pool of variables, the important variables related to a study. Variables that are interrelated in terms of their correlations can be grouped, thereby possibly identifying some otherwise hidden concept(s). The variables that group or cluster together can be combined into a weighted linear combination called a factor, which can then be used to measure concepts not otherwise directly observable. Thus factor analysis can facilitate the reduction of focus to a smaller set of variables, facilitate concept identification, and facilitate measurement of these concepts

The various techniques of factor analysis differ in the manner in which the weights for the variables constituting the factors are determined. The most widely used method for determining factors is that of *principal component* analysis, which is the method used in analysing the responses to the user satisfaction questionnaire as described in Chapter 8. In the sequel the term factor analysis is used as a synonym for principal component analysis.

Factor analysis can be used both for exploratory and confirmatory studies. The use of factor analysis for concept identification illustrates how the technique can be used in an exploratory manner. It is used in a confirmatory sense when, for example, the factor analysis solution is compared to some *a priori* postulation concerning the grouping of the variables into factors. In our study it was used for exploratory purposes.

Once the analyst has identified the variables that are to be analysed, there are three main computational steps to the factor analysis, namely, the construction of a correlation matrix, the extraction of initial factors and the rotation of the initial factors.

Correlation matrix

In factor analysis the starting point is to convert the observations on the variables to a correlation matrix whose elements are the pairwise correlations among the variables being factor analysed. For a factor analysis to be worthwhile in terms of grouping the variables into a smaller number of factors the elements of the correlation matrix should generally display significant correlation. A measure that can be used to decide whether to proceed with a factor analysis is the Kaiser-Meyer-Olkin (KMO) statistic. The KMO is a function of the pairwise correlations between the variables.

Should the calculated KMO be 0.80 or more the factor analysis is likely to lead to substantial simplification of the data set. Should the KMO be below 0.50 then it is unlikely that much will be gained from performing a factor analysis.

Initial factor extraction

The aim of the initial factor extraction is to determine the extent to which the original set of variables, p (say), can be summarised into a much smaller set of factors, m (say), where each of the factors is a linear combination of the original variables. The method of factor extraction described here is that of principal component analysis. The factors are constructed so that they are uncorrelated with one another or as it is sometimes expressed, 'orthogonal to one another'.

Thus through the application of principal component analysis the set of correlated variables is transformed into a set of uncorrelated factors which are themselves linear combinations of the original variables.

The extraction of the principal components or factors can be viewed as being derived in a sequential manner from the original X variables. The model used to extract the principal component factors is (see Lehmann, 1989)

$$F_j = I_{j1}X_1 + I_{j2}X_2 + ... + I_{jp}X_p$$

where

$F_j = j - th$ principal component factor

I_{ji} = the coefficient linking the i-th variable to the j-th factor

$$(j = 1,2,...,p; i = 1,2,...,p)$$

Invariably it is the standardised variables rather than the original variables X that are subjected to a principal component analysis. This approach is particularly important should the original variables be measured on different scales. The standardisation procedure reduces all variables to the same units so that the standardised variables all have mean zero and unit standard deviation. When we use standardised variables the principal components procedure is essentially extracting factors from the correlation matrix. In this case the factor loading coefficients I_{ji} are the ordinary correlation coefficients between the i-th variable and the j-th factor. Thus it is possible in this case to talk in terms of statistical significance and non-significance of the factor loadings. For example for a sample of 100 respondents to a questionnaire a factor loading of 0.30 will be statistically significant at the 5% level. Thus factor loadings of 0.30 or more can be considered significant.

The components are extracted sequentially in the following manner. The first component is the linear combination of the original variables that explains the most variation in the sample, the second that linear combination that explains the second most variance and so on for the other factors. It is possible to extract as many principal component factors as there are variables.

Practical considerations require that the number of factors to be retained is determined, as well as those factors that load 'significantly on' or 'belong to' the retained factors. Some guidelines are provided.

First the importance of the derived factors must be defined and measured. The importance of a factor is determined by the amount of the total variance that it explains, usually expressed as a percentage. The variance of a factor is related to its so-called eigenvalue. For example the eigenvalue for factor j, which is denoted by l_j is the sum of the squared factor loadings l_{ji} of the original variables with the factor. Thus,

$$l_j = \sum_{i=1}^{p} l_{ij}^2$$

where $j = 1,2,\ldots,p$

When working with the standardised variables the sum of the p extracted eigenvalues must equal the number of variables p. The j-th principal component will explain $\left((l_j / p) * 100\right)\%$ of the total variance. Also we have,

$$\sum_{j=1}^{p} l_j = p$$

This information can then be used to determine how many factors to retain. There is however no hard and fast rule as to how many factors should be retained. Three approaches are frequently used in practice. Approaches include the following (Lehmann, 1989):

1 Retain those factors which have an eigenvalue greater than 1. Since we are working with standardised variables this im-

plies that each standardised variable on its own can be expected to explain $((1/p)*100)\%$ of the variance and so the eigenvalue greater than 1 rule will at least ensure that the newly created variable or factor will explain more variance than any one of the original variables on its own.

2 Retain those factors that collectively explain a pre-specified proportion of the total variance.

3 Factors are extracted sequentially until they begin to explain an 'insignificant' amount of the still unexplained variance.

4 The most frequently used approach is the eigenvalue greater than 1 rule. This is the default option on most statistical software packages, of which SPSS is one.

Rotation of factors

In situations where two or more factors are retained by the principal component analysis we invariably find that the manner in which the variables load onto the factors does not lend itself to interpretation that makes sense. The reasons for this are that we are likely to find that most of the variables load highly on the first principal component or that variables are highly correlated with (i.e. load onto) more than one factor. This is an artefact of the mathematical procedure that determines the factors.

It can be shown that when there are more than two factors retained, neither the factors nor their loadings are unique with respect to orthogonal transformations. There are numerous methods for performing orthogonal rotations with the *Varimax* procedure the most widely used.

The purpose of the rotation is to facilitate interpretation by redistributing the variance among the retained factors so that there is little or no ambiguity concerning the factor onto which the original variables load. Thus after *varimax* rotation one is likely to find that if a variable loads highly on one factor then it is likely to load lowly on the other factors. Opinion differs as to what is to be considered a high loading. The authors have found that using loadings of 0.50 or larger regularly leads to satisfactory results. Some practitioners consider loadings of 0.30 as their cut-off.

In practice the meaning of the factor is usually established by identifying the variables that load 'significantly' on the factor and then trying to establish, usually through brainstorming, with those who are knowledgable in the area being studied, what underlying characteristic is most likely to provide the link between them.

Summary

In order to factor analyse the responses to a questionnaire on user satisfaction, the following steps should be taken:

1 Calculate the correlation matrix. A study of the correlation matrix will provide a 'feel' for how the variables are likely to group.

2 Look at the Kaiser-Meyer-Olkin (KMO) statistic. If the statistic is in excess of 0.70 then it is likely that the factor analysis will lead to substantial reduction in the data. If less than 0.50 there is no need to proceed with factor analysis.

3 Extract factors using the principal components procedure.

4 Decide on the number of factors to be retained. Retain only those factors which have an eigenvalue greater than 1.

5 Rotate the initial solution using the *varimax* routine. Rotation of the factors precedes interpretation and naming of the factors.

6 Interpret the factors for measuring. Interpretation is facilitated by focusing attention on those variables that load heavily on it. Concentrate only on variables with a loading of

0.5 or more, and then establish, possibly by 'brainstorming' with experts, what it is that links these variables together.

7 Name the factors. An output from the interpretation phase described in 6 above is that each of the retained factors is given a generic name.

Appendix E

Sample sizing scenarios

Scenario one

International Enterprises plc

International Enterprises plc is an extensive user of personal computers with more than 12,000 installed worldwide. In the United Kingdom alone there are more than 9500 in use.

The firm wishes to conduct a survey to establish how their users regard the personal computer service offered by the firm. It is realised that the total number of personal computer users is too large to be able to survey them all. Therefore it is agreed to use a sampling technique.

After much discussion it was decided that in the first instance only the office system OA2000 would be surveyed. There are 2750 users of this system.

Management have asked the survey team to design the measuring procedure so that they can have 95% confidence that their results will be accurate to within 2%.

1 How big a sample will they need to measure the OA2000 system?

2 How will the sample size change if management change their mind and want to have 99% confidence that their results are accurate to within 1%?

3 After completing the OA2000 review International Enterprises plc want to extend the survey to include all the other users in the United Kingdom. How big must the sample be if management want 5% accuracy and a confidence level of 95%?

There are two ways in which a sample size needs to be calculated. First there is the issue of measuring a percentage of a population, and second there is the issue of measuring a mean on a scale.

International Enterprises plc solution

Size of sample required giving management 2% accuracy and 95% confidence.

Sample size to estimate a percentage

In the first instance calculate a sample size assuming an infinite population as described in Chapter 12, section 12.4.8.

$$n = \frac{3.84 \times 50(100 - 50)}{2^2} = \frac{3.84 \times 2500}{4} = 2400$$

Check whether the calculated sample size exceeds 10% of the population size. As it does, then a correction must be made to reduce the sample size.

Apply the sample size correction factor to calculate the appropriate sample size under these circumstances.

$$n' = n \times \left(\frac{N}{N + n - 1} \right)$$

where n' is the appropriate sample size.

$$n' = 2400 \times \left(\frac{2750}{2750 + 2400 - 1} \right)$$
$$n' = 2400 \times (0.534$$
$$n' = 1281$$

Therefore if 1281 responses are received and the percentage of the sample that holds a particular view is calculated and quoted, then we can be 95% confident that the percentage quoted is accurate to within 2%.

Sample size to estimate the mean response:

Again we start by applying the formula assuming infinite population size.

Thus, $n = \dfrac{3.84 \times S^2}{E^2}$

We need to estimate S, the standard deviation, assuming a 4-point scale on the questionnaire:

$$S = \frac{Max(X_i) - Min(X_i)}{4} = \frac{4-1}{4} = 0.75$$

Therefore $S^2 = (0.75)^2 = 0.5625$

Now we need to express E in terms of the measurement scale's units.

The measurement scale goes from 1 to 4.

Take $E = 2.5 \times 0.02$. (0.02 corresponds to 2%, which is the required accuracy.) Thus $E = 0.05$.

Hence, $n = \dfrac{3.84 \times 0.5625}{(0.05)^2} = \dfrac{2.160}{0.0025} = 864$

Again the calculated sample size does exceed 10% of the population size, so a correction must be made to reduce the sample size.

The sample correction factor is applied, giving:

$$n' = 864 \times \left(\frac{2750}{2750 + 864 - 1} \right) = 864 \times (0.761) = 658$$

Therefore 658 responses to the questionnaire are required in order to estimate the mean response to 2% accuracy with 95% confidence.

Size of sample required giving management 1% accuracy and 99% confidence.

Sample size for percentage p – 99% confidence; 1% accuracy.

Proceed as before, but using the appropriate formula.

$$n = \frac{6.66 \times p(100 - p)}{E^2} = \frac{6.66 \times 50(50)}{1^2} = 16,650$$

(The 6.66 represents 2.58 standard deviations. Some sources use 3 standard deviations, in which case the multiplication factor would be 9 and not 6.66.)

However, 16,650 is more than 10% of the population size, therefore applying the correction factor we get

$$n' = 16,650 \times \left(\frac{2750}{2750 + 16,650 - 1}\right) = 2,360$$

Sample size determination for the mean – 99% confidence; 1% accuracy.

Proceed as above, but using the appropriate formula

$$n = \frac{6.66 \times S^2}{E^2} = \frac{6.66 \times (0.75^2)}{(0.025)^2} = 5994$$

Again there is a need to apply the sample correction formula.

$$\text{Thus, } n' = 5994 \times \left(\frac{2750}{2750 + 5994 - 1}\right) = 1886$$

Size of sample required giving management 5% accuracy and 95% confidence.

Sample size to estimate percentage

Applying the formula as before the required sample size is 384.

Thus, $\dfrac{n}{N} \times 100 = \dfrac{384}{9500} \times 100 = 4\%$

Since the sample size is less than 10% of the population size there is no need to apply the correction formula.

Sample size to estimate the mean

In this case we need to express E in terms of the measurement scale units. Thus we have $E = 2.5 \times (0.05)$. (0.05 corresponds to the 5% required accuracy.)

Also the standard deviation $S = 0.75$.

Hence, $n = \dfrac{3.84 \times (S^2)}{E^2} = \dfrac{3.84 \times (0.5625)}{0.0156} = 138$

Scenario two

Engineers Unlimited plc

Engineers Unlimited plc is a large engineering design and consulting firm in the Midlands. The firm has a long tradition of using computers but was relatively slow to acquire personal computers. It has been using various forms of end user computing for the past five years, but throughout this period there have always been continual complaints.

Engineers Unlimited plc decided to conduct a survey to establish exactly what the end users felt about the systems which were installed and also to find out what new systems the staff felt they should acquire.

There are about 985 end users in Engineers Unlimited plc and a 20-page questionnaire was sent out to all of these individuals. Only 315 completed questionnaires were returned.

1 The firm would now like to know the degree of accuracy and the degree of confidence that it may associate with the results of the questionnaire.

2 It is believed that with a reasonable amount of effort another 75 questionnaires could be rounded up. How would this affect the accuracy and the confidence level?

Engineers Unlimited plc - Solutions

The total population is denoted by N and the number of returned questionnaires is n'. Therefore $N = 985$, $n' = 315$ and thus $n' > 10\%$ of N, so the correction factor must be applied.

Estimating the percentage accuracy associated with 95% confidence, sample size n'

$$E = \sqrt{\frac{3.84p(100 - p)}{n'} \times \frac{(N - n')}{N - 1}}$$

$$E = \sqrt{\frac{3.84(2500)}{315} \times \frac{(985 - 315)}{985 - 1}}$$

$$E = \sqrt{\frac{(9600)}{315} \times \frac{(670)}{984}}$$

$$E = 4.6\%$$

(Note: if n' is small relative to N then $\dfrac{N - n'}{N - 1} = approximately\ 1$)

Therefore the percentage accuracy associated with 95% confidence is 4.6% for a sample size of 315.

Accuracy achieved when estimating the mean.

$$E = \sqrt{\frac{3.84(0.5625)}{315} \times \frac{(985 - 315)}{985 - 1}} = \sqrt{0.0047} = 0.07\ units$$

Therefore if the sample mean is 2.5, the estimate of the true mean is accurate to 0.07 units with 95% confidence.

Accuracy achieved when estimating the percentage using and additional 75 questionnaires.

$$E = \sqrt{\frac{3.84(2500)}{390} \times \frac{(985 - 390)}{985 - 1}}$$

$$E = \sqrt{14.89} = 3.86\%$$

Therefore the percentage accuracy if another 75 questionnaires are included is 3.86%

Accuracy achieved when estimating the mean.

$$E = \sqrt{\frac{3.84(0.5625)}{390} \times \frac{(985 - 390)}{985 - 1}} = \sqrt{0.0033} = 0.06 \text{ units}$$

Therefore the additional 75 questionnaires improves the accuracy of the estimate of the mean from 0.07 to 0.06 units.

Appendix F

Measurement of IS effectiveness – a questionnaire

PART A

Please supply the following information about your position:

1   In which department or section do you work (Tick one)?

Inland Operations	
Operations Services	———
Infrastructure Planning	———
Strategic planning	———
Public Affairs	———
Information Services	———
New Works	———
Analytical Services	———
Process Services	———
Geographic Information Systems	———
Finance & Administration	———
Human Resources	———
Other, Please Specify	———
	———

2   How many years' have you been working in the organisation?   ____

3   How many years experience have you had working with a PC or terminal?   ____

4   How many years' experience have you had working with a PC network or mainframe?   ____

5   How many hours per week do you use a PC or a PC network or mainframe?   ____

PART B – Expectations under ideal circumstances

Please respond by ticking the number that corresponds to how much you agree or disagree with the following statements of expectation, *given an ideal situation*.

		Strongly Disagree								Strongly Agree
1	I expect ease of access to computing facilities.	1	2	3	4	5	6	7	8	9
2	I expect up-to-date hardware.	1	2	3	4	5	6	7	8	9
3	I expect up-to-date software.	1	2	3	4	5	6	7	8	9
4	I expect access to external databases.	1	2	3	4	5	6	7	8	9
5	I expect a low percentage of hardware and software downtime.	1	2	3	4	5	6	7	8	9
6	I expect a high degree of technical competence from systems support staff.	1	2	3	4	5	6	7	8	9
7	I expect to have a high level of confidence in the systems I use.	1	2	3	4	5	6	7	8	9
8	I expect to have a high degree of personal control over the systems I use.	1	2	3	4	5	6	7	8	9
9	I expect the ISD to be responsive to my changing needs.	1	2	3	4	5	6	7	8	9
10	I expect confidentiality for my own data.	1	2	3	4	5	6	7	8	9
11	I expect a provision for disaster recovery.	1	2	3	4	5	6	7	8	9
12	I expect piracy avoidance procedures to be in place.	1	2	3	4	5	6	7	8	9
13	I expect excellent system's response time.	1	2	3	4	5	6	7	8	9
14	I expect excellent technical training.	1	2	3	4	5	6	7	8	9
15	I expect fast response time from support staff to remedy problems.	1	2	3	4	5	6	7	8	9
16	I expect to participate in the planning of system technology requirements.	1	2	3	4	5	6	7	8	9
17	I expect a positive attitude from support staff.	1	2	3	4	5	6	7	8	9
18	I expect overall cost-effectiveness from information technology.	1	2	3	4	5	6	7	8	9

		Strongly Disagree								Strongly Agree
19	I expect the use of IT to improve my personal productivity.	1	2	3	4	5	6	7	8	9
20	I expect the use of IT to enrich my working experience.	1	2	3	4	5	6	7	8	9
21	I expect standardisation of hardware.	1	2	3	4	5	6	7	8	9
22	I expect excellent documentation to support technical training.	1	2	3	4	5	6	7	8	9
23	I expect help to make the most of my application software.	1	2	3	4	5	6	7	8	9
24	I expect to be able communicate by e-mail with colleagues.	1	2	3	4	5	6	7	8	9
25	I expect to have access to the World Wide Web.	1	2	3	4	5	6	7	8	9
26	I expect to find the time to learn the systems I use.	1	2	3	4	5	6	7	8	9
27	I expect there to be a service level agreement in place.	1	2	3	4	5	6	7	8	9
28	I expect IS professionals to monitor their performance in delivering IT services.	1	2	3	4	5	6	7	8	9
29	I expect prompt processing of requests for changes to existing systems.	1	2	3	4	5	6	7	8	9
30	I expect IT to be aligned to the overall corporate plan.	1	2	3	4	5	6	7	8	9
31	I expect there to be short lead times for the development of new systems.	1	2	3	4	5	6	7	8	9
32	I expect systems analysts to understand my business requirements.	1	2	3	4	5	6	7	8	9
33	I expect a high degree of flexibility in the system with regards data and reports.	1	2	3	4	5	6	7	8	9
34	I expect the portfolio of software applications available to me to be continually increased.	1	2	3	4	5	6	7	8	9
35	I expect the benefits derived by myself from the systems I use to be measured.	1	2	3	4	5	6	7	8	9

PART C – Actual performance

Please respond by ticking the number that corresponds to how much you agree or disagree with the following statements of performance, *i.e. what actually happens*.

		Strongly Disagree — Strongly Agree
1	I have easy access to computing facilities.	1 __ 2 __ 3 __ 4 __ 5 __ 6 __ 7 __ 8 __ 9 __
2	I have up-to-date hardware.	1 __ 2 __ 3 __ 4 __ 5 __ 6 __ 7 __ 8 __ 9 __
3	I have up-to-date software.	1 __ 2 __ 3 __ 4 __ 5 __ 6 __ 7 __ 8 __ 9 __
4	I have access to external databases.	1 __ 2 __ 3 __ 4 __ 5 __ 6 __ 7 __ 8 __ 9 __
5	I experience a low percentage of hardware and software downtime.	1 __ 2 __ 3 __ 4 __ 5 __ 6 __ 7 __ 8 __ 9 __
6	I experience a high degree of technical competence from systems support staff.	1 __ 2 __ 3 __ 4 __ 5 __ 6 __ 7 __ 8 __ 9 __
7	I experience a high level of confidence in the systems I use.	1 __ 2 __ 3 __ 4 __ 5 __ 6 __ 7 __ 8 __ 9 __
8	I have a high degree of personal control over the systems I use.	1 __ 2 __ 3 __ 4 __ 5 __ 6 __ 7 __ 8 __ 9 __
9	The ISD is responsive to my changing needs.	1 __ 2 __ 3 __ 4 __ 5 __ 6 __ 7 __ 8 __ 9 __
10	I have confidence in the confidentiality for my own data.	1 __ 2 __ 3 __ 4 __ 5 __ 6 __ 7 __ 8 __ 9 __
11	I am satisfied with the provisions made for disaster recovery.	1 __ 2 __ 3 __ 4 __ 5 __ 6 __ 7 __ 8 __ 9 __
12	I am satisfied with the provisions made for piracy avoidance.	1 __ 2 __ 3 __ 4 __ 5 __ 6 __ 7 __ 8 __ 9 __
13	I experience excellent system's response time.	1 __ 2 __ 3 __ 4 __ 5 __ 6 __ 7 __ 8 __ 9 __
14	I receive excellent technical training.	1 __ 2 __ 3 __ 4 __ 5 __ 6 __ 7 __ 8 __ 9 __
15	I experience fast response time from support staff to remedy problems.	1 __ 2 __ 3 __ 4 __ 5 __ 6 __ 7 __ 8 __ 9 __
16	I participate in the planning of system technology requirements.	1 __ 2 __ 3 __ 4 __ 5 __ 6 __ 7 __ 8 __ 9 __
17	I experience a positive attitude from support staff.	1 __ 2 __ 3 __ 4 __ 5 __ 6 __ 7 __ 8 __ 9 __

		Strongly Disagree								Strongly Agree
18	I am satisfied with the overall cost-effectiveness of our information technology.	1	2	3	4	5	6	7	8	9
19	The use of IT improves my personal productivity.	1	2	3	4	5	6	7	8	9
20	The use of IT enriches my working experience.	1	2	3	4	5	6	7	8	9
21	I have standardisation of hardware.	1	2	3	4	5	6	7	8	9
22	I receive excellent documentation to support technical training.	1	2	3	4	5	6	7	8	9
23	I receive help to make the most of my application software.	1	2	3	4	5	6	7	8	9
24	I am able to communicate by e-mail with colleagues.	1	2	3	4	5	6	7	8	9
25	I have access to the World Wide Web.	1	2	3	4	5	6	7	8	9
26	I find the time to learn the systems I use.	1	2	3	4	5	6	7	8	9
27	There is a service level agreement in place.	1	2	3	4	5	6	7	8	9
28	IS professionals monitor their performance in delivering IT services.	1	2	3	4	5	6	7	8	9
29	I experience prompt processing of requests for changes to existing systems.	1	2	3	4	5	6	7	8	9
30	IT is aligned to the overall corporate plan.	1	2	3	4	5	6	7	8	9
31	I experience short lead times for the development of new systems.	1	2	3	4	5	6	7	8	9
32	Systems analysts do understand my business requirements.	1	2	3	4	5	6	7	8	9
33	I experience a high degree of flexibility in the system with regards data and reports.	1	2	3	4	5	6	7	8	9
34	The portfolio of software applications available to me continually increases.	1	2	3	4	5	6	7	8	9
35	The benefits derived by myself from the systems I use are measured.	1	2	3	4	5	6	7	8	9

PART D

Please rate your *overall opinion* of the computer services offered by the information systems department.

	Strongly Disagree								Strongly Agree
On the whole our information systems are excellent	1 __ 2 ____ 3 ___ 4 ___ 5 ___ 6 ___ 7 ___ 8 ___ 9 ___								

Please supply any further comments you wish concerning the effectiveness of your computer network system.

_____

_____

_____

_____

_____

_____

_____

_____

_____

_____

Appendix G

Active benefit realisation – a questionnaire

Part 1 – The business opportunity or problem identification and validation

1 Does your organisation have a formal procedure for identifying business opportunities or problems?

Yes ☐   No ☐

2 If the answer to question 1 is yes, briefly describe how this formal procedure operates.

_____

3 If the answer to question 1 is no, how are business opportunities or problems identified?

_____

4 How frequently does IT play a role in assisting your organisation to exploit a business opportunity or to solve a business problem?

All the time   ☐

Some of the time   ☐

Occasionally   ☐

Hardly ever   ☐

5 If IT is hardly ever perceived as a facilitating agent to assist your organisation with its business opportunities or problems, what do you regard as the main purpose or function of your information technology?

_____

6 When IT is identified as an important aspect of the solution to the business problem or opportunity, who normally points out the role which IT can play?

IT staff   ☐

Eventual users of the system   ☐

Administrators   ☐

Consultants   ☐

Others (Please specify)   _____

7 Does your answer to question 6 differ depending on the size of the project or the type of application?

Yes   ☐   No   ☐

8 If the size of the project is critical is that size measured in terms of person years, money amounts or other?

_____

9 Is a formal definition of a business problem or opportunity produced?

Yes   ☐   No   ☐

10 If the answer to question 9 is yes, what does the formal definition look like?

Half-page written description   ☐

Calculation of cost reduction or profit improvement   ☐

Other (please specify) _____

11 Proposed or suggested IT projects may sometimes be inappropriate, i.e. too expensive or inconsistent with the organisation strategy. How do you check to see if the proposed IT system is relevant and appropriate?

_____

12 In performing a relevance and appropriateness check which of the following do you use?

Strategic alignment test   ☐

Internal benchmarking   ☐

External benchmarking   ☐

Brainstorming techniques   ☐

Some other technique (please specify)

_____

Part 2 – Stakeholder issues

13 How many different types of stakeholders are typically involved or concerned with a major IT project?

_____

14 Although each project will have a different set of stakeholders, are there certain groups of stakeholders which will be involved in almost all projects? If so who are these?

_____

15 How are appropriate stakeholders identified and who does this identification?

_____

16 Are formal stakeholder meetings convened?

Yes ☐   No ☐

17 If the answer to question 16 is yes, how frequently are these meetings held?

_____

18 On the assumption that there are primary and secondary stakeholders of the IT project, which stakeholders would you normally regard for a typical project as primary and which as secondary?

_____

19 Are the eventual users of the systems always included among the stakeholders?

Yes ☐   No ☐

20 If the answer to question 19 is yes, how influential is the eventual owner in the project decision making?

_____

21 Do you attempt to involve top management (someone at director level or someone reporting to a director) as a stakeholder?

Yes ☐   No ☐

22 If the answer to question 21 is yes, would you attempt to sustain the attention of top management throughout the project and if so how would you do this?

_____

23 How important is the issue of partnership between the stakeholders?

Essential ☐

Very ☐

Quite ☐

Not at all ☐

24 If you consider the issue of partnership to be essential or very important how do you attempt to create a partnership approach and how successful are you in this endeavour?

_____

25 Who makes the final decision whether to proceed with an IT project?

Senior managers ☐

Eventual users ☐

IT staff ☐

Accountants and administrators ☐

Others, (please specify) _____

26 At what stage in the project is the eventual ownership of an information systems project identified?

At the outset ☐

When the project is authorised ☐

During project production ☐

At testing ☐

When the project is commissioned ☐

27 How are the eventual owners of the information system identified?

_____

Part Three – Feasibility study issues

28 Does your organisation generally perform a formal information systems feasibility study?

Yes   ☐   No   ☐

29 If the answer to question 28 is yes, are information systems costs and benefits estimated?

Yes   ☐   No   ☐

30 If the answer to question 29 is no, how are the decision criteria for approving an information systems project presented?

_____

31 If the answer to question 29 is yes, how are these cost estimates obtained?

Vendor supplied   ☐

From internal know-how   ☐

Use consultants   ☐

Others, (please specify) _____

32 When benefits are estimated, how is this done?

Stated as financial numbers in the form of single point estimates   ☐

Stated as financial numbers in the form of range estimates   ☐

Stated as business issues such as higher customer satisfaction   ☐

Other, (please specify) _____

33 If benefits are stated as business Issues such as higher customer satisfaction how will it be established whether these benefits have been, in due course delivered?

_____

34 Are any benefits, either financial or business, validated as appropriate by establishing whether they are aligned with the organisation's corporate CSF?

_____

35 If financial figures are used in the feasibility study which investment indicator is calculated?

Payback   ☐

ROI   ☐

NPV   ☐

IRR   ☐

Other, (please specify) _____

36 Are solution alternatives considered as part of the process of deciding whether or not to proceed with a project?

_____

37 At what stage, if ever, do your project management procedures address the question of risk?

_____

38 Could risks be identified and associated with different benefits, different CSFs and different stakeholders?

_____

39 Does the feasibility study or any other aspects of the preparation process for a project require an outcome statement?

_____

Part Four - Culture gap issues

40 Sometimes there are language difficulties in discussing information systems, especially when information systems staff and eventual users have to exchange ideas about a system. How do you attempt to minimise communication problems between these groups?

41 At the time of the project being initiated which of the following issues have been resolved?

The budget ☐

Who the system's champion will be ☐

The system delivery date ☐

The test data ☐

User's responsibility ☐

System's ownership ☐

Strategic implication of the system ☐

Other, (please specify) _____

42 How long does it typically take (in months) from system's concept initialisation to project approval?

Appendix H

Issues addressed in effectiveness surveys

Functioning of existing transaction/reporting systems

The following represents the issues on which the 38 questions in the Miller-Doyle effectiveness measurement instrument are based.

- ♦ Completeness of output information
- ♦ Accuracy of output information
- ♦ Presence of monitoring systems
- ♦ Relevance of report contents
- ♦ Currency of output information
- ♦ Volume of output information
- ♦ Report availability and timeliness
- ♦ More exception systems

Linkages to strategic processes in the organisation

- ♦ Top management involvement
- ♦ Strategic IS planning
- ♦ Business-related systems priorities

♦ Using database technology

♦ Overall cost-effectiveness of IS

♦ Use of steering committee

Amount and quality of user involvement

♦ Users' feeling of participation

♦ Users' control over IS services

Communication between IS and user management

♦ Users' understanding of systems

♦ User confidence in systems

Responsiveness to new systems needs

♦ Prompt processing of change requests

♦ Short lead time, new systems development

♦ Responsiveness to changing user needs

♦ IS support when users prepare new systems proposals

♦ Flexibility of data and reports

End user computing

♦ More analysis systems

♦ More enquiry systems

♦ Effective training of users

♦ Ease of user access to systems

Quality of IS staff

♦ User-oriented systems analysts

♦ Competence of systems analysts

♦ Technical competence of IS staff

♦ Larger IS effort to create news systems

- Positive attitude to IS by users

Reliability of service

- Low percentage of hardware and systems downtime

- Efficient running of current systems

- Data security and privacy

Appendix I

Bibliography and reading list

Adelman, C. (1996) 'Anything goes: evaluation and relativism', *Evaluation*, vol. 2, no. 3, pp 291–305.

Bannister, F. and Remenyi, D. (2000) 'Acts of faith: instinct, value and IT investment decisions', *Journal of Information Technology*, vol. 15, no. 3.

Barua, A., Kriebel, C.H. and Mukhopadhyay, T. (1995) 'Information technologies and business value: an analytical and empirical investigation', *Information Systems Research*, vol. 6. no. 1.

Benzecri, J.P. (1969) *Data, Methodologies of Pattern Recognition*, Academic Press, New York.

Berelson, A. (1980) cited in Krippendorf K., *Content Analysis*, Sage Publications, Thousand Oaks, CA.

Brown, S.W. and Swartz, T.A. (1989) 'A gap analysis of professional service quality', *Journal of Marketing*, April.

Brunner, I. and Guzman, A. (1989) 'Participatory evaluation: a tool to assess projects and empower people', in R.F. Conner and M. Hendricks (eds) *International Innovations in Evaluation Methodology: New Directions for Evaluation Methodology*, Jossey-Bass, San Francisco.

Brynjolfsson, E. (1993) 'The productivity paradox of information technology: review and assessment', *Communications of the ACM*, December.

Brynjolfsson, E. and Hitt, L. (1995) ' Information technology as a factor of production: the role of differences among firms', *Economics of Innovation and New Technology*, vol. 3, no. 4.

Checkland, P. (1986) *Systems Thinking, Systems Practice*, John Wiley and Sons, Chichester.

Churchill, G.A. (1987) *Market Research: Methodological Foundations*, 4th Edition, Dryden Press, Chicago.

Churchill, G.A. (1994) *Market Research: Methodological Foundations*, 6th Edition, Dryden Press, Chicago.

Churchman, C.W. (1971) *The Design of Inquiring Systems*, Basic Books, New York.

Davenport, T.H. (1993) *Process Innovation: Reengineering Work through Information Technology*, Harvard Business School Press, Cambridge, MA.

Davenport, T.H. (1997) *Information Ecology*, Oxford University Press, New York.

Dillon, W.R., Madden, T.J. and Firtle, N.H. (1997) *Market Research in a Marketing Environment*, 2nd Edition, Irwin, Chicago.

Drucker, P. (1999) ' The Drucker interview', *Financial Times*, 10 April, p. 30.

Economist, (1991) ' IT Investment', 24 August p. 75.

Edison, T. (1995) attributed by Johnson, M. in *Managing in the Next Millennium*, Butterworth–Heinemann, Oxford, p. 117.

Evans, C. (1981) *The Making of the Micro – A History of the Computer*, Victor Gollancz, London.

Evans, P. and Wurster, H. (1999) *Blown to Bits: How the New Technology of Information Transforms Strategy*, Harvard Business Press, Cambridge, MA.

Ezingeard, J-N. and Race, P. (1996) ' A survey of current practice of value assessment in the management of manufacturing information and data systems', *Proceedings of the 2nd International Conference on Management Integrated Manufacturing*, 26-28 June, Leicester University, pp. 407-414.

Farbey, B. Land, F. and Targett, D. (1993) *IT Investment: A Study of Methods and Practices*, Butterworth-Heinemann, Oxford.

Farbey, B. Land, F. and Targett, D. (1995) 'A taxonomy of information systems application: the benefits' evaluation ladder', *European Journal of Information Systems*, vol. 4, no. 4.

Finne, H., Levin, M. and Nilssen, T. (1995) 'Trailing research: a model for useful program evaluation', *Evaluation*, vol. 1, no. 1, July.

Fortune, J. and Peters, G. (1995) *Learning from Failure, The Systems Approach*, John Wiley and Son, New York.

Gonin, R. and Money, A.H. (1989) *Nonlinear L_p-norm Estimation*, Marcel Dekker,

Gould, S.J. (1992) *The Mismeasure of Man*, Penguin Books, London, p. 27.

Greenacre, M.J. (1984) *The Theory and Application of Correspondence Analysis*, Academic Press,

Hamilton, S. and Chervany, N.L. (1981 a) 'Evaluating information system effectiveness – part II: comparing evaluation approaches', *MIS Quarterly*, vol. 5, no. 4, December.

Hamilton, S. Chervany, N.L. (1981 b) 'Evaluating information system effectiveness – part I: comparing evaluation approaches', *MIS Quarterly*, vol. 5, no. 3, September.

Handy, C. (1998) *The Hungry Spirit*, Random House, London.

Hewett, T.T. (1986) 'The role of iterative evaluation in designing systems usability', in M. Harrison and D. Monk (eds) *Proceedings of the 2nd BCS HCI Specialist Group Conference, People and Computers: Designing for Usability*, British Computer Society, York.

Hochstrasser, B. (1992) 'Justifying IT Investments', in *Proceedings of the conference on Advanced Information Systems; The new technologies in today's business environment*, Imperial College, London, pp. 17-28.

Hogbin, G. and Thomas, D.V. (1994) *Investing in Information Technology: Managing the Decision Making Process*. McGraw-Hill/IBM Series, Cambridge, UK.

Hopwood, A.G. (1983) 'Evaluating the real benefits', in H.J. Otway and M. Peltu (eds) *New Office Technology, Human and Organisational Aspects*, Chapman and Hall, London.

Irani, Z., Ezingeard, J-N. and Grieve, R.J. (1998) 'Costing the true costs of IT investments: a focus during management decision making', *Logistics and Information Management*, vol. 11, no. 1, pp. 38-43.

Johnson, N.L. and Kotz, S. (1970) *Distributions in Statistics: Continuous Univariate Distributions*, vols. 1 and 2, Houghton Mifflin, New York.

Keen, P.W.G. (1991) *Shaping the Future: Business Design through Information Technology*, Harvard Business School Press, Cambridge, MA.

Kerlinger, F.N. (1969) *Foundations of Behavioral Research*, Holt Rinehart and Winston, New York.

Kim, K. (1990) 'User information satisfaction: toward conceptual clarity', in J. de Grosse, M. Alavi and H. Oppelland (eds) *Proceedings of 11th International Conference on Information Systems*, Copenhagen, pp.183–191.

Lacity, M. and Hirschheim, R. (1995) *Information Systems Outsourcing - Myths, Metaphors and Realities*, John Wiley and Son, Chichester.

Lehmann, D.R. (1989) *Marketing Research Analysis*, 3rd Edition, Richard D. Irwin, Chicago.

Lincoln, T. (1990) *Managing Information Systems for Profit*, John Wiley and Sons, Chichester.

McKeen, J.D., Smith H.A. and Parent, M. (1999) 'An integrative research approach to assess the business value of information technology', in M.A. Mahmood and E.J. Szewczak (eds) *Measuring Information Technology Investment Payoff: Contemporary Approaches*, Idea Group Publishing, Hershey, PA.

Miller, J. and Doyle, B.A. (1987) 'Measuring the effectiveness of computer-based information systems in the financial services sector', *MIS Quarterly*, vol. 11, no. 1, March.

Money, A.H., Tromp, D. and Wegner, T. (1988) 'The quantification of decision support benefits within the context of value analysis', *MIS Quarterly*, vol. 12, no. 2, June.

Mooney, J.G., Gurbaxaniand, V. and Kraemer, K.L. (1995) 'A process oriented framework for assessing the business value of information technology', in J. de Grosse, G. Ariav, C. Beath, R. Hoyer and C. Kemerer (eds) *Proceedings of the Sixteenth International Conference on Information Systems*, December 10-13, Amsterdam.

Nugus, S. (1997) *Financial Planning using Spreadsheets*, Kogan Page, London.

Parasuraman, A. (1991) *Market Research*, 2nd Edition, Addison-Wesley, Reading, MA.

Parasuraman, A, Zeithaml, V. and Berry, L.A. (1985) 'Conceptual model of service quality and its implications for research', *Journal of Marketing*, vol. 61, no. 3, Fall.

Parasuraman, A., Zeithaml, V. and Berry, L. (1988) 'SERVQUAL: a multi-item scale for measuring consumer perceptions of quality', *Journal of Marketing*, vol. 64, no. 1, Spring.

Parker, M.M. and Benson, R.J. (1987) 'Information economics: an introduction', *Datamation*, December.

Parker, M.M and Benson, R.J. (1989), 'Enterprise-wide information economics: latest concepts'. *Journal of Information Systems Management*, vol. 6, no. 4, pp.7–13.

Parker, M.M, Benson, R.J and Trainor, H.E. (1988) *Information Economics: Linking Business Performance to Information Technology*. Prentice Hall, Englewood Cliffs, NJ.

Porter, M.E. (1985) *Competitive Strategy Techniques for Analysing Industries and Competitors*, Free Press, New York.

Remenyi, D. (1996) 'Ten common information systems mistakes', *Journal of General Management*, vol. 21, no. 4, pp. 78–91.

Remenyi, D. (1999) *IT Investment – Making a Business Case*, Butterworth-Heinemann, Oxford.

Remenyi, D. and Money, A.H. (1993) 'Service quality and correspondence analysis as diagnostic tools in determining the problems associated with the effective use of computer services', in D. Remenyi and E. Whitley (eds) *Proceedings of the First European Conference on Information Systems*, Henley Management College, Henley-on-Thames, March.

Remenyi, D., Sherwood-Smith, M. and White, T. (1997) *Achieving Maximum Value with Information Systems*, John Wiley and Son, Chichester.

Shadish, W.R., Cook, T.D. and Leviton, L.C. (991) *Foundations of Program Evaluation: Theories of Practice*, Sage Publications, Newbury Park, CA.

Soh, C. and Markus, L. (1995) 'How IT creates business value: a process theory synthesis', in J. de Grosse, G. Ariav, C. Beath, R. Hoyer and C. Kemerer (eds) *Proceedings of the Sixteenth International Conference on Information Systems*, December 10-13, Amsterdam.

Solow, R.M. (1987) 'Review of S.S. Cohen and J Zysman "Manufacturing matters: The myth of the post-industrial economy"', *New York Book Review*, 12th July.

Strassmann, P.A. (1985), *Information Payoff: The Transformation of Work in the Electronic Age*, Free Press, New York.

Strassmann P.A. (1990) *The Business Value of Computers*, Information Economics Press, , CT.

Strassmann, P.A. (1997) *The Squandered Computer*, Information Economics Press, New Canaan, CT.

Svendsen, A. (1998) *The Stakeholder Strategy*, Berrett-Koehler, San Francisco.

Symons, V. (1991) 'A review of information systems evaluation: Content, Context and Process', *European Journal of Information Systems*, vol. 3, no. 1, pp. 205-212.

Walsham, G. (1993) *Interpreting Information Systems in Organisations*, John Wiley and Son, Chichester.

Ward, J., Taylor, P. and Bond, P. (1996) 'Evaluation and realisation of IS/IT benefits: an empirical study of current practices', *European Journal of Information Systems*, vol. 5, no. 4, pp. 214–225.

Wheatley, M. (1997) 'Hidden costs of the humble PC', *Management Today*, January, pp. 52–54.

Wheatley, M. J. (1992) *Leadership and the New Science*, Berret Koehler, San Francisco.

Wick, C. and Leon, L. (1993) *The Learning Edge: How Smart Managers and Smart Companies Stay Ahead*, McGraw Hill, New York.

Willcocks, L. and Lester, S. (1993) 'How do organisations evaluate and control information systems investments? Recent UK survey evidence', in D. Avison, J. Kendall and J. DeGross (eds), *Human, Organisational and Social Dimensions of Information Systems Development*, North Holland, Amsterdam.

Wiseman, C. (1985) *Strategy and Computers – Information Systems as Competitive Weapons*, Dow-Jones Irwin, Homewiid, IL.

Wittgenstein, L. (1914) *Notebooks, Entry for November 1*, J. Anscombe (ed.), cited in the Columbia Dictionary of Quotations, 1998, Columbia University Press.

Wittgenstein, L. (1980) *Culture and Value*, G.H. von Wright with Heikki Nyman (eds), cited in the Columbia Dictionary of Quotations, 1998, Columbia University Press.

Zehnder, C. A. (1990) *Développement de Project en Informatique*, Presses Polytechniques Romandes, Lausanne, Switzerland.

Zuboff, S. (1988) *In the Age of the Smart Machine: The Future of Work and Power*, Basic Books, New York.

Index